# US Immigration in the Twenty-First Century

## Making Americans, Remaking America

# Dilemmas in American Politics

Series Editor: **Craig A. Rimmerman,** *Hobart and William Smith Colleges*

If the answers to the problems facing U.S. democracy were easy, politicians would solve them, accept credit, and move on. But certain dilemmas have confronted the American political system continuously. They defy solution; they are endemic to the system. Some can best be described as institutional dilemmas: How can the Congress be both a representative body and a national decision-maker? How can the president communicate with more than 250 million citizens effectively? Why do we have a two-party system when many voters are disappointed with the choices presented to them? Others are policy dilemmas: How do we find compromises on issues that defy compromise, such as abortion policy? How do we incorporate racial and ethnic minorities or immigrant groups into American society, allowing them to reap the benefits of this land without losing their identity? How do we fund health care for our poorest or oldest citizens?

Dilemmas such as these are what propel students toward an interest in the study of U.S. government. Each book in the *Dilemmas in American Politics Series* addresses a "real world" problem, raising the issues that are of most concern to students. Each is structured to cover the historical and theoretical aspects of the dilemma but also to explore the dilemma from a practical point of view and to speculate about the future. The books are designed as supplements to introductory courses in American politics or as case studies to be used in upper-level courses. The link among them is the desire to make the real issues confronting the political world come alive in students' eyes.

# BOOKS IN THIS SERIES

# US Immigration in the Twenty-First Century

## Making Americans, Remaking America

**Louis DeSipio**
University of California, Irvine

**Rodolfo O. de la Garza**
Columbia University

**WESTVIEW PRESS**

A Member of the Perseus Books Group

WESTVIEW PRESS was founded in 1975 in Boulder, Colorado, by notable publisher and intellectual Fred Praeger. Westview Press continues to publish scholarly titles and high-quality undergraduate- and graduate-level textbooks in core social science disciplines. With books developed, written, and edited with the needs of serious nonfiction readers, professors, and students in mind, Westview Press honors its long history of publishing books that matter.

Published by Westview Press,
A Member of the Perseus Books Group
2465 Central Avenue
Boulder, CO 80301
www.westviewpress.com

Every effort has been made to secure required permissions for all text, images, maps, and other art reprinted in this volume.

Westview Press books are available at special discounts for bulk purchases in the United States by corporations, institutions, and other organizations. For more information, please contact the Special Markets Department at the Perseus Books Group, 2300 Chestnut Street, Suite 200, Philadelphia, PA 19103, or call (800) 810-4145, ext. 5000, or e-mail special.markets@perseusbooks.com.

Designed by Jack Lenzo and Cynthia Young

A CIP catalog record for the print version of this book is available from the Library of Congress.
LCCN: 2014954088
PB ISBN: 978-0-8133-4473-7
EBOOK ISBN: 978-0-8133-4474-4

10 9 8 7 6 5 4 3 2 1

*To our families' immigrant heritage*

*Luigi Ricca, great-grandfather*
*Clara Richieda, great-grandmother*
*Gioachino DeSipio, grandfather*
*Italians by birth*

*Laurence Walton, great-great-great-great-grandfather*
*English by birth*

*Sofia Oropeza, mother*
*Mexican by birth*

*Adelaida Traveria, mother-in-law*
*Serafin Corbelle, father-in-law*
*Ileana Corbelle, wife*
*Cubans by birth*

*and others unknown*
*Americans by choice*

# Contents

# 6 *Conclusion: US Immigration Policy for the Twenty-First Century* 203

# Boxes and Tables

## Boxes

. . . . . . . . . . . . . . . . . . . . . . . . . . . . . . . . . . . . . . . . . . . . . . . . . . . . .

## Tables

. . . . . . . . . . . . . . . . . . . . . . . . . . . . . . . . . . . . . . . . . . . . . . . . . . . . .

# Preface

AS WE BEGAN THIS PROJECT, WE ANTICIPATED THAT WE WOULD be writing a somewhat different book. The nation is long overdue for a major reform to its immigration policies, and the outline of what a new system could look like has been clear for nearly a decade. With these conditions in place, our expectation was that Congress and the executive branch would find the compromises necessary to craft a major, comprehensive immigration reform bill, and that our study of immigration and immigrant incorporation policy would conclude with an assessment of this new piece of legislation itself, as well as a study of the political and policy calculus that allowed the necessary compromises to be achieved.

We were wrong. Instead, Congress has not been able to agree on a new direction for US immigration in the twenty-first century, and it is increasingly likely that Congress will remain in the current legislative stalemate at least into the early 2020s. For the past fifteen years, Congress (particularly the US Senate) and the two most recent presidents—Republican George W. Bush and Democrat Barack Obama—have actively debated immigration policy and have identified a bipartisan set of changes and reforms to the current immigration law. However, no bill has been sent to either president for his review and signature. With the exception of added border and interior enforcement measures, Congress has been unable to pass even narrow immigration legislation. Left unaddressed are the needs of highly organized segments of US society, such as the business community, which claims it cannot meet its labor needs under the current system, or the needs of segments of the unauthorized immigrant community, such as the young adults who entered the United States unauthorized as children and subsequently went on to succeed in US society, and who have a compelling claim to legal status.

Dissatisfaction with the status quo characterizes the dominant opinions about contemporary US immigration policy across many sectors of US society—the business community, state and local governments, immigrant/ethnic communities, native populations fearful of the size and diversity of the immigrant populations, US allies abroad, and some in the national security community. Yet the status quo has survived and will for the foreseeable future.

Certainly, these sectors of US society do not agree on all aspects of immigration reform and any new immigration law will have to be a compromise for all. However, although their positions may be firm, they are not intransigent. The desire for comprehensive reform has created new alliances to advocate for it that were largely unimaginable a decade ago, such as an agreement between business interests and the nation's leading trade union on a guest worker program that would be acceptable to both. However, even these new alliances have been insufficient to ensure Congressional action. In this book, we examine why it has been impossible to achieve a resolution to this debate and we assess what compromises will ultimately be necessary to reform US immigration law.

Despite not being able to offer an initial review of a new immigration bill—which would be the foundation of US immigration policy for the early twenty-first century—we anticipate that this volume will still be of use to analysts, students, and policymakers by grounding the contemporary debates and issues surrounding immigration in the history of US immigration and immigrant incorporation policies. This history offers lessons on how the United States has previously approached immigration policy conflicts within US society on who should be admitted and under what circumstances in the past. It also demonstrates how the United States has overcome these conflicts to restructure, and frequently expand, opportunities to immigrants, and how it has handled providing immigrants with the resources to become full and equal members of US society.

Policymakers often neglect the issue of immigration incorporation, though it tends to be the focus of those who oppose immigration. We consider immigrant incorporation to be of considerable importance and assess paths to immigrant incorporation from several perspectives in this book. We look at the formal process of how immigrants attain full membership in the polity: naturalization. We also assess the distinctions in rights and privileges between US citizens and non-naturalized immigrants, and between legal permanent residents and unauthorized immigrants. Finally, we assess how immigrants (and their US-born children) are exercising their political voice, both in the United States and in their countries of origin or ancestry. We believe that it is this immigrant agency that will ultimately ensure that an inclusive immigration reform bill is achieved. When immigrants organized en masse in 2006 and spoke out to defend their interests, they fundamentally changed the policy debate.

Although recent events could easily lead to pessimism about the prospects of immigration reform, it is clear that US interests in the issues surrounding immigration policy are simply too great for the status quo—which dissatisfies more Americans than it satisfies—to endure in perpetuity. We conclude, then, with a discussion of what will need to change in Congress and in the executive branch in order to see passage of a new immigration bill, though we now suspect that these changes will not appear until early in the 2020s. Predictions, of course, are dangerous in the political and policymaking worlds. There will undoubtedly be more mass and elite organizing around immigration reform between now and the early 2020s, which could change some of the dynamics that we discuss in this book. However, the coalitions that have formed to influence immigration policy and the issues around which they are willing and unwilling to compromise are sufficiently clear that we can anticipate, with some certainty, the shape of the ultimate reform.

If we began this project with the anticipation of an earlier resolution in Congress than has appeared, we are certainly now more pessimistic about the speed of the ultimate resolution. However, about the core issues that must be resolved and the shape of the compromises that will need to be reached, we are as confident as we were at the project's inception.

*Louis DeSipio*
*Rodolfo O. de la Garza*

# *Introduction*

IN 2006, AS MANY AS 5 MILLION PEOPLE PROTESTED US IMMI-gration policies in up to 150 cities nationwide. Most who protested called for an expansion in immigration opportunities, and specifically for an opportunity for unauthorized immigrants to legalize their status. But theirs was not the only voice seeking to influence US immigration policy. Although less public in their concerns, a large share of the general public demanded a very different policy solution—enhanced immigration enforcement, and limited or no opportunities for unauthorized immigrants to legalize. A plurality of Americans also advocated a reduction in current levels of legal immigration. Some who advocated restriction also joined volunteer militias along the US-Mexico border to demonstrate their dissatisfaction with federal enforcement of US immigration laws.

Other organized interests in American society also sought to shape the future of US immigration policy. Some state governments signaled their dissatisfaction with the current policies by passing an unprecedented number of laws seeking to regulate immigration and shape immigrant incorporation at the state level. However, some other states responded by expanding the rights and opportunities of immigrants, including unauthorized immigrants, to use state services. Many in the business community sought increases in immigration, of both skilled and unskilled workers. These demands most often focused on *guest workers*, immigrants who would be allowed to work for a number of years in the United States but who would not have the eventual opportunity to become permanent residents and, later, US citizens.

Each of these voices sought to shape Congressional debates in 2005, 2006, 2007, 2010, and 2013 to make significant, perhaps wholesale, changes to US immigration law. As important as immigration policy has become, the many voices seeking to shape policy have not sought compromise. On the contrary, for reasons that we will discuss, interests have

1

become more hardened over this period of mass organizing and Congressional debate (Voss and Bloemraad 2011; Tichenor and Rosenblum 2012). Perhaps not surprisingly, Congress has yet to find a compromise despite encouragement from both the George W. Bush and Barack Obama administrations on the changes necessary to build a new, comprehensive immigration structure for the United States (DeSipio 2011a). Instead, the US immigration system that engendered this popular protest and public concern in the first place nonetheless remains national policy, and apparently will for the foreseeable future.

Our goal in this book is to analyze historic and contemporary US immigration policy with an eye to the decisions that Congress and the nation will have to make to reform immigration and immigrant incorporation policies for the twenty-first century. As should be evident even from our brief introduction, it will not be easy to find a balance of policies that will satisfy the many voices and interests seeking to change US policies. Key actors seek very different outcomes from immigration policy and there is frequently no obvious middle ground between these positions.

## Terminology

Before we get too deeply into the debates over comprehensive immigration reform, we need to define several terms and concepts that appear repeatedly throughout our discussion.

The beginning of the immigration process is a decision by an individual or a family to migrate. *Migration* is movement from one place to another. In the United States, we take migration largely for granted. People migrate from city to city or region to region for education, for employment, and often just for a change of scene. When migration—movement—crosses an international frontier, it is called by different names—emigration and immigration—though, at a fundamental level, it is also still migration. *Emigration* means leaving one country; *immigration* refers to entering another.

Because emigration and immigration require that a migrant cross an international frontier, the migrant must usually get the permission of the country of origin, of the receiving country, or of both. Historically, some countries have restricted emigration, though that is rare today (North Korea is an exception). Countries that restrict emigration do not want to lose the labor, skills, knowledge, experiences, or other assets of potential emigrants. Some countries also restrict emigration for symbolic reasons; they do not want to give the appearance to other countries in the world that their subjects are not satisfied living in that country.

Although formal restrictions on emigration have diminished, the potential for migration is not equal in all parts of the world. Transportation links make migration easier from some parts of the world than from others. Patterns of previous migration from a region increase the likelihood that new migrants will come from that same region. Migration is often not an individual act, so the previous immigration experiences of friends or family members shape where subsequent emigrants go and how they adapt to the receiving society. Employers recruit labor abroad and relationships often develop between employers in an immigrant-receiving country and migrants in a city or region of an immigrant-sending country. Finally, emigration is limited to those who can afford the cost of international transit and who have a reasonable expectation of being able to survive in the receiving country. Immigrants, unlike the common stereotype assigned them, are usually not the poorest of the poor in their sending countries. The poorest usually cannot afford the cost of migration or do not have the skills to find work in the receiving society. Instead, immigrants are usually relatively more successful members of the sending society who feel that their skills and resources are not sufficiently rewarded in that society. Because there are many risks associated with migration, migrants often have a family member or friend in the receiving society who can offer assistance on arrival.

Compared to emigration, immigration is much more highly restricted. Few countries accept large numbers of immigrants each year. Even fewer accept large numbers of immigrants with the promise that these immigrants can become full members of the receiving society. The four countries that routinely accept the most immigrants annually are the United States, Canada, Australia, and New Zealand. Each of these countries offers many of its immigrants the opportunity not just to live there permanently but also to join the country as a full member—that is, as a citizen. The United States offers "permanent residence" to approximately 1.1 million immigrants annually.

Each country accepts immigrants according to its own standards. Broadly, these standards involve three types of potential immigrants: those with blood ties, those with specific skills or wealth, and those with ideological congruence. The largest of these categories is blood ties, whether immediate or fictive. That is, some countries look for individuals who are related to citizens in the receiving country. Others seek people who share a common ethnic background or a common religious background with societal groups. The second category for immigrant admissions grants a higher likelihood of admission to people with specialized job skills or with wealth that can be transferred to the new country. Even countries that admit few immigrants rarely reject the wealthy seeking a new home, particularly when those wealthy immigrants are willing to invest their wealth. Although the truly rich are relatively few (and often not interested in migration), the educated and technically skilled make up a larger pool of potential migrants who are often welcomed as immigrants. The United States has always sought these migrants but is facing increased competition with other countries to win their loyalties today. The final category of people who are sometimes granted immigration eligibility includes those in ideological agreement with the leaders of the receiving state. So, for example, during the Cold War, some residents of Communist countries could migrate to the Soviet Union for purposes of education or technical training; in this same period, the United States welcomed scientists fleeing Eastern Europe and the Soviet Union, even if they had previously worked in Nazi Germany. As the salience of the world's dominant ideologies has declined, this category of potential immigrants has also declined. Nevertheless, for some countries it remains an explanatory factor for high-profile immigrants (for example former National Security Agency analyst Edward Snowden was able to migrate to Russia after he released classified data on US surveillance programs abroad).

With immigration often restricted to family members, the rich, the skilled, or ideologues, many potential immigrants are not eligible for formal or legal immigration. This leads to a second stream of international migrants, those who enter a country without the legal authorization to remain permanently. In the United States, we identify these immigrants as illegal, undocumented, or (the term that we use in this book) *unauthorized immigrants*.

Unauthorized immigrants in the United States are heterogeneous. Some are family members of US citizens or permanent residents. Others are people who have migrated to the United States to seek work opportunities. Some of these workers are in unskilled or semiskilled positions that are shunned by US citizens, but others have advanced technical skills and find work in positions desired by Americans. Still other undocumented immigrants are fleeing political persecution or economic privation in their home countries. Some crossed borders without legal permission, whereas others entered with legal, but short-term, immigrant visas and stayed in the United States after their visas expired. Clearly, these categories of undocumented immigrants overlap. Economic or political persecution in sending countries can encourage undocumented immigration. US immigration policy often unwittingly encourages undocumented immigration by allowing some family members to immigrate as permanent residents even while denying other family members access to legal immigration. Legal immigrants, then, often facilitate the unauthorized migration of their families.

Based on our discussion of international migration thus far, the two main categories of immigrants—permanent residents and unauthorized immigrants—should encompass all immigrants, because an immigrant is either in the receiving country with the permission of the receiving country or not. Alas, international migration is, in reality, much more complex. For example, some countries admit immigrants solely for labor-related reasons. These immigrants are permitted to stay in the receiving country only as long as they perform the job that spurred their entry and as long as the receiving society needs their labor. These are *guest workers*. The United States currently admits guest workers in agriculture, entertainment and recreation activities (such as amusement parks in the summer and ski resorts in the winter), child care, and skilled workers in technology industries.

A second category of immigrant having neither the rights nor opportunities of the permanent resident, at least initially, nor the statutory exclusion of the undocumented, is the refugee or asylee. *Refugees* are individuals who emigrate in the face of persecution in their home countries. *Asylees* are immigrants already present in the United States who cannot return to their home countries because they fear persecution upon return. Most countries find it very difficult to define what level of persecution merits these statuses. Political considerations in the receiving country often cloud the objective factors that should guide the award of refugee or asylee status.

Most countries offer a form of short-term immigration for the purposes of tourism and commerce. Most tourists and businesspeople who travel internationally are not intent on staying in the receiving country and, hence, do not meet our definition of "immigrants," but some immigrants intentionally use the opportunity to obtain short-term visitor or business visas as a ruse to enter a country and then stay on illegally. Although it might seem as if modern, technologically adept countries like the United States should be able to control these visa overstayers, many, including the United States, do not have this capacity.

Each of these three possible routes to immigration other than permanent residence or undocumented immigration—that is, guest workers, refugees and asylees, and those who overstay their visas—shares two characteristics: they do not offer immigrants the opportunity to attain a permanent status in the receiving country, and they offer some period during which immigrants may live legally in the receiving country and access opportunities to stay and, perhaps, seek to change their status to something more permanent if they are eligible. Thus, although these short-term or conditional statuses do not offer the opportunities of permanent residence or the risks of undocumented immigration, they do expand the pool of potential immigrants in the receiving society.

A final category of migrant also meets part of our definition: people who are forced to move internationally. These are people who are removed from their homes to new nations for labor-related purposes. Specifically, these are people sold into forms of slavery and transported abroad to perform that labor. We refer to slaves in our discussions as *involuntary immigrants*. As we will suggest, it is important to recognize that they are part of the immigrant flow during the period of their transport. In the United States, for example, the legal importation of slaves until 1808 (and, in violation of US law afterward) reduced the demand for voluntary immigrants. Since 1808, the United States has officially eliminated involuntary immigration. It, however, remains a component of international migration, including international migration to the United States. The US State Department (2005) estimated that 600,000 to 800,000 men, women, and children are trafficked annually across international borders worldwide. Approximately 80 percent are women and girls and up to 50 percent are children. The majority of involuntary migrants are trafficked into commercial sexual exploitation.

The diversity of legal statuses held by immigrants obscures one fundamental division: that between immigrants who have the right to become citizens of the receiving country and those who do not. Naturalization requirements vary from country to country. In the United States, most immigrants who become permanent residents may apply for naturalization after five years of legal residence.

Throughout our discussion, it is important to keep in mind this simplified outline of the transition from migrant to naturalized citizen that we have provided here. The complexity of the legal barriers and personal and familial change that accompany the move to the United States ensures that each immigrant likely faces many detours and false starts. Nevertheless, the basic pattern remains. We should also note that the path is not unidirectional. Many immigrants never attain permanent resident status. Others become permanent residents but never naturalize. Some of these return to the home countries, others emigrate to third countries, and still others die as *denizens*—long-term residents who are not citizens—in the United States.

## Overview of the Book

Congress has invested considerable time and energy in debating a comprehensive revision to American immigration policy in 2006, 2007, and 2013, and made more limited efforts in 2010, but it has failed to agree on a bill that it could send to the president. Congress passed some immigration legislation in the first decade of the twenty-first century, but this legislation primarily focused on one small component of the overall policy—enforcement—and has failed to satisfy the many public voices and business interests that have become increasingly dissatisfied with US immigration policy. In Chapter 1, we use these Congressional debates as a point of departure to analyze the various dimensions of "comprehensive" immigration reform. We assess why many in US society are dissatisfied with current immigrant law, what Congress has tried to do to create a new immigration policy for the twenty-first century, and the major components that will need to be addressed to enact comprehensive immigration reform. This discussion of contemporary debates serves as a foundation for the rest of the book. In Chapter 2, we examine the historical evolution of US immigration and immigrant settlement policies. In Chapter 3, we look at the rights and responsibilities of immigrants, immigrant settlement, and the relationships between immigrants and natives. In Chapter 4, we provide an overview of naturalization policy, and in Chapter 5, we discuss immigrant civic and political engagement.

In the Conclusion, we return to the question of the structure of a new US immigration policy in the twenty-first century. As will be evident, some of the issues that will need to be addressed for a comprehensive reform are central to the current popular debate over immigration, but others are not. Despite the consensus among executive and legislative branch leaders that the nation's immigration system needs considerable reform, we do not mean to suggest that Congress will necessarily reform all aspects of immigration simultaneously. In fact, history would suggest otherwise (Tichenor 2002; Zolberg 2006). Instead, these pieces will eventually need to be addressed by legislators and policymakers, perhaps over a period of years. Whether or not they are addressed in Congress's next effort at immigration reform, they will continue to be a part of the public debate over immigration and immigrant incorporation in the United States for many years to come.

# 1

····································································

# Current Immigration and Immigrant Incorporation Debates: How Did We Get Here?

To understand the issues at stake for Congress and the nation in the debates over comprehensive immigration reform, it is necessary to understand the current immigration policies of the United States as well as why many in American society feel that those policies are not serving the needs of the nation. As will be evident in our discussion in this chapter and in Chapter 3, the many criticisms of immigration policy and its implementation often conflict with each other and reflect very different visions for the future of the nation and its peoples. For this reason, compromises on immigration reform are hard to achieve and the search for acceptable compromises has long vexed Congress and presidents.

Our goal in this chapter is to identify key existing policies, the concerns about these policies felt by organized interests in US society, and the possible resolutions to these perceived failings that have been or are being debated by Congress. With this contemporary public policy debate as a foundation, we conclude the discussion in this chapter by identifying the key compromises that will need to be addressed by Congress as part of a comprehensive immigration reform bill. A *comprehensive bill* is a piece of legislation that addresses multiple aspects of immigration policy in a single bill and is, by definition, a compromise that addresses the policy goals of multiple interests in US society. Because comprehensive bills are compromises, they require most advocates of the bill to accept provisions that they oppose as well as provisions that they support to ensure passage. We make no predictions as to when Congress (and the president) might make the compromises and enact foundational legislation for US immigration policy in the twenty-first century, but we are confident that the issues identified here will be critical to that legislation.

## The Statutory Foundation of Contemporary US Immigration Policy

Although the roots of the contemporary system of immigration and immigrant incorporation policy can be traced to the nation's earliest days, the statutory foundation was immigration reform legislation passed in 1965. We examine this bill and its implementation in depth in Chapter 2, but for our purposes of examining today's immigration debates it is important to recognize two elements of this watershed law. First, it created the legal basis for large numbers of legal immigrants to migrate to the United States each year. Each decade, immigrants grow the country by nearly eleven million people, or roughly 3.5 percent of the national population (315 million). Most new legal immigrants are from Latin American or Asia and so are ethnically distinct from the current majority of Americans.

Second, the 1965 immigration bill signed into law by President Lyndon Johnson tells many people throughout the world that they will *never* be able to immigrate to the United States because they do not meet any of its standards for establishing permanent residence. Immigrants include short-term visitors and others who cannot stay permanently, such as guest workers (discussed later). Generally when we speak of immigrants colloquially, we mean immigrants to permanent residence. The 1965 law, however, did not create an enforcement mechanism sufficient to prevent unauthorized migration. Although enforcement resources have increased considerably in the years since 1965, the incentives to unauthorized migration (family members in the United States, job opportunities, civil strife in immigrant-sending countries, for example) have proved strong enough to overcome the barriers imposed on unauthorized migrants. The best estimates are that approximately 11.7 million unauthorized migrants lived in the United States in 2012, down from a high of nearly 12 million in 2007 (Passel, Cohn, and Gonzalez-Baker 2013). Approximately 51 percent of these unauthorized migrants are from Mexico. Other countries that send sizeable unauthorized populations to the United States include El Salvador, Guatemala, Honduras, the Philippines, India, and Korea.

In sum, the 1965 immigration law guarantees that large numbers of immigrants—both legal and unauthorized—who are ethnically distinct from the American majority will immigrate to the United States each year and that this number will continue to grow in the future. This virtually guarantees that immigration policy in the United States will continue to be contentious. And although it is less discussed by political leaders or the punditry, the 1965 immigration legislation also means that successful immigrant incorporation policies are critical to the future of the nation.

This ongoing contestation about immigration policy has led to several major amendments to the 1965 immigration legislation, none of which has changed its basic design. We discuss these amendments in greater depth in Chapter 2, but here it is important to identify them briefly as background to outlining key concerns about the structure of US immigration policy held by the general public and legislative leaders alike. To a significant extent, the public's perception that these earlier reforms have failed makes Congress's efforts more difficult today.

In 1986, Congress passed and President Ronald Reagan signed into law the Immigration Reform and Control Act (IRCA). The act sought to reduce unauthorized migration by requiring employers to document within the first few days of employment the eligibility of all new employees to work in the United States. The legacy of this legislation is the I-9 form that all employees complete when they start a new job. The IRCA was a compromise and was passed only after several years of negotiation. This compromise provided for legalization of approximately 2 million long-term unauthorized workers (immigrants who had been resident in the United States for five or more years).

Another key lesson we can take from the debates surrounding immigration policy in the mid-1980s and the passing of the IRCA is the importance of agricultural interests in shaping immigration policy. In fact, the agricultural lobby continues to use its influence to ensure that it has access to immigrant labor. The IRCA included provisions for nearly one million unauthorized immigrants with short periods of residence who had worked in agriculture. Although the IRCA is often portrayed as a failure because it did not stem unauthorized migration, it did prove quite successful at ensuring that previously unauthorized migrants were able to make the transition to permanent residence. By 2001 approximately one-third of formerly unauthorized immigrants had naturalized as US citizens (Rytina 2002).

Congress also passed major immigration reforms in 1990 and 1996. These reforms focused both on immigration to achieve permanent residence (legal immigration) and unauthorized migration. In 1990, Congress examined whether there should be an annual cap on the total number of legal immigrants admitted to the United States. It concluded that there shouldn't be, and enacted a "flexible cap," clever wording that meant there would be no limits for certain immediate family members of US citizens. Congress also enacted the Diversity Immigrant Visa Program (discussed later) to expand the range of countries of origin of legal immigrants to the United States. That program has served as an engine for new streams of family-based migration since its enactment. Finally, in 1990, Congress expanded the grounds for deportation of immigrants resident in the United States, making it easier to deport non-naturalized immigrants who have committed crimes in the United States.

The 1996 reform sought to reduce the cost of recent legal immigrants to US society (though without much evidence that recent immigrants were, in fact, a financial burden). It added some means testing to immigration eligibility, making it more difficult for poor would-be migrants to immigrate to the United States, regardless of family connections in this country. It also increased the expectation that the immigrant's sponsor—the family member or company who sponsored the immigrant—would pay the government for any public benefits the immigrant used. Finally, the 1996 immigration and welfare reform legislation also barred recent legal immigrants from eligibility for US social welfare programs for the poor.

Although these 1990s reforms shaped the lives of many immigrants and potential immigrants, they did not fundamentally limit growing public concerns about immigration. Public and legislative debates over immigration increasingly came to focus on the size of the unauthorized immigrant population in particular, the changes that immigrants were perceived as bringing to American culture and society, the potential national security threats from specific immigrants, and the costs of immigrants to US society and to native workers.

## Immigration Reform in the George W. Bush Years

These growing national concerns and the increasing frequency of immigration reform legislation led to public and Congressional expectations that the George W. Bush administration would craft a more substantial comprehensive reform. These expectations were the result of several factors. First, the public was increasingly dissatisfied with enforcement of immigration policy, and was particularly concerned about the growing numbers of unauthorized migrants in the United States. Second, immigrants (both legal and unauthorized) were increasingly migrating to parts of the country, such as the South and the agricultural Midwest, that had seen few immigrants in a century or longer. Third, Bush had premised his candidacy and his presidency on a greater understanding of immigrants and Latinos than more nativist Republicans who perceived threats to the American economy and society posed by immigration, and who had dominated the party leadership in the 1990s (DeSipio and de la Garza 2005). Bush thus promised a more compassionate approach to immigrants while also making the more traditional Republican promise of ensuring that the business and agricultural communities would have access to the inexpensive labor they needed.

Early in his administration, President Bush appeared to be moving forward on his commitment to tackle immigration. However, in July 2001 an internal White House memo leaked to the *New York Times* indicated that the Bush administration was considering a proposal to legalize what was then estimated to be 3 million unauthorized Mexicans in the United States (Schmitt 2001). This proposal was a piece—undoubtedly the most controversial piece—of a comprehensive set of proposed reforms that focused on new border enforcement strategies, cooperation with Mexico over binational migration, and the creation of a guest worker program that would allow temporary residence and employment for foreign workers.

This memo appeared on the front page of a *New York Times* Sunday edition. It was evidently leaked by an opponent of the reform proposal, which demonstrates how controversial even these possible reforms were. Advocates of legalization quickly indicated that they would not support a program targeted only at Mexicans, and they opposed a guest worker program. The Bush administration had not fully developed these plans or yet built support among Congressional leaders, so it had to backpedal quickly and, at least for a short time, withdraw the proposal from internal debate. But even with the leak and the backpedaling, a discussion this early in the Bush administration indicated that immigration reform would likely move forward in some form. That possibility ended abruptly with the September 11, 2001, terrorist attacks.

The Bush administration did not return to addressing immigration reform until 2004. Even then many felt that it was only the upcoming

2004 presidential election that prompted the administration's resurrection of the subject (Bumiller 2004). Critics from the right saw the revised Bush proposal—which focused on increased border security and a guest worker program, with no explicit discussion of a legalization program— as a poorly designed effort to win Latino votes in the election, which failed to prevent future authorized migration (DeSipio and Leal 2010). Critics on the left maintained their opposition to a guest worker program, a position that they might have been willing to compromise on in exchange for an explicit commitment to opportunities for guest workers to move toward legal status at the end of their "guest" period.

Had the Bush administration been as committed in 2004 to immigration reform as it had been in 2001, its new proposals might have served as the foundation for Congressional action. Admittedly, though, the proposals would likely have had a difficult time passing both the Republican-controlled Senate and House of Representatives, which was growing increasingly resistant to Bush's leadership on key issues. By this point, however, Bush and his senior advisors were not focused on immigration or building positive relations with Mexico, which had been part of their goal with the 2001 proposal. Instead, the war on terror and the wars in Afghanistan and Iraq were absorbing their energies. The 2004 proposals put immigration back on the table, but neither the Bush administration nor Congress made it a priority. Immigration ended up not being a major policy issue in the 2004 presidential race (de la Garza, DeSipio, and Leal 2010).

As the White House moved away from a leadership role on immigration in this period, public dissatisfaction continued to grow. Security fears from the September 11, 2001, events and the steady influx and dispersion of unauthorized migrants amid the strong economy of the mid-decade added to public demands for action. Leaders in Congress seized this challenge beginning in 2005.

### Criminalization: An Effort to Control the Legislative Debate

In late 2005, the House of Representatives passed H.R. 4437, an enforcement-focused bill. The bill passed the House 239–182, with most of the support coming from Republican members. The bill's primary sponsor, Colorado representative Tom Tancredo, the chair of the House Immigration Reform Caucus, used his advocacy of the bill as the foundation for unsuccessful runs for the Republican nomination for the presidency in 2008 and the Colorado governorship in 2010.

The provisions of the bill were heavy on criminalization and enforcement, including

- Criminalization of unauthorized status in the United States. (This is currently a civil violation rather than a criminal offense.)
- Criminalization of providing assistance to unauthorized immigrants. ("Assistance" would include transporting unauthorized immigrants or concealing them from authorities.)
- An eighteen-month deadline for the Department of Homeland Security to obtain "operational control" over US borders.
- Authorization for the construction of a double security fence along highly trafficked parts of the US-Mexico border.
- Requiring apprehended unauthorized immigrants to be held in custody until their deportation hearings (in place of the more common policy of releasing unauthorized immigrants without criminal records on bond until their hearings).
- Reassigning deportation reviews of unauthorized, non-Mexican immigrants from immigration judges to non-judicial staff persons of Immigration and Customs Enforcement (ICE).
- Requiring that employers screen all new employees through a Homeland Security database of work eligibility within two years of the law's enactment.
- Eliminating the Diversity Visa program.
- Withholding federal funding for state and local police forces in jurisdictions that maintain policies that prevent their police forces from reporting unauthorized immigrants or working with federal authorities on immigration matters.

This bill was an effort by the House of Representatives to shift the legislative debate in a more restrictive direction and to ensure that the more inclusive Senate did not set the terms of the debate. Although the bill could be seen as a legitimate response from the House of Representatives to the steadily increasing numbers of unauthorized immigrants in the United States, few expected the bill to become law. Some parts of the legislation would have been impossible to implement and legislative leaders realized that the Senate would insist on more balance in any legislation it considered. As Arizona Republican representative Jim Kolbe observed, "after we pass this, we send it off to the Senate and that's the end of it" (*Congressional*

*Quarterly* 2006). Kolbe was correct from a legislative perspective. The bill did not receive Senate approval and did not become law. When the Senate took up immigration reform in 2006, it did not approve the House bill or even include many of its provisions in the version considered by the Senate. However, that was hardly "the end of it." The House bill engendered a massive public response, perhaps the largest set of public protests that the nation had ever seen. What was even more surprising about these protests is that many who took part were themselves immigrants and in many cases unauthorized immigrants, a group in US society that is least able to risk challenging authority.

### The 2006 Protests and Congressional (In)Action in 2006 and 2007

The 2006 immigrant rights protests were unprecedented in their scope. Estimates suggest that these marches included as many as five million people who marched in more than 150 cities (Woodrow Wilson Center for Scholars 2007). The protests were spurred in large part by H.R. 4437, which would have criminalized unauthorized status, thus ensuring that any unauthorized immigrant convicted of this new crime would *never* be able to immigrate legally. The consequences were felt not just by unauthorized immigrants but also by family members who are in many cases legal immigrants or even US citizens (many immigrant households include immigrants in various legal statuses). The provisions criminalizing assistance to unauthorized immigrants would have subjected legal immigrants and US citizens to prosecution (and possible deportation) for helping family members or for simply housing them.

Immigrants and their family members were not the only ones with concerns about H.R. 4437, though they made up the vast majority of those who protested in the streets in 2006. Employers and immigrant advocates realized how unlikely it was that the government would be able to develop the database of eligible workers within the two-year window established in the bill. The prototype of the database (what would ultimately become E-Verify, discussed later) was rife with errors and had particular difficulty with ethnic names, often failing to identify legal workers accurately because of alternate spellings of names. Civil libertarians objected to the notion of a national record of all citizens and permanent residents that could be abused for other purposes. The Department of Homeland Security did not have detention space to hold all immigrants awaiting deportation hearings. The goal of "operational control" of the border seemed far-fetched, even to its proponents, and was left largely undefined in the bill. Few in Washington—including Republican leaders in the House of Representatives who saw H.R. 4437 as a platform on which Republicans could run in 2006, rather than as a serious legislative proposal—expected this bill to become law. Immigrant communities, however, could not be so certain that the bill would not pass. They needed to ensure that criminalization of unauthorized status was taken out of the political debate.

How did this fear among immigrants and their families translate into such massive protests? This national mobilization was made possible by a new organizational coalition that included some traditional immigrant rights organizations but added new institutional players: state federations of immigrant hometown associations, service sector unions, ethnic radio, and some religious organizations that had not previously been involved in immigrant organizing (Bada, Fox, and Selee 2006; Benjamin-Alvarado, DeSipio, and Montoya-Kirk 2009; Pallares and Flores-González 2010; Voss and Bloemraad 2011). These groups cooperated to send a common message to immigrant populations nationwide: action needed to be taken immediately, Congress would listen, and activism would be safe so long as protests were peaceful and patriotic. The lesson of early protests, beginning in March 2006, served as a model for later and larger protests that continued until May. Almost all 2006 protests were family affairs, with several generations of families attending. They were peaceful and the dominant patriotic image was of the US flag and not images from immigrant-sending countries. At the larger protests, the message was sent to wear white, as it was a nonthreatening color. Most of the protestors were Latino, though large urban areas saw somewhat more multicultural participants. In the largest cities, the immigrants' rights protestors received explicit and verbal encouragement from local political leaders (Barreto, Manzano, Ramírez, and Rim 2009).

The organizational efforts ensured widespread participation, and protestors achieved their short-term goal of blocking the enactment of H.R. 4437 and its criminalization of unauthorized status. As the protests were taking place, House Republican leaders publicly backed away from this most contentious aspect of the law. They had been privately circumspect about criminalization for months, but the rank-and-file members of the Republican caucus were much more committed. The marches also shaped the behavior of Democratic members of Congress. They began speaking up on behalf of immigrants' rights and proposing policy alternatives to the House of Representatives' focus on enforcement, such as legalization of unauthorized immigrants. Up until the marches, Democrats preferred to allow immigration policy to divide Republicans and to make them appear more radical. Thus, the marches succeeded in removing criminalization from the political debate for several years. At the national level, talk of criminalization has not been heard since, but in 2010, Arizona resurrected criminalization as an issue on the state level.

The 2006 protests and, more broadly, public concern about the tenor of the House proposals spurred the Senate to seek a more comprehensive solution to the nation's immigration and immigrant incorporation policies. A bipartisan coalition in the Senate passed more inclusive legislation that explicitly rejected the criminalization provisions of the House legislation and provided, among other things, for several paths to permanent residence for the unauthorized. For unauthorized immigrants who had been residing in the United States since April 2001, S. 2611 allowed for an "earned adjustment" to legal status. Immigrants applying under this provision would have to work in the United States for six years after the bill's enactment, pass a background check, pay back taxes, learn civics and English, and pay a $2,000 fine. For unauthorized immigrants who came to the United States after April 2001, S. 2611 would have allowed for a three-year deferred mandatory departure status, at the end of which the formerly undocumented immigrants could apply for permanent resident status. They would be subject to the same requirements as the applicants who had been residing in the United States longer. S. 2611 would also have allowed up to 200,000 guest workers to enter the country annually, initially with three-year temporary visas. After being present (and working) in the United States for four years (and after having renewed their temporary visas once), guest workers would have the opportunity to establish permanent residence (opportunities that were narrowed somewhat during floor debates on the bill).

However, like the House bill, S. 2611 failed to become law. The bipartisan coalition that had proposed S. 2611 held firm and it passed the Senate 62–36 with only minor amendments. The supporters included twenty-three Republicans and most Senate Democrats. The House held firm on their bill, H.R. 4437 (and tapped popular sentiment to add to the border enforcement provisions), leading to a stalemate that prevented any legislation from passing in 2006. President Bush largely stayed out of the debate, in part to protect Republican candidates in the 2006 election, but all indications were that he would sign a bill similar to the legislation passed in the Senate. House leaders not only refused to engage in a deliberation with the Senate, they sought to use immigration and their enforcement-focused strategies to assist party candidates in the fall elections.

As the election neared, Republican leaders in both houses of Congress (including supporters of the more inclusionary bill in the Senate and the exclusionary bill in the House) realized that they needed to pass some immigration legislation focused on border enforcement. The early indications were that the Republicans would lose their legislative majorities in the 2006 elections. Each house broke up its bills into smaller pieces. The only one of these to pass both houses was Pub. L. 109-367, which authorized a seven-hundred-mile fence on the southern border of the United States and added staffing to the Border Patrol. This legislation passed overwhelmingly in each house: 80–19 in the Senate and 283–138 in the House of Representatives. Each house later supported appropriations legislation to pay the cost of building the border fence, which was largely complete by 2009.

The election of Democratic House and Senate majorities in the 2006 midterm elections raised expectations that Congress would be able to pass a comprehensive immigration bill in 2007 (and well enough in advance of the 2008 races to insulate some members from their votes). Congressional leaders, figuring that the debate in the House of Representatives would likely be more contentious, scheduled debates on immigration legislation first in the Senate. S. 1348 was the result of ongoing conversations between Democratic and Republican senators and representatives of the Bush administration. Overall, S. 1348 was considerably more restrictive, and arguably proposed more fundamental changes to the structure of US immigration law than the 2006 Senate bill. Senate leaders hoped that this would allow for a compromise that would bring in moderate Republican votes in both the House and the Senate.

Like the 2006 Senate bill, S. 1348 included provisions for legalization of unauthorized immigrants. Any legalization, however, would be put on hold until the newly legislated enforcement provisions were in place. These enforcement provisions included completing at least 370 miles of border fence (out of the approximately 700 miles that was to be built), developing a fraud-proof system to verify worker eligibility, and doubling the size of the Border Patrol. In S. 1348, access to legalization was also more restrictive than in the 2006 bill. Once the new border enforcement provisions were in place, unauthorized immigrants who had been residing in the United States since January 1, 2007, would be eligible for legalization, and would have one year to register with the government. They could apply for a temporary visa that would last for eight years, at which point they could apply for permanent residence. During this period, they could work legally in the United States but couldn't travel internationally. Each of these transitions would require the payment of fees and fines that would amount to several thousand dollars per immigrant. To attain legal permanent resident status, applicants would need to demonstrate that they could speak English. This legislation, then, would require a wait of at least fourteen years (and, most likely, several years more) for an unauthorized immigrant to be eligible for application for naturalization. S. 1348 also provided initially for at least 400,000 temporary worker visas that would allow guest workers to work in all parts of the economy. Unlike under the 2006 Senate bill, these temporary workers would not have a direct path to permanent residence at the end of their service as guest workers and they would have to return to their countries of origin.

The 2007 Senate bill also included more profound changes to the structure of US immigration. If it had passed, it would have changed the allocation of visas for immigration to permanent residence to a system that would better reward education, job skills, and English-speaking ability, and reduce the importance of family ties to US citizens and permanent residents. It would have created a "point system" for the award of visas that would assign a specific number of points for each of these desired traits (education, English-speaking ability, etc.). Each year, the government would set a minimum threshold for the number of points necessary to obtain a visa, which would create the potential for annual raising or lowering of the number of immigrants, based on national economic needs. Family connections to a US citizen or permanent resident would likely no longer suffice to qualify a potential migrant for a visa. This would represent a significant change in the structure of immigration to permanent residence established in the 1965 Immigration and Naturalization Act, but this point was largely neglected in the public awareness or media discussion of S. 1348.

Ultimately, the bill failed to overcome a *filibuster* (the legislative rule in the United States Senate that allows for unlimited debate on a bill, thus postponing a vote on the bill). The vote in favor of *cloture* (a vote of sixty members of the Senate to end a filibuster) was just forty-six votes, however, suggesting that even in a purely majoritarian system, the bill was facing an uphill struggle in the Senate (not to mention the House, where it would have faced an even more difficult path). Senators proposed 351 amendments to the bill, many of which were designed to reduce the likelihood of Senate passage.

One interesting fact revealed by these votes on cloture and on the amendments was that the Senate had changed in the year between 2006 and 2007. In simple partisan terms, the Senate should have become more receptive to comprehensive immigration reform. By gaining six seats, the Democrats gained control of the body with a one-seat majority. Certainly, immigration is not a strictly partisan issue, and the Senate votes on the 2006 immigration bill were not strictly partisan. Approximately 40 percent of Senate Republicans had voted for the passage of S. 2611 in 2006 (and several Democrats voted against the bill). The 2006 election, however, made support for inclusive immigration legislation riskier for all senators and particularly for Republicans. Newly elected Democratic and Republican senators, who had faced the electorate during the 2006 immigration debates, were consistently more resistant to legalization and guest worker provisions of S. 1348 than were the senators elected in earlier years (DeSipio 2011). Of equal importance, Senate Republicans largely moved away from support of the bill and in many cases into outright opposition. The most prominent of these cases was one of the bill's former lead cosponsors, Senator John McCain of Arizona, who in preparation for his 2008 presidential run appeared to oppose his own bill as often as he supported it, particularly as it became evident that he would not be able to count on support from many of his fellow Republicans.

A comprehensive immigration bill was never considered by the House of Representatives in 2007. Although the Democrats had also gained the majority in the House as a result of the 2006 elections, Democratic leaders knew that they could not count on support for a comprehensive bill from many moderate Democrats (including many of the Democratic surprise winners in the 2006 election) and that few Republicans would cross party lines to support a comprehensive immigration bill. Liberal Democrats were very resistant to the guest worker provisions that did not ensure a path to permanent residence but instead placed a high number of barriers to legalization for the unauthorized. Considering that President Bush supported the bill, this failure to achieve any sort of bipartisanship in either the House or the Senate indicated the low degree of presidential influence at this late stage of his administration.

After the comprehensive bill failed to overcome filibuster, supporters of immigration reform tried to divide the bill to further its most popular pieces as separate legislation, such as a provision to allow minor children who had joined their parents in unauthorized migration to legalize if they attended college or joined the military for two years, as well as a guest worker provision for agriculture. This first of these small pieces of legislation was known as the Development, Relief, and Education for Alien Minors Act, or DREAM Act. These piecemeal efforts at immigration reform also failed to receive sufficient support to overcome filibuster. After the failure of the cloture vote on the bill to provide legalization for the children of unauthorized immigrants (the DREAM Act), John McCain observed, "we are not going to resolve this issue until 2009. . . . It's a moot point" (*Congressional Quarterly* 2008).

McCain was correct that the 2008 presidential campaign would move immigration out of Congressional debates; he was not so prescient about the likelihood of a debate or resolution in 2009. The absence of immigration reform legislation from the Congressional docket in 2008 can be seen as a tactical calculation by leaders of both parties to remove a controversial issue from debate in an election year. This served members facing reelection bids as well as the presidential candidates whose positions on many controversial aspects of immigration were more similar than different. McCain paid a price in the Republican primaries for his support of immigration reform (which he had cosponsored with Republican nemesis Senator Edward Kennedy of Massachusetts), but he tried to use his past support of the bill, no matter how tepid in 2007, to win Latino votes in the general election.

## Immigration Reform in the Obama Years

With the Obama victory in 2008 and the expansion of Democratic majorities in the House and Senate, immigration reform activists had high expectations for an early debate on a comprehensive immigration reform. This expectation was reinforced by Obama himself during the campaign when he promised in a speech before the League of United Latin American Citizens that immigration reform would be a "top priority" in his first year in office (Hotline on Call 2008). This deadline, however, slipped in the face of other priorities, including health care reform, economic stimulus, and Wall Street reforms, as well as international commitments.

In 2010, as the Democrats were preparing for midterm elections in which substantial Democratic losses were predicted, President Obama and the Democratic Congressional leadership did promise that Congress would take up a comprehensive immigration reform bill in 2010 after the elections, in what is known as the "lame duck" session before the new Congress is sworn in. Lame duck sessions are notoriously poor venues for controversial bills, however, particularly after the party in power has lost a large number of seats, so this commitment was seen more as a political gambit to retain support from Latino voters for Democratic candidates.

Both houses of Congress ultimately did debate an immigration bill, the DREAM Act. The act would have provided permanent residence to young adults who were between the ages of twelve and thirty-five (subsequently lowered to twenty-nine) at the time of the enactment of the law, who had arrived in the United States before the age of sixteen, and who could provide documentation of continuous residence in the United States for at least five consecutive years. To be eligible, these young adults would also have to have graduated from high school in the United States or have earned a General Education Development certificate. Applicants would have to be of good moral character, which covers a number of behaviors, the most important of which is not having been convicted of serious crimes (the specific crimes that would bar eligibility were outlined in the legislation). They would have to pay fees for their applications. Finally, applicants would also have to register with Selective Service (for the military draft).

The House of Representatives passed the DREAM Act. In the Senate, in a near party-line vote, the DREAM Act received fifty-five votes but failed to reach the sixty votes necessary to overcome a Republican-led filibuster. The failure to pass the DREAM Act in the Senate came on a day that otherwise will be remembered for its civil rights accomplishments: the Senate earlier that day repealed the "Don't Ask Don't Tell" prohibition on gays and lesbians serving openly in the US military.

Recognizing that the new Republican-controlled House of Representatives in 2011 would not pursue any comprehensive immigration reform legislation, the Obama administration began to explore regulatory strategies that it could implement without Congressional action. In 2011, it redirected immigration enforcement activities to focus on unauthorized aliens who had committed crimes or who had previously been given a deportation order. The Obama administration justified this change in focus by recognizing that immigration enforcement resources were limited and that the available resources should be focused on unauthorized aliens who posed the greatest risk to society. As part of this policy, the Obama administration asked that pending deportation cases against young adults who would have qualified for the DREAM Act had it passed be reviewed and held in abeyance pending legislative action or regulatory changes (US Citizenship and Immigration Services 2010).

In 2012, using its discretionary powers under the existing immigration law, the Obama administration established a new short-term immigrant visa with work authorization for young adults who would meet the qualifications for the DREAM Act. This program is called Deferred Action for Childhood Arrivals (DACA). Upon review and acceptance of their applications and a $465 fee, DACA recipients are eligible to work in the United States for two years and would not be subject to removal for simply being in the United States without legal status. Initially, their status would expire after this two-year window, so, while offering some short-term protections from deportation and the ability to work legally, this regulatory change simply delayed a decision about their ultimate status in the United States. In 2014, President Obama extended DACA for an additional two years and expanded the populations eligible to apply.

The 2012 DACA did not address the immigration status of younger or older unauthorized immigrants or of young adult unauthorized immigrants who had dropped out of school and had not earned a GED. Although the estimates for the number of immigrants who would be eligible for this policy change varied from 800,000 to 1.4 million, just 581,000 were awarded DACA status in the program's first two years (Migration Policy Institute 2012; US Citizenship and Immigration Services 2014).

President Obama's reelection coalition included large majorities of the Latino and Asian American electorate, a vote sealed by Obama's DACA program and the anti-immigrant tone of the Republican primary. Although the 2012 Republican nominee—former Massachusetts governor Mitt Romney—said little about immigration during the general election campaign, his language from the primary followed him throughout the race. Perhaps most memorable to many immigrants and their advocates was his support for "self-deportation" as a strategy to reduce the number of unauthorized immigrants in the United States. Obama's growing success with minority voters led many leading Republicans to seek to temper the party's strident tone on immigration reform. Perhaps most notable among these was House Speaker John Boehner, who indicated in the days after the election that Congress needed to pass comprehensive immigration reform.

Boehner, however, did not control the House Republican caucus, and a majority of its members continued to block any consideration of a comprehensive immigration bill. Periodically, Boehner indicated that the House would move on immigration, but he was never able to develop a consensus among his caucus on how to approach this issue. Had Boehner really wanted to pass a bill, he could have done so with the Democrats in the House and a minority of the Republican members. This would necessarily have resulted in a more liberal bill than one passed primarily with Republican votes—and would probably have ended the Boehner speakership. Ultimately, Speaker Boehner did not pursue this path.

The Senate was more active on immigration reform at the beginning of Obama's second term, though without the cooperation of the House of Representatives, it was unable to send a bill to the president. In 2013, after several months of bipartisan negotiations by leading senators of both parties (the so-called Gang of Eight), the Senate passed a comprehensive immigration reform modeled on the 2007 Senate bill with added enforcement provisions. The Border Security, Economic Opportunity, and Immigration Modernization Act (S. 744) passed by a vote of 68 to 32; the majority included the votes of fourteen Republicans, which should be seen as a remarkably bipartisan vote in what are very partisan times in Washington.

Like the 2006 and 2007 Senate bills, S. 744 comprehensively addressed a range of immigration issues. It changed the basis for legal immigration away from the standards enacted in 1965; created a new terminal guest worker program that would allow the new guest workers to move from job to job while their guest worker visas were in effect; required all new employees to verify their work eligibility through a national database; provided a path to legal status and US citizenship for many of the 11.7 million unauthorized immigrants in the United States (and a speedier path to legal status for DREAMers); expanded the due process guarantees and right to counsel for immigrants facing deportation; and increased the funding for immigration enforcement. It also included a provision to hold any legalization in abeyance until the new enforcement provisions were in place (see Immigration Policy Center 2013 for a detailed discussion of S. 744's provisions).

How was this bill able to pass (and with fourteen Republican votes)? At the last minute, Senate leaders added a significant enforcement component. This included $46.3 billion in additional spending on immigration enforcement for technology, an additional seven hundred miles of border fencing, and a doubling of the size of the Border Patrol. It is not clear that Congress was willing to appropriate this much additional spending or that it would have had the anticipated effect (nearly half of unauthorized immigrants enter the country legally but then overstay their visas), but this commitment to enforcement offered enough cover for moderate senators of both parties to support the bill. Senators were also aware that were the House to pass an immigration bill, it would undoubtedly be different from the Senate bill, which would necessitate the creation of a conference committee and thus allow for another opportunity to vote on the bill.

But the passage of S. 744 did not spur action by the House of Representatives. Speaker Boehner's interest in passing some legislation was certainly also felt by Republican Party leaders, but this desire to move beyond simply debating the issue of immigration so that the GOP could make some inroads with Latino and Asian American voters was not felt by many of the GOP's rank-and-file members in the House. They had few minority constituents and did not rely on minority votes for reelection. Instead, they had to hold on to the votes of members of the Republican base, who strongly opposed any immigration reform that allows for legalization of unauthorized immigrants.

This message was reinforced for many Republican members of the House in a surprising 2014 Republican primary outcome. In Virginia's Seventh District, Eric Cantor, the House majority leader (the second most powerful position in the House), was defeated by a poorly funded, largely unknown challenger. Among Cantor's weaknesses in the eyes of Republican primary voters was a seeming openness to the DREAM Act, specifically (and not more broadly to comprehensive immigration reform). Cantor's opponent criticized him as supporting "amnesty" for undocumented immigrants and that charge was sufficient to weaken Cantor in a conservative district where he had been repeatedly elected (Kim 2014; Silver 2014). Few Republican incumbents wanted to risk a similar outcome, despite the message they were getting from their party's leadership on the importance of immigration reform to the future of the party.

In the absence of Congressional action, President Obama could do little to address popular demands for immigration reform. Consequently, despite the demands for immigration reform from throughout the country and a willingness by some (such as unions, liberal Democrats, and the business community) to make considerable compromises, Congress remained stalemated, as it has been since at least 2006.

## State Initiatives to Spur Federal Action

The failure of Congress to find the compromises necessary to achieve comprehensive immigration reform did not subdue popular concerns about immigration policy. Immigrants and immigrant advocacy organizations pushed President Obama and the Democratic leadership of the House and Senate to live up to Obama's commitments to pass a comprehensive immigration reform that included a legalization plan. Their advocacy not only focused on the need to reform immigration but also contained an implied threat of dire consequences at the polls for the Democrats if Congress failed to engage the debate.

Although the size of the unauthorized immigrant population declined somewhat in the wake of the economic downturn of 2007, many in America remained concerned about the size of the unauthorized population and the apparent failure of border enforcement initiatives enacted over the previous decade. Immigration debates became much more partisan in this period, with few Republicans willing to focus on any aspect of immigration other than enhanced enforcement.

Business interests continued to seek change. Some were initially tempered in their demands by the weakened economy, but sectors that had traditionally depended on immigrant labor, such as agriculture, light manufacturing, the service sector, and technology industries, continued to press Congress for targeted expansion in immigration. As the economy recovered, business interests increased their demands for more open immigration, particularly for skilled workers and for new guest worker programs. Additionally, there were concerns that immigrants were not adapting to American society quickly enough. Some taking this position simply sought to reduce immigration; others called for state and federal programs to facilitate immigrant incorporation.

With no action on immigration at the federal level, some states began to initiate policy on their own. In 2009, state legislatures passed 333 pieces of legislation related to immigration or immigrant incorporation policy.

This was up from just 32 in 2005 (Gorman 2010). In 2010, forty-five state legislatures considered bills on immigration, most of them further restricting the rights of immigrants or beefing up state enforcement of federal immigration laws. The most controversial of these was Arizona's S.B. 1070, which directly challenged what had traditionally been a federal prerogative to enforce immigration laws.

S.B. 1070 criminalized alien presence in Arizona for immigrants without federal immigration documents. To enforce this provision, it obligated all state and local police in Arizona to verify the status of immigrants (and, arguably, potential immigrants) during a "lawful stop, detention, or arrest made by a law enforcement official." In addition, S.B. 1070 criminalized the hiring of unauthorized aliens from a stopped vehicle so as to prevent the hiring of day laborers. Like H.R. 4437 (the 2005 immigration bill passed in the House of Representatives), Arizona S.B. 1070 also criminalized the following: (1) encouraging or inducing unauthorized migration, (2) giving shelter to unauthorized migrants, and (3) transporting or attempting to transport unauthorized migrants. Federal law already prohibits encouraging unauthorized migration, but S.B. 1070 went further by criminalizing the "harboring" of unauthorized aliens. These provisions meant that the family members of unauthorized immigrants and advocacy organizations protecting the rights of unauthorized immigrants could potentially have been categorized as criminals.

S.B. 1070 can be seen as a direct descendant of H.R. 4437, with a key difference. States, in this case Arizona, have law enforcement resources absent at the federal level, so if implemented, the effects would potentially be felt immediately in immigrant communities. It also placed state and local police at the center of national immigration policy enforcement. It was, in part, these provisions that caused the federal courts to suspend the implementation of the Arizona law during a period of review of the law by the courts.

The Arizona legislature overwhelmingly passed S.B. 1070, along largely partisan lines. The Republican governor of the state—Jan Brewer—who was running for election in 2010, signed the bill into law and became one of its chief advocates in the media. The bill proved immediately controversial. Advocates saw it as a concrete and necessary step to control unauthorized migration, given the failure of the federal government to meet its responsibilities in managing immigration. Although proponents recognized the dangers in the requirement that police seek documents from

potential unauthorized immigrants, they believed that with proper training of police, racial profiling could be controlled. Aside from the specifics
of the bill, its advocates understood its political importance. Republican
Party leaders and candidates saw the bill as a rich opportunity to distinguish themselves from Obama and the Democrats.

Opponents of the bill, on the other hand, raised constitutional as well
as practical concerns (Meissner and Ziglar 2010). Article I of the US Constitution specifies the legislative powers of Congress. Among these explicitly enumerated powers is establishing "a uniform rule of naturalization,"
thus placing responsibility for naturalization in the hands of the federal
government. When the Constitution was ratified, there was no sense that
immigration could be regulated (see Chapter 2), but the courts have interpreted Congress's constitutionally delegated power over naturalization
as applying to immigration policy as well. Opponents of the Arizona law
were also concerned that racial profiling would be the only possible outcome of the bill, regardless of police training. Police would be unlikely
to ask all Arizonans for evidence of immigrant status or citizenship and,
thus, would focus their questions on Latinos and Asian Americans. This
raised other Constitutional issues of possible violations of the "due process" guaranteed by the Fifth Amendment to the Constitution and "the
equal protection of the laws" guaranteed by the Fourteenth Amendment.

In 2012, the Supreme Court heard the case testing the Arizona law. It
upheld one part of the law and overruled others on both Constitutional
and statutory grounds (Liptak 2012). The Court upheld the central provision of the law that allowed state and local police to request evidence of
legal presence in the United States. The Court majority saw this provision
as commensurate with national law and not an effort to create state-level
immigration laws. However, it also recognized that the implementation
of this provision could later be challenged in light of evidence that these
provisions are being implemented in a discriminatory manner. The Court
rejected the parts of the law that subjected unauthorized aliens to criminal penalties for their presence in Arizona or for failing to report their
status to the federal government (*Arizona et al. v. United States* 2012). The
Court majority saw these provisions as efforts to create state-level immigration law that went further than federal law.

The Supreme Court's partial resolution of the Constitutional questions
raised by S.B. 1070 should not, however, obscure the political and policy
questions that pushed Arizona to pass such legislation in the first place.

The concern and anger expressed by many Arizonans over unauthorized immigrants, which were then endorsed by the state legislature in its passing of S.B. 1070, grew from the steady failure of the federal government to act on its constitutional authority to enact needed reforms to US immigration policy. Opponents of S.B. 1070 reacted quickly, challenging the legislation and winning a partial victory in the Supreme Court, but they, too, would have preferred to focus their energies on a national resolution of weaknesses in immigration and immigrant incorporation policies. All involved in the debate were well aware that Arizona's effort was simply the first of many state-level reforms that would need to be contested in the courts until Congress offered a more comprehensive resolution of immigration and immigrant incorporation issues. In fact, in the years between Arizona's passage of S.B. 1070 and the Supreme Court's ruling, five additional states passed laws modeled on Arizona's, and several more states have debated enacting similar legislation (we discuss these state efforts in greater depth in Chapter 3).

Although less common, some states sought to pressure federal action by *expanding* the rights of unauthorized immigrants. The most common of these state-level efforts were to offer driver's licenses to unauthorized immigrants and to provide in-state college tuition (and, in fewer cases, state financial aid) to unauthorized immigrants who had graduated from high schools in the state. Each of these initiatives proved very controversial, even in states with strong Democratic legislative majorities.

## "Comprehensive" Immigration Reform: What Does This Entail?

What might comprehensive immigration reform look like, and what might it take to achieve it (de la Garza 2011; Tichenor and Rosenblum 2012)? To be truly comprehensive, immigration reform would require that Congress address each of the following issues:

- Redesigning the rules for immigration to permanent residence in order to meet the labor needs of sectors of the economy most dependent on immigrant labor.
- Guaranteeing the labor rights of immigrants, including the right to organize.
- Regulating more rigorously the flow of unauthorized migration.

- Legalizing some (or many or most) of the unauthorized immigrants resident in the United States at the time of the law's passage.
- Protecting the civil and human rights of immigrants.
- Ensuring that national security needs and global interests are met through US immigration and immigrant incorporation policies.
- Restructuring fiscal policy so that costs of immigration are shared equitably by local, state, and federal authorities.
- Developing programs to ensure that immigrants—particularly immigrants to permanent residence and any newly legalized immigrants—have the training and encouragement needed to speed their entry and incorporation into US society.

Each of these issues was addressed by Congress in its failed efforts to reform immigration between 2005 and 2007. Compromise will need to be reached in each before US immigration policy can be reformed in a meaningful way.

## Meeting the Labor Needs of the US Economy

At its core, US immigration policy has always been designed to ensure that the nation's economy will grow (Zolberg 2006). Relative to other advanced democracies, the United States has always had a relatively low people-to-land ratio and, consequently, has needed labor from abroad to ensure that its economy continues to grow. In 2007, the United States had approximately 27 people per square kilometer of land area (United Nations 2010b). For purposes of comparison, globally there are approximately 42 people per square kilometer, and most of the other advanced democracies against which the United States competes economically have a higher share of people in their territories. Germany, for example, has 233 people per kilometer and the United Kingdom has 244. Of the advanced democracies, only the countries that also receive large shares of immigrants have lower population densities than the United States, including Canada (3.2 per km), Australia (2.5 per km), and New Zealand (15 per km).

Immigration policy, however, is not designed simply to increase the number of people in the country but to ensure that the people who are added to the country are those most needed to build the economy. Historically, this has meant entrepreneurs and laborers, including agricultural workers. Today, the most desired immigrant would have higher levels of education or training and, ideally, advanced technical skills. In this search for skilled migrants, the United States competes with many other nations, some of which are much more aggressive in recruiting the most skilled or richest immigrants.

The 1965 immigration law, however, is not necessarily designed to ensure that the United States makes immigration opportunities available to the immigrants who would most benefit the US economy. Under current law, approximately one-third of immigrants who gain permanent residence attain eligibility to immigrate through employment-based visas because they have skills that are certified by the US Department of Labor to be in short supply within the American workforce. Most of the remaining two-thirds of visas are awarded to close family members (parent, child, or spouse) of a US citizen or permanent resident. These "family preference" visas often end up going to lower-skilled workers and their immediate family members.

Throughout the nation's history, immigration practices and rules have always privileged some immigrants and discouraged or prohibited others. It seems unlikely that the current balance between employment- and family-based visas will remain in the future. This is certainly not to say that only workers in critical industries are likely to be offered admission in the future; the nation has long realized that unless family members are also admitted, immigrants will not come. Comprehensive immigration reform, however, will likely privilege skilled migrants over unskilled migrants more than the current law does.

A small share of visas (up to 50,000 annually) are awarded through the Diversity Immigrant Visa Program (DV program), an international mail lottery open to residents of countries "other than the principal sources of current immigration to the United States" (see http://travel .state.gov/content/dam/visas/DV_2014_Instructions.pdf for further information on this program). Applicants may apply once each year; visas are awarded to applicants selected randomly by a computer program. In 2014, eligibility included residents of all countries other than Bangladesh, Brazil, Canada, China (mainland-born, excluding Hong Kong, Macau, and Taiwan), Colombia, the Dominican Republic, Ecuador, El Salvador, Haiti, India, Jamaica, Mexico, Pakistan, Peru, the Philippines, South Korea, the United Kingdom (except Northern Ireland) and its dependent territories, and Vietnam, because each of these countries had sent more than 50,000 immigrants to the United States between 2009 and 2013. Applicants for these visas must have either a high school degree or two years of work experience in the previous five years in a job that requires at least two years of training experience to perform. This program is controversial, because it does not recruit the most highly skilled immigrants and because the recently immigrated permanent residents and US citizens from this program then seek immigration for their eligible relatives, putting further pressure on the demand for family preference immigration visas. The DV program may well be sacrificed as part of a more comprehensive reform.

When the US Senate debated immigration in 2007, it looked to replace this mixture of skill-, employment-, and family-based visas, as well as diversity visas, with a point system to measure relative eligibility to immigrate to the United States. However, because Senate debates in 2007 did not delve deeply into this proposal, it is not possible to present a concrete sense of how a point system would replace the current system. Canada uses a point system for its immigration program, allocating some points for family connections to Canada, but more points for higher education, for English- or French-language skills, and for specific job skills (Reitz 2004). A comparable system implemented in the United States might give more points for family connections than Canada does simply because the United States receives a higher number of immigrants each year. But it is likely that a reform of US immigration laws will increasingly favor skilled immigrants and their family members over less skilled immigrants, and favor immigrants with traits that facilitate quick incorporation, such as English-language skills, over immigrants without those traits. Another advantage of a point system is that the number of points for immigration eligibility can be adjusted in accord with overall economic conditions; in today's system, however, immigration levels are largely unrelated to the broader economy.

Employers will argue that this allocation system is simply not sensitive enough to respond to their needs for the kinds of labor unavailable in the US workforce, particularly low-skill labor. These claims, and the strong influences that US corporations can have on Congress, have spurred the establishment of the various short-term labor programs that admitted 3 million guest workers to the United States in 2012. These programs targeted specific industries, including agriculture and agriculture processing, technology, seasonal employers, and child care. As part of immigration reform debates, it is likely that employers will seek broader authority to hire workers for set periods of time. However, guest workers would not necessarily have the guarantee of staying in the United States after their guest status ends. In the 2006 debate in Congress, guest worker status was a precursor to a legal and, ultimately, permanent status, but the 2007 and 2013 debates included a guest status that did not necessarily lead to permanent status. Aside from what the law would say, there is considerable evidence that previous guest worker programs in both the United States and Europe have created increased opportunities for unauthorized migration after the end of the guest worker period (Castles, with Booth and Wallace 1984; Castles 1985; Calavita 1992). Organized labor in the United States has traditionally opposed new guest worker programs, particularly guest worker programs that do not limit the workers to specific industries. Interestingly, in 2013, the American Federation of Labor indicated its openness to a guest worker program that does not lead to legal status as part of a comprehensive immigration reform as long as protections for American workers are built into the bill.

Each of these potential reforms to the structure of legal immigration will add pressure to other components of comprehensive immigration reform. For example, the DV program was designed in part to offer a path to legal status for unauthorized Irish immigrants in the United States in 1990 (a constituency of particular importance to Senator Ted Kennedy of Massachusetts who, at the time of the bill's passage, was the leading advocate of immigration reform among the Senate Democrats). Now that the program has been in place for twenty years, it has allowed for immigration from many parts of the world that did not previously send immigrants to the United States. However, the DV immigrants now expect that they will be able to bring over their immediate relatives, joining the group of immigrants from the "traditional" countries who have been waiting many years for the opportunity to unify their families—and thereby increasing the number of requests for family-based visas. This, in addition to any new restrictions immigration reform might place on family-based visas, will add to the incentives for family members who cannot get a legal immigrant visa to migrate without authorization. Similarly, guest worker programs might provide temporary migration opportunities for workers who do not have the skills sought in a newly designed visa allocation system. After a few years in the United States, temporary workers might come to believe—as have previous generations of temporary workers—that they would be able to stay and work in the United States even without legal status. And employers have historically demonstrated that they are more than willing to continue to hire former guest workers with whom they have worked, even after the workers' legal status has ended.

Substantial reforms in legal immigration or establishment of new guest worker programs will likely face strong opposition in the general public due to the perception that immigration will thereby increase. As we discuss in Chapter 3, the American public is generally divided on the question of whether immigration should be maintained at current levels or should decrease. Few, however, support increases in immigration. So, as Congress searches for reforms to meet national labor needs, it will need to frame those reforms in terms of maintaining current immigration levels and establishing greater control over immigration so that immigrants contribute to national economic growth but don't compete with native workers.

## New Regulation and Enforcement to Reduce or Eliminate Future Unauthorized Migration

To ensure popular support for any new immigration legislation, a key element will need to be a convincing assurance that the proposed reform will slow or stop future unauthorized migration and prevent the need for a legalization program in the future. In this, new legislation will not be any different from other major immigration legislation passed since the concept of unauthorized migration first appeared early in the 1900s. With successive failures to control unauthorized migration, it has become ever more difficult for Congress to convince the public that enforcement will work.

This is the area of immigration policy that Congress and the executive branch have been most able to find agreement on over the past two decades. Enforcement along the US-Mexico border has increased considerably, in terms of both technology and personnel. Based on legislation passed in 2006, a wall has been built along approximately one-third of the US southern border. Much of the rest of the border relies on a "virtual" fence that marries belowground, ground-level, and aerial surveillance technologies. These technologies are supported through a dramatic increase in personnel along the border. Beginning in the early 1990s, each successive Congress has added to the funding and staffing for the Border Patrol. Staffing has increased from approximately 4,500 Border Patrol agents in 1990 to more than 21,000 in 2013 (Meissner and Kerwin 2009).

Funding for the Border Patrol more than doubled between 2004 and 2014 from approximately $6 billion to nearly $12.9 billion.

The federal government has also focused on interior enforcement, though with less intensity than its efforts along the border. The Bush administration pursued raids against likely employers of large numbers of unauthorized immigrants (Camayd-Freixas 2013). The Obama administration shifted away from raids at employment sites to a twin policy of verifying employer records of employee work eligibility and pursuing unauthorized immigrants convicted of minor crimes (immigrants who were convicted of major crimes had always been deported). These efforts by the Obama administration resulted in an average of 400,000 deportations annually through its first five years in office, which is an increase over the levels from the last year of the Bush administration policies (Horsley 2010; Simanski and Sapp 2012). Both the Bush and Obama administrations also developed an employer-focused employment verification technology—E-Verify—which is designed to offer a comprehensive database of US citizens, permanent residents, and others eligible to work in the United States. Although this technology has yet to prove sufficiently reliable to mandate its use for all workers newly hired by employers nationwide, some states are requiring that businesses use E-Verify as part of the process to verify their employees' work eligibility (Preston 2009).

Despite this huge investment in resources, staffing, and technology, unauthorized immigrants and the businesses that seek to employ them have proven resilient. Until the 2007 economic downturn slowed demand for immigrant labor, the pool of unauthorized immigrants grew by about 500,000 annually. In part, this growth in unauthorized migration, at least until the economic downturn, reflected a failure to focus enforcement resources effectively. The best estimates suggest that as many as half of long-term unauthorized migrants enter the United States legally on short-term visas (such as tourist, student, or work visas) and then overstay their visas. The United States does not monitor all emigration, so it does not necessarily know when many short-term immigrants leave the country. Most enforcement resources are targeted at the border and not on interior enforcement that could identify visa overstayers. This is partly due to Congressional and popular pressure to focus on the perceived problem at the border. But even the resources dedicated to the border have not proved effective at deterring unauthorized migration. Instead, rather than simply deciding not to migrate to the United States, unauthorized migrants are crossing in more distant and more dangerous locations (Cornelius and Lewis 2007). Once in the United States, unauthorized migrants are not returning home, so as not to have to cross the border again, ensuring that the "permanent" unauthorized population grew more rapidly in the 2000s even as enforcement efforts grew.

We can assume that as part of any future comprehensive immigration reform Congress and the executive branch will continue to seek technological solutions to control future unauthorized migration. Eventually, however, policy strategies in this arena may also directly involve native-born and naturalized citizens—something that Congress has been unwilling to consider in the past. Specifically, national concerns about immigration may force a debate about developing a non-counterfeitable national identification card and requiring its use for certain activities, such as starting a new job. Civil libertarians and ethnic advocates would probably oppose such a solution, but the availability of such a resource would reduce the ability of employers to claim that they were unaware that a specific worker was not eligible for employment. Many in the business sector would likely also oppose the requirement of such an identification card. The business community would criticize the cost to business of having to rely on a government database prior to all hiring, and would express concern that they would not be able to hire staff quickly to meet short-term business needs.

Finally, debates about appropriate strategies to restrict new unauthorized migration would need to address the role of guest workers in the United States and the likelihood that guest workers would return to the countries of origin at the end of their labor service. Over the past thirty years, Congress has enacted several targeted guest worker programs and there is increased demand to expand the programs. Congress may well accede to this request as part of a comprehensive reform and sell this reform to the public as a strategy to control unauthorized migration—President George W. Bush made this argument in both 2001 and 2004. Without effective controls on unauthorized workers, however, Congress would simply create a longer-term problem, because guest workers and their employers tend not to want to sever the relationship at the end of the contract, which contributes to unauthorized migration.

Organized labor has traditionally opposed any program that allows guest workers to work in any sector, though this position may be in flux as unions increasingly represent unauthorized immigrants who seek legal status as part of a comprehensive immigration reform. Though not as vociferous as organized labor, ethnic advocacy organizations also tend to oppose these programs, unless the proposed programs end in a path to permanent residence and provide the guest workers with the protection of US labor laws. Ultimately, popular concerns about the long-term plans of guest workers will probably limit the viability of guest worker programs as a policy option, whether the programs are for limited terms only or provide a path to permanent residence.

### Legalization of Unauthorized Immigrants in the United States

Although considerably more controversial than increased enforcement of US immigration law, a path to immigrant legalization and citizenship is necessary in any comprehensive immigration reform bill. This is true for political reasons, as no reform can pass without the votes of liberal Democrats, who will likely support only a bill that includes some form of legalization, but also because it would reflect the generally inclusive nature of US immigration policy. When the United States has previously faced large numbers of unauthorized immigrants, it has created a path to legal status. This happened in the 1920s, 1940s, 1950s, and 1980s.

What would legalization look like as part of a comprehensive immigration bill? As the 2006 and 2007 Senate debates should suggest, there is no clear answer to this question. The comprehensiveness and viability of a new legalization program would depend on several factors:

- The number of years of residence Congress would require for legalization of immigrants, and the standards for what would constitute continuous residence. For example, would short visits to their countries of origin eliminate eligibility?
- The skills that immigrants would need in order to be eligible for legalization, such as English-language abilities or knowledge of civics. Would applicants have to possess these skills at the time of application or could they be pursuing them at the time of application?
- The expectations for legalizing immigrants, such as the number of years of employment or tax records that would need to be

provided as part of the application. Could gaps in these records, such as failure to have paid taxes in some years, be remedied retroactively prior to the legalization application?

- The administrative standards for legalizing immigrants. Will would-be immigrants need to return to their countries of origin in order to obtain a visa? If so, will all family members need to return or just the head of household?
- The status of legalizing immigrants. Would there be a period of temporary residence (with work and border crossing eligibility) prior to attaining permanent resident status? If so, how long would this "temporary" status last?
- The cost of applying for temporary residence and ultimately permanent residence. Would this cost simply be an application fee or would there be fines for previously violating the law? Would these fees and fines apply to all family members or just to adults?
- Are all unauthorized immigrants applying for legalization treated the same or are there faster paths for some unauthorized immigrants, such as the DREAMers?

As politically necessary as legalization is to comprehensive immigration reform, it is highly controversial in the media and among the general public. Tarred as a "path to citizenship" and "amnesty," its critics fail to note the many steps that immigrants would need to go through to earn permanent residence, let alone citizenship. Had the 2007 or 2013 Senate bill become law, for example, it would have taken an unauthorized immigrant at least fourteen years to be eligible to naturalize as a US citizen.

The American public has not formed a cohesive opinion on legalization and reacts differently depending on how such a program is discussed. The majority of Americans oppose "amnesty" but support an earned path to legal immigration for long-term unauthorized immigrants. Congress will need to employ finesse in designing and marketing this area of comprehensive immigration reform, because any new immigration bill is unlikely to pass unless it gives a sizeable share of today's unauthorized immigrants the opportunity for legalization and a path toward US citizenship. As mentioned previously, liberal Democrats and ethnic advocates will likely support only a bill that includes legalization, to balance what will likely be added enforcement and changes to the allocation of legal resident visas.

## Ensuring That Immigration and Immigrant Incorporation Policies Meet US National Security Needs and Global Interests

In the period since World War II, US immigration policy has needed to serve American geopolitical interests as well as meet national labor needs. Most important, US immigration law and practices need to deal with refugees and asylees, both to meet US treaty obligations and to promote US relationships abroad. However, these geopolitical interests have never been central to immigration policymaking and are frequently neglected by policymakers and legislators. In 2012, for example, the United States admitted approximately 76,000 refugees and asylees to permanent residence, which is only around 6.9 percent of all immigrants. Although asylum policy likely will not be as central to the immigration debates as the issues of meeting national labor needs, enhancing enforcement mechanisms, and legalizing unauthorized immigrants, it will nevertheless still need to be part of the discussion.

We discuss asylum in greater depth in Chapter 2, but for now, it is important to note that, like most developed countries, the United States is hesitant to admit large numbers of refugees. Historically, the United States has used refugee admissions to reward political migrants from countries that the United States had once supported, but that had seen a change in government that made them more opposed to US interests (such as Cuba and Vietnam in the 1970s, or Nicaragua in the 1980s). In contrast, it has resisted admitting refugees from governments allied to the United States (El Salvador in the 1980s and 1990s, or Haiti in the 1990s). Comprehensive immigration reform would include asylum policies that place less emphasis on the political connections of refugees and more emphasis on their fear of persecution, which is the standard used by the United Nations.

Immigration policy has also increasingly been subject to concerns about US national security (Givens, Freeman, and Leal 2009). This was made particularly apparent to the American public after the events of September 11, 2001, when it was revealed that each of the hijackers had entered the United States as a legal, but temporary, visitor, and that most of them had overstayed their visas. Since 9/11, much more attention has been paid to the political loyalty and organizational connections of immigrants to the United States. Undoubtedly, this attentiveness would continue whether there is comprehensive immigration reform or not.

What is changing, though, is the range of beliefs and organizational loyalties that would put an immigrant at legal risk once in the United States. Loyalty to a foreign government with whom the United States is at odds has long been prohibited in US law (and can lead to denaturalization), but the United States is increasingly subjecting an immigrant's organizational attachments and beliefs to scrutiny. Should having organizational ties and beliefs deemed contrary to US interests become prohibited by law, this would reflect a considerable change in America's policy toward its immigrants and naturalized citizens, and one that would raise questions about how effectively the US can monitor belief systems.

All evidence would suggest that the vast majority of permanent residents and naturalized US citizens are loyal to the United States and adopt its civic and political culture willingly and quickly (see Chapters 4 and 5). For only a handful out of the many tens of millions who have immigrated to the United States in the past four decades is this not necessarily the case. Any permanent resident who violates US law is subject to deportation, but with a few exceptions, this is not the case for naturalized US citizens. Congress has begun to question this distinction and may well reduce some rights of naturalized citizens when it next takes up immigration legislation (Corbin 2010). In a geopolitical environment shaped by a new and poorly understood enemy, it is unlikely that there will be organized voices speaking up to defend the breadth of rights that immigrants and naturalized citizens have traditionally exercised.

### Providing Immigrants with Training and Encouragement Needed for Entry into US Society and the Polity

The question of how well immigrants incorporate into their new homelands is arguably the most important one that an immigrant-receiving society can face. If immigrant incorporation is successful, then the other questions of immigration policy should be of less concern. However, if immigrant incorporation appears to be failing, then the entire policy needs to be reevaluated. One truism of US immigration history is that the success of immigrant incorporation is continually questioned as it is taking place, but in the long run it appears to have succeeded. If we define successful immigrant incorporation as the acculturation of the immigrant generation and the social, political, and economic integration of the children and grandchildren of immigrants, then the available evidence

suggests that incorporation of post-1965 immigrants has been successful (Portes and Rumbaut 2001; Alba and Nee 2003; Bean and Stevens
2003; DeSipio and Uhlaner 2007; Wong et al. 2011; Fraga et al. 2012; Crul
and Mollenkopf 2012). These past successes, however, are no guarantee
of future success. As society grows more complex and the demands on
all residents increase, immigrant-receiving societies must be increasingly
attentive to ensuring that immigrants (and their children) have the skills,
motivation, and resources to thrive.

Historically, the federal government has had few immigrant-specific
policies to ensure the incorporation of immigrants. States, on the other
hand, have been more attentive to the unique policy needs of immigrants.
Programs designed to serve the needs of the native population—most
notably public K–12 and higher education—also served the needs of immigrants and allowed the descendants of immigrants to achieve on levels
comparable to those of natives. Exceptions to this rule certainly occurred,
but the relative disadvantage that immigrants faced in these exceptions
were often the result of intergenerational discrimination in which racial or
ethnic populations were not given equal access to the rights and privileges
enjoyed by native-born citizens (Takaki 1993; Omi and Winant 1994).

This neglect that has traditionally characterized federal government policies will need to change in order to ensure that new immigrants and their
descendants incorporate as successfully as previous generations. We suspect
that policies that had traditionally been the responsibilities of states will
shift to the federal government as immigration becomes a more national
phenomenon. These federal incorporation policies would need to include
language training, job training and retraining, and programs to assist with
conversion of professional licensing and professional degree requirements
earned abroad. In addition, cost-saving strategies, such as excluding immigrants from eligibility for federal programs, will need to be reevaluated.
Civic training will also be necessary to ensure that immigrants become
active participants in the political world. The long-term national policy of
not promoting naturalization among legal immigrants also should be reas-
sessed. We examine these policies in greater depth in later chapters.

Immigrant incorporation policies will also need to be attentive to the
children of immigrants, some of whom are US citizens by birth and others of whom are not. Most important in this area is ensuring that the
decline of the quality of public K–12 education in the United States and

the decline in public funding for public higher education do not dispro-portionately limit the opportunities of second-generation immigrants. The success of incorporation across generations requires that the children of immigrants have opportunities comparable to those of the children of the native-born. Immigrants tend to reside around other immigrants and are more likely to reside in urban areas than the population as a whole. Urban schools have declined considerably in quality in the past decades. This decline, though not a conscious set of policies to disadvantage immi-grants, is another challenge for the next generation of immigrant incor-poration. Public higher education was the engine of economic advance for the children of turn-of-the-twentieth-century immigrants. Today, public higher education is increasingly out of reach for working poor families, a category that includes many immigrant households.

For a restructured incorporation policy to be successful, it would need to remedy what has become an increasing challenge in immigrant incor-poration in the period since 1965: the lack of federal funding and services for immigrants. The best evidence indicates that immigrants are a net financial plus to government. In other words, the taxes they pay exceed the cost of the services they use. The fiscal benefit of the immigrant pres-ence in the United States, however, goes almost entirely to the federal gov-ernment, whereas most of the costs are paid by the states. Immigrants pay federal taxes and Social Security taxes to the federal government, but receive few federal benefits. Most of the services that immigrants and their children receive—public education, public safety, and social ser-vices—are provided by the states and localities. Central to any successful immigrant incorporation policy would be recognizing that immigration is a federal policy and that the costs as well as the benefits of immigration should rest with that level of government.

As we indicated at the beginning of this discussion, incorporation pol-icies are rarely central to policymaker discussions of immigration policy. Thus, the issues we raise here may well not be a part of a comprehen-sive immigration reform debate, but they will continue to lurk below the surface. For immigration reform legislation truly to succeed, the native population must perceive that immigrants are a net plus to US society. Unfortunately, extensive conversation about policies to ensure that immi-grants will likely succeed and thrive in the United States would under-mine popular support for new immigration reform.

## Conclusion

Immigration continues to change the United States fundamentally. More than a million legal immigrants annually join our society. More than 500,000 become US citizens each year. With their willingness to join American society, immigrants and their children energize the economy and the polity, helping to fuel the engine of national growth. By most measures, immigrants are successfully merging into the larger society and ensuring that the United States lives up to its national rhetoric of being a nation of immigrants.

Yet, there is widespread dissatisfaction with US immigration policy from many groups within American society. Much of this dissatisfaction focuses on one aspect of immigration—unauthorized migration—but there are doubts about immigration more generally, voiced by a variety of groups. For example, economic interests are concerned that employers will not be able to obtain the labor they need and ethnic groups are afraid that US society will reduce opportunities for immigration and immigrant incorporation. Considering all of these concerns, the 2006 protests appear less as an immigrant-specific movement seeking a specific change in US policies and more as a societal demand for a comprehensive debate over the future of US immigration policy, so that some long-term policy questions can be more completely resolved.

# 2

. . . . . . . . . . . . . . . . . . . . . . . . . . . . . . . . . . . . . . . . . . . . . . . . . . .

# *Defining Who We Will Be: The History of US Immigration Policy*

THROUGHOUT US HISTORY, CITIZENS AND LEADERS HAVE accepted, praised, and revered immigrants. The symbolic notion of a "nation of immigrants" is richly entwined in the mythology of the United States. Intermittently, however, the public has also reacted against immigration and immigrants. Indeed, each of the major periods of welcome and acceptance has been shattered by popular reactions against immigration. Among the most famous reminders of these periods of anti-immigrant sentiment are the Alien and Sedition Acts (1798), the American ("Know-Nothing") Party (1850s), and the Red Scares at the end of World War I (1919–1920). Another wave of anti-immigrant sentiment began in the mid-1990s, which continues to impede contemporary efforts to craft comprehensive immigration reform.

Despite these cycles of long-term acceptance of immigration and periodic anti-immigration fervor, the reverence for immigrants remains strong—reflected in the notion that the United States is a nation of immigrants and that the nation's success has been and continues to be built on the labor and dreams of immigrants. However, the attacks of September 11, 2001, and the continuing flow of unauthorized immigrants from Latin America and Asia eroded this pro-immigrant sentiment for many Americans (a topic we explore in greater depth in Chapter 3).

In this chapter, we examine this seeming contradiction between love of immigrants and periodic opposition to immigration throughout history. We will also look at how this contradiction set the stage for the major ongoing challenge in the creation and implementation of US immigration policy—that is, the twin questions of how many immigrants the nation should admit and what characteristics they should have. These questions were not asked, at least not by policymakers, until the 1860s, when Chinese immigration began to be limited, culminating in the Chinese Exclusion Act of 1882. Since then, deciding who and how many should be allowed to immigrate has become a crucial ongoing debate for the polity, and has in turn shaped the composition of immigrants in the United States at various stages of our history. Because there can be no doubt that the nation will continue to experience immigration, it is not an understatement to say that the answers to these questions will influence the future of the nation.

Once government establishes restrictions on immigration, it must decide who should enforce the restrictions and what should be done with people who migrate in violation of restrictions. Although seemingly simple, this is actually a complex question. Not only does it raise moral and human rights issues, but given the federal structure of our government, it creates major political, legal, and jurisdictional issues centered on which level of government (federal, state, or local) sets and enforces policy. Although the Supreme Court ruled in 1875 that states had no power to regulate immigration in a manner inconsistent with federal policy (see *Chy Lung v. Freeman*, 92 U.S. 275, 1875), today there are at least 1,500 formal agreements between the federal government and state and local criminal justice agencies empowering state and local officials to enforce immigration laws. In principle, none of these agreements allows states to initiate policies that contradict federal standards. However, enforcing this boundary requires continuous vigilance and negotiation, especially because immigration policy comes into conflict with domestic policies, particularly those concerning labor, education, and health, as well as foreign policy. Faced at times with seeming federal inaction in enforcing immigration laws, states have begun to express their dissatisfaction by passing laws like Arizona's S.B. 1070 that usurp what had traditionally been a federal government responsibility. We analyze the extent to which such state efforts to implement immigration policies, and the rise in anti-immigrant sentiment evident in public debates over unauthorized migration, may signal a permanent shift in the nation's response to immigration.

## Ebbs and Flows of Immigration to the United States

As Oscar Handlin noted, the history of America is the history of the immigrant (1951: 3), and as he would have predicted, the story of American immigration in many ways presents an overview of the major phases of American history. Broadly, then, this chapter focuses on the question of deciding who we will be by looking at the ebbs and flows of immigration to the United States and the way the nation has restricted access to its borders through various eras of immigration. This discussion of the history of US immigration policies provides a context for understanding the larger issues being debated by Congress in its search for comprehensive immigration reform. The outcomes of those debates will serve as a foundation for America's immigration law for the early part of the twenty-first century.

The first era covers the country's earliest experiences with immigration and immigrants, events that in some cases occurred before the founding of the country. These early experiences shaped the way the Constitution approached immigration and settlement policy. The second era includes the first of the great waves of immigration to the United States, in the period between 1841 and 1860, when populations perceived as different from the dominant populations entered the country in large numbers. In this First Great Wave of immigration, more than 1 million Irish and Germans entered the United States. The third phase begins with the end of the Civil War and continues to World War I, and is known as the Second Great Wave of immigration. The fourth begins formally in 1965 with the civil rights movement and extends to September 11, 2001. The final era begins with the national response to 9/11 and is ongoing today.

For each era of immigration history, we examine who was immigrating and in what numbers, where these immigrants settled in the United States, what their similarities and differences from previous immigrants and from the US-born population were, and what economic and social opportunities were open to these immigrants. In addition, we look at how the American public and institutions have responded to large-scale immigration. Each of these periods has witnessed high, and increasing, numbers of immigrants who are often ethnically or racially distinct from the majority of native-born Americans, and each era concludes with a reaction against large-scale immigration and a national effort to eliminate some of the immigration flow. Further, for each of these periods, we look at the institutional and regulatory changes implemented to further restrict immigration and increase selectivity of immigrants. We examine who makes and enforces immigration policy and what happens when immigrants violate the immigration law. Throughout US history, Congress and the people have continually revisited these ongoing challenges in immigration policy—how many immigrants the nation should admit, what characteristics they should have, what rights they should have, and how those who enter illegally should be treated. We summarize major federal legislation concerning immigration in all five eras in Table 2.1.

TABLE 2.1. Summary of Major Federal Immigration Laws, 1788–2014

| 1788–1875: Minimal Federal Regulation Focusing Primarily on Transportation of Immigrants | |
|---|---|
| 1798 | "Alien and Seditions Acts" authorized deportation of aliens dangerous to the United States and established reporting requirements for captains of passenger vessels. |
| 1819 | Ship captains must deliver passenger lists to customs officials (immigration data begin with the implementation of this law). |
| 1847 | "Passenger Acts" legislation to protect passengers, including immigrants, on passenger vessels. |
| 1855 | Required ship captains to provide separate reporting of immigrants arriving for permanent residence and immigrants arriving for temporary residence. |
| 1862 | Prohibited transportation of Chinese "coolies" on American vessels. |
| 1864 | Created a "Commissioner of Immigration" in the State Department and permitted labor contracting in which the immigrant exchanged future labor for the cost of transportation. |
| **1875–1965: Immigration Restriction and National Origin Quotas** | |
| 1875 | Prohibited the immigration of criminals, prostitutes, and "Orientals" who did not freely and voluntarily consent to immigration. |
| 1882 | Suspended the immigration of Chinese laborers for ten years (subsequently extended until 1943) and added to the restricted categories for non-Chinese immigrants to exclude persons likely to become a public charge. |
| 1885 | "Contract Labor Law" prohibited the immigration of those who had been contracted to perform specific services (exceptions were made for temporary immigrants). |
| 1891 | Bureau of Immigration established in the Treasury Department; prohibited immigration of persons suffering from contagious diseases as well as felons, polygamists, and aliens whose passage was paid by others; empowered secretary of treasury to establish rules for inspection along US land borders; and directed deportation for immigrants who entered the United States in violation of US law. |
| 1903 | Prohibited the immigration of anarchists and mandated deportation of immigrants who became public charges within two years of immigration. |
| 1907 | Prohibited immigration of imbeciles, feebleminded persons, persons with physical or mental defects, children unaccompanied by their parents, and women coming to the United States for immoral purposes. |
| 1917 | Prohibited the immigration of the illiterate and created the "barred zone" that excluded all Asians from immigration. |
| 1921 | First "National Origin Quota" law established cap of 350,000 immigrants annually and allocated immigration visas based on the number of foreign-born persons of each nationality in the 1910 census; exempted the Western Hemisphere from these restrictions. |

TABLE 2.1. *(continued)*

| 1924 | Second "National Origin Quota" law set annual quota at 164,667 and allocated visas based on the 1890 census (later changed to 150,000 and the 1920 census); established preference quota system to facilitate the immigration of immediate family members of US citizens and residents; and established consular control system to issue visas abroad. |
|------|---|
| 1929 | Registry established to legalize unauthorized immigrants resident for eight years. |
| 1937 | Mandated the deportation of immigrants who secured visas by fraudulent marriages to US citizens. |
| 1940 | Mandated registration of all immigrants in the United States. |
| 1943 | Established "Bracero Program" to provide short-term agricultural labor and made Chinese eligible for immigration (their initial quota was 105 annually). |
| 1945 | Waived visa requirements for war brides. |
| 1948 | First refugee law provided for immigration of up to 205,000 persons displaced by World War II. |
| 1950 | Prohibited the immigration of current and former members of the Communist Party, the Nazi Party, and other totalitarian organizations. |
| 1952 | Criminalized facilitating unauthorized immigration or harboring unauthorized immigrants (employing an unauthorized immigrant was not classified as harboring); expanded powers of the Border Patrol to investigate unauthorized immigration; amended national origin quotas to base the quota on the 1920 census and all persons of each national ancestry or origin with each Asian country awarded no more than 2,000 visas. |
| 1957 | Modified refugee admissions so that a surge in one year would not have to be mortgaged against immigration from that country in future years. |
| 1961 | Eliminated ceiling of 2,000 visas from Asian countries. |
| 1964 | Terminated "Bracero Program." |

**1965–2001: Family Preferences, Controlling Refugee/Asylee Admissions, and Controlling Unauthorized Immigrations**

| 1965 | Abolished "National Origin Quota" system and replaced it with a first-come, first-served system rewarding potential immigrants with immediate family in the United States and with special or needed job skills; established per-country limit of 20,000 immigrants (immediate family members did not count against this limit); exempted Western Hemisphere from per-country limit, but established regional limit of 120,000. |
|------|---|
| 1976 | Applied 20,000-per-country limit to the Western Hemisphere; eliminated the regional limit for the Western Hemisphere. |
| 1980 | First comprehensive legislation to address refugee admissions eliminated refugees as a category in the preference system. |

TABLE 2.1. *(continued)*

| 1981 | Further expanded Immigration and Naturalization Service (INS) powers to combat unauthorized immigration, including the ability to seize property used to facilitate unauthorized immigration. |
|------|------|
| 1986 | Immigration Reform and Control Act of 1986 authorized "legalization" for unauthorized immigrants who had resided in the United States since before January 1, 1982, and agricultural workers with shorter residences; created sanctions for employers knowingly hiring unauthorized immigrants and established requirement to prove work eligibility before starting a job; increased enforcement at the borders; and provided for new agricultural labor immigration during periods of agricultural labor shortage.<br>Established two-year "conditional" permanent residence for aliens deriving their immigrant status through marriage to US citizens (to control marriage fraud). |
| 1990 | Increased total preference immigration to a flexible cap of 675,000 and expanded border enforcement and grounds for deportation. |
| 1996 | Expanded and sped up removal process for unauthorized immigrants and asylum applicants denied asylee status; made immigrant sponsorship legally enforceable and raised the financial level necessary to sponsor an immigrant; terminated permanent resident eligibility for most federal social welfare programs (both for immigrants already resident in the United States and for those who would immigrate after the law was enacted); and reduced judicial oversight of asylum and deportation proceedings. |
| 1997 | Supplemental Security Income program eligibility restored for permanent resident immigrants. This was made possible when Illegal Immigration Reform and Immigrant Responsibility Act (IIRIRA) legislation was incorporated into the Immigration and Nationality Act (INA) (Pub. L. 82-414), Section 287(g). This legislation authorized the federal government to enter into voluntary agreements with state, county, and local law enforcement agencies to train officers to help identify individuals who are in the country illegally. The program, supervised by Immigration and Customs Enforcement (ICE), formerly the INS, was originally conceived with the narrow mandate of arresting fugitive aliens, that is, unauthorized immigrants already subject to outstanding warrants of deportation. |

**2001–2012: Searching for "Comprehensive" Immigration Reform in an Era Shaped by Concerns over International Terror**

| 2001 | In response to the September 11, 2001, attacks on the World Trade Center and the Pentagon, Congress passed the USA Patriot Act (Uniting and Strengthening America by Providing Appropriate Tools Required to Intercept and Obstruct Terrorism Act of 2001), which included several provisions to strengthen US border enforcement and to prevent the immigration of individuals providing material support for terrorist organizations. The INS was directed to identify criminal aliens with pending orders of deportation but who had not been deported, and to improve the technology monitoring of who was entering and, particularly, exiting the United States. |
|------|------|

TABLE 2.1. *(continued)*

| | |
|---|---|
| | The Justice Department apprehended 2,000 aliens suspected of terrorist connections and detained more than 700. Attorney General John Ashcroft ordered that their names be kept secret. Of these, approximately 134 were detained on criminal charges and 99 were convicted or pled guilty. Many of the others were deported. Efforts by the Justice Department to hold secret deportation hearings were held to be illegal in most states (the exception, the Sixth Judicial Circuit, comprising Tennessee, Michigan, Ohio, and Kentucky). |
| 2002 | The Homeland Security Act of 2002 transferred the Immigration and Naturalization Service from the US Department of Justice and established in its place the two agencies within the newly established US Department of Homeland Security: the US Citizenship and Immigration Services and Immigration and Customs Enforcement.<br><br>The Justice Department finalized administrative rules based on the 1996 immigration bill that allowed state and local police to detain individuals for immigration violations, formerly a prerogative of the federal government. INS also fully implemented another provision of the 1996 laws that established a database to track students with student immigrant visas (the Student and Exchange Visitor Information System, SEVIS). |
| 2003 | Attorney General John Ashcroft issued an administrative ruling that unauthorized immigrants could be detained indefinitely whether they had ties to terrorist groups or not. |
| 2005 | House of Representatives passed legislation (which was not passed in the Senate and did not become law) that would have criminalized unauthorized presence in the United States; made it a crime to "assist, encourage, direct, or induce" people to enter the country illegally; mandated detention of apprehended unauthorized immigrants; and expedited the removal of unauthorized immigrants by expanding the range of administrative officers who could authorize such removal. Although this legislation did not become law, it mobilized many to enter the "comprehensive" immigration reform debate and limited options for legislators seeking compromise. |
| 2006 | Congress authorized and appropriated funds for a 700-mile fence along the US-Mexico border. |
| 2006–2015 | Local jurisdictions and states pass ordinances seeking to enforce national immigration law and requiring local officials to determine the legal status of immigrants. When challenged in the federal courts, these local and state laws have been held to be unconstitutional because they are preempted by federal legislation in an area recognized by the courts as one where the federal government has primary authority. Challenges of local and state lawmaking in federal courts continue. |
| 2007 | Workplace enforcement expands considerably and relies increasingly on large, highly publicized raids of workplaces, particularly in the agricultural processing sector. |

TABLE 2.1. *(continued)*

| 2009–2010 | In the absence of Congressional action on immigration reform, the Obama administration used its administrative authority to implement several changes in US immigration policy. These included: prioritizing the removal of unauthorized immigrants who pose a "danger to national security or a risk to public safety"; seeking to dismiss deportation proceedings for unauthorized immigrants who appear to be immediately eligible for permanent resident status based on pending applications; choosing not to initiate deportation proceedings against unauthorized students who might be eligible for a targeted legalization aimed at young adults who migrated with their parents and who pursued higher education (the DREAM Act); and shifting workplace enforcement from large public raids to employers who hire unauthorized immigrants. |
|---|---|
| 2012 | President Obama, using administrative authority, implemented Deferred Action for Childhood Arrivals to provide two-year residence authorization and work permits for young adults who migrated to the United States as children and completed high school, served in the military, and were enrolled in educational institutions. Obama extended this program for two additional years in 2014. |

*Source:* Compiled by authors. For a complete index of immigration legislation in 1790–1999, see US Immigration and Naturalization Service (2000: Appendix 1).

Immigration steadily increased between 1820, when governmental efforts to collect immigration data began, and 1920. Early in this period, Northwestern Europeans were dominant, but by the period's end, Southern and Eastern Europeans had become most common among US immigrants. From the 1920s through the 1950s, the United States saw a much lower level of immigration than in the preceding decades. The 1930s, for example, witnessed the lowest levels of immigration since the 1830s. Although Europeans continued to be the most frequent immigrants, for the first time Mexico was among the countries sending the most emigrants to the United States.

Beginning in the 1960s—particularly after 1965—and continuing until today, the absolute level of immigration is the highest in American history. The composition of this immigration has also changed markedly. Mexico, Latin America in general, and the Philippines, China, Korea, and Asia in general are the sources of the majority of immigrants to the United States. The number of immigrants, and the four largest immigrant-sending countries, by decade from the 1820s to the present, are shown in Tables 2.2 and 2.3. Table 2.2 also indicates the share that immigrants from each decade added to the US population at the beginning of the next decade.

TABLE 2.2. Immigration to the United States, by Decade, 1820s–2010s

| Decade | Immigrants | Previous Decade's Immigrants as Share of National Population (%)[1] |
|---|---|---|
| 1820s | 128,502 | 1.0 |
| 1830s | 538,381 | 3.2 |
| 1840s | 1,427,337 | 6.2 |
| 1850s | 2,814,554 | 9.0 |
| 1860s | 2,081,261[2] | 5.2 |
| 1870s | 2,742,137 | 5.5 |
| 1880s | 5,248,568 | 8.3 |
| 1890s | 3,694,294 | 4.8 |
| 1900s | 8,202,388 | 8.9 |
| 1910s | 6,347,380 | 6.0 |
| 1920s | 4,295,510 | 3.5 |
| 1930s | 699,375 | 0.5 |
| 1940s | 856,608 | 0.6 |
| 1950s | 2,499,268 | 1.4 |
| 1960s | 3,213,749 | 1.6 |
| 1970s | 4,248,203 | 1.9 |
| 1980s | 6,224,379 | 2.5 |
| 1990s | 9,775,398 | 3.5 |
| 2000s | 10,299,430 | 3.3 |
| 2010 | 1,042,645 | |
| 2011 | 1,063,040 | |
| 2012 | 1,031,631 | |
| 2013 | 990,553 | |

*Sources:* US Bureau of the Census (2010); US Department of Homeland Security (2013).

[1] Immigrants from the previous decade, percentage as calculated at the beginning of the next decade.
[2] Until 1867, the federal government recorded only people who arrived at seaports as immigrants.

TABLE 2.3. Four Largest Immigrant Nationalities, by Decade, 1820s–2000s

| Decade | Country | Number of Immigrants | Decade's Immigrants (%) |
|---|---|---|---|
| 1820s | TOTAL | 128,502 | |
| | Ireland | 51,617 | 40.2 |
| | United Kingdom | 26,336 | 20.5 |
| | France | 7,694 | 6.0 |
| | Germany | 5,753 | 4.5 |
| 1830s | TOTAL | 538,381 | |
| | Ireland | 170,672 | 31.7 |
| | Germany | 124,726 | 23.2 |
| | United Kingdom | 74,350 | 13.8 |
| | France | 39,330 | 7.3 |
| 1840s | TOTAL | 1,427,337 | |
| | Ireland | 656,145 | 46.0 |
| | Germany | 385,434 | 27.0 |
| | United Kingdom | 218,572 | 15.3 |
| | France | 75,300 | 5.3 |
| 1850s | TOTAL | 2,814,554 | |
| | Ireland | 1,029,486 | 36.6 |
| | Germany | 976,072 | 34.7 |
| | United Kingdom | 445,322 | 15.8 |
| | France | 81,778 | 2.9 |
| 1860s | TOTAL | 2,081,261 | |
| | Germany | 723,734 | 34.8 |
| | United Kingdom | 532,956 | 25.6 |
| | Ireland | 427,419 | 20.5 |
| | Canada and Newfoundland | 117,978 | 5.7 |
| 1870s | TOTAL | 2,742,137 | |
| | Germany | 751,769 | 27.4 |
| | United Kingdom | 578,447 | 21.1 |
| | Ireland | 422,264 | 15.4 |
| | Canada and Newfoundland | 324,310 | 11.8 |

TABLE 2.3. *(continued)*

| | | | |
|---|---|---|---|
| 1880s | TOTAL | 5,248,568 | |
| | Germany | 1,445,181 | 27.5 |
| | United Kingdom | 810,900 | 15.4 |
| | Ireland | 674,061 | 12.8 |
| | Norway-Sweden | 586,441 | 11.1 |
| 1890s | TOTAL | 3,694,294 | |
| | Italy | 603,791 | 16.3 |
| | Germany | 579,072 | 15.7 |
| | Austria-Hungary | 534,059 | 14.5 |
| | Russia[1] | 450,101 | 12.2 |
| 1900s | TOTAL | 8,202,388 | |
| | Austria-Hungary | 2,001,376 | 24.4 |
| | Italy | 1,930,475 | 23.5 |
| | Russia | 1,501,301 | 18.3 |
| | United Kingdom | 469,518 | 5.7 |
| 1910s | TOTAL | 6,347,380 | |
| | Italy | 1,229,916 | 19.4 |
| | Austria-Hungary | 1,164,727 | 18.3 |
| | Russia | 1,106,998 | 17.4 |
| | Canada and Newfoundland | 708,715 | 11.2 |
| 1920s | TOTAL | 4,295,510 | |
| | Canada and Newfoundland | 949,286 | 22.1 |
| | Italy | 528,133 | 12.3 |
| | Mexico | 498,945 | 11.6 |
| | Germany | 386,634 | 9.0 |
| 1930s | TOTAL | 699,375 | |
| | Canada and Newfoundland | 162,703 | 23.3 |
| | Germany | 119,107 | 17.0 |
| | Italy | 85,053 | 12.2 |
| | United Kingdom | 61,813 | 8.8 |

TABLE 2.3. (continued)

| 1940s | TOTAL | 856,608 | |
|-------|-------|---------|---|
| | Canada and Newfoundland | 160,911 | 18.8 |
| | United Kingdom | 131,794 | 15.4 |
| | Germany | 119,506 | 14.0 |
| | Mexico | 56,158 | 6.6 |
| 1950s | TOTAL | 2,499,268 | |
| | Germany | 576,905 | 23.1 |
| | Canada and Newfoundland | 353,169 | 14.1 |
| | Mexico | 273,847 | 11.0 |
| | United Kingdom | 195,709 | 7.8 |
| 1960s | TOTAL | 3,213,749 | |
| | Mexico | 441,824 | 13.7 |
| | Canada and Newfoundland | 433,128 | 13.5 |
| | United Kingdom | 220,213 | 6.9 |
| | Germany | 209,616 | 6.5 |
| 1970s | TOTAL | 4,248,203 | |
| | Mexico | 621,218 | 14.6 |
| | Philippines | 337,726 | 7.9 |
| | Cuba | 256,497 | 6.0 |
| | Korea | 241,192 | 5.7 |

# Colonization of the New World and the Revolutionary Era

All Americans, with the exception of Native Americans, trace their ancestry to immigrants, though even the Native American has migrant forebears in Asia. The arrivals of the earliest European and African immigrants are relatively well documented. The historical record notes the arrival of the Spanish missionaries at St. Augustine in 1565, the Spanish settlement of the New Mexico colony in 1598, the founding of Jamestown by English settlers in 1607, and the arrival of the first African slave in

TABLE 2.3. *(continued)*

| | | | |
|---|---|---|---|
| 1980s[2] | TOTAL | 6,244,379 | |
| | Mexico | 1,009,586 | 16.2 |
| | Philippines | 502,056 | 8.0 |
| | Korea | 322,708 | 5.2 |
| | India | 231,649 | 3.7 |
| 1990s | TOTAL | 9,775,398 | |
| | Mexico | 2,757,418 | 28.2 |
| | Philippines | 534,338 | 5.5 |
| | China[3] | 458,952 | 4.7 |
| | Russia | 433,427 | 4.4 |
| 2000s | TOTAL | 10,299,430 | |
| | Mexico | 1,704,166 | 16.5 |
| | China | 649,294 | 6.3 |
| | India | 590,464 | 5.7 |
| | Philippines | 545,463 | 5.3 |

*Source:* US Department of Homeland Security (2013: Tables 1 and 2).

---

[1] Prior to 1919, the Russia category included immigrants from parts of today's Poland.

[2] Recipients of legalization under the Immigration Reform and Control Act of 1986 appear as legal immigrants in the year in which they obtained legal permanent resident status. For most IRCA recipients this occurred between 1989 and 1993.

[3] China includes Hong Kong beginning in 1990.

Virginia in 1619. Though celebrated as a national symbol of early immigration, the arrival of the Pilgrims in Massachusetts in 1620 was late in the period of initial European colonization of territory that later became the United States.

By the 1630s, however, immigration to what was to become the United States was so common that individual arrivals and even the total number of immigrants went unrecorded. This was the case for nearly two centuries, during which immigration to the colonies and then to the new United States was largely unregulated by these receiving governments. Immigration during this first phase of American immigrant history differs somewhat from the periods that followed, yet patterns developed in this period that were to repeat themselves throughout US history (Zolberg 2006).

### Prerevolutionary Immigration, 1630–1776

Approximately 600,000 immigrants moved to North America in the seventeenth century. The majority of them settled outside of the territory that would become the United States. The best available estimates indicate that between 1630 and 1700, approximately 155,000 English immigrated to the British colonies (Altman and Horn 1991: 4). These English immigrants accounted for approximately 90 percent of European immigrants to the colonies. The next largest group of future Americans, the African slaves who began to populate the Southern plantations, were forced into their status. Although they were involuntary immigrants, the slaves, once freed after the Civil War, presented incorporation dilemmas for the polity much like those posed by voluntary immigrants. Furthermore, their forced immigration reduced the demand for the labor of voluntary migrants from Europe.

Immigration levels increased vastly in the eighteenth century. During a rare period without European wars between 1713 and 1765, approximately 350,000 Europeans and Africans settled in the British colonies in North America. Approximately 40 percent of these prerevolutionary eighteenth-century immigrants were involuntary—Africans destined for slavery. The Europeans who immigrated in this period were much more diverse in origin than those of the previous century. They included approximately 100,000 Irish, who themselves included the descendants of Scottish Presbyterians who had migrated to Ireland in the sixteenth century. The Germans, the next largest nationality among the prerevolutionary immigrants, numbered approximately 65,000. Dutch and Scottish immigration was also significant.

These groups by no means make up the full range of immigrants to the territories that would become the United States. Spanish colonies in Florida and the Southwest, and French colonies in the Louisiana Territory, thrived in this period. These settlements, however, never developed the population density that the British colonies did. Instead, both France and Spain established vast territorial claims based on networks of fortified trading posts and missions. By 1720, these networks covered two-thirds of what is today the continental United States. Still, there was little to attract immigrants to these areas, so its European- and African-origin populations, whether foreign-born or American-born, never exceeded 50,000.

In addition to nationality, the major distinction among European immigrants to the British colonies before the Revolutionary War related to how they afforded passage to the colonies. Some immigrated based on their own or family resources. These included governmental officials, clergy, merchants, artisans, farmers, gentry, and lesser nobility seeking to make their way in the New World. Generally, these immigrants had skills or capital, or worked in one of a narrow set of professions. Those with capital, for the most part, became landholders. Most immigrants, however, were indentured laborers or convicts. The indentured servants were required to perform between two and eight years of labor to repay the price of their passage. The convicts faced different requirements, based both on their sentences and on the types and locations of their labor in the colonies. For the most part, the indentured servants and convicts had no capital and few skills, other than their ability to perform arduous labor. The lack of capital forced many of the seventeenth-century indentured servants to continue to work beyond the term of their original contract. However, as land in the West became available and safe from raids by Native Americans, indentured servants (both those under contract and those who had fulfilled their contractual responsibilities) began to discover other opportunities. These opportunities in the expanding frontier steadily reduced the appeal of indentured servants to many landholders, and African slaves were used in greater numbers instead.

Indentured servitude represents an early form of labor recruitment as an incentive to immigration. Even after the decline of indentured servitude, labor recruitment continued to be an important source of immigrants to the United States well into the twentieth century. When Congress began to explore ways to limit immigration in the nineteenth century, one of its early targets was immigrants who had been recruited abroad for jobs in specific industries or regions in the United States.

The immigrants of different legal statuses and nationalities did not spread evenly across the colonies. For example, the immigration patterns of indentured servants and slaves were focused on the Middle Colonies (Pennsylvania, New York, New Jersey, Delaware) and the South, respectively. Most New England immigrants were free and of English or Welsh origin. New York City and the Hudson Valley had large Dutch populations. German immigrants dominated the flow to Philadelphia and eastern Pennsylvania. Convicts were most likely to end up in the Chesapeake Bay region. Finally, the South saw concentrations of Africans, Germans, Scots, and Scots-Irish.

Each of these immigrant populations found a home in the New World but initially sought to cultivate cultural links to the world they had left behind, including retaining the languages of their homelands. The Germans, in particular, sought to maintain their mother tongue by establishing German-language schools. These early immigrants also maintained a religious bond with their roots through their local churches. Many of the early colonists were religious minorities in their home countries who sought a greater religious freedom in their adopted home. Tolerance varied from colony to colony, but the effect was to create a religious mosaic throughout the territories, which eventually necessitated the constitutional guarantee of religious freedom.

The large-scale immigration generated a range of responses from the several colonies where immigrants settled. Foreshadowing conflicts that have characterized immigration throughout American history (Schrag 2010), the Pennsylvania legislature passed a tax on foreigners entering the territory. Though quickly repealed, this tax sought to undermine the efforts by the territorial governor to promote immigration, particularly of Germans. In this debate, the governor saw the economic advantage of new settlers, whereas the legislature represented mass concerns about cultural change and economic competition (Muller 1993: 18–19). In several other colonies, anti-Catholic sentiments shaped people's thinking about immigration. Interestingly, this religious bigotry, though pervasive, did not result in successful efforts to prevent Catholic immigration. Instead, it manifested itself in efforts to limit the civil rights of Catholic immigrants once they had arrived. In this era, there was little sense that immigration could be restricted by government action.

Overall, despite some objections to specific groups of immigrants and their unequal treatment upon arrival, the British colonies actively sought new immigrants. The availability of land and the need for labor reduced the popular opposition to immigration. Moreover, a slow shift in British policy away from promoting immigration to the colonies in the years leading up to the Revolution contributed to the colonial sentiment that separation from Britain was necessary. The popular desire for continued immigration appears in the Declaration of Independence. One of the charges against King George III was that "he has endeavored to prevent the population of these states; for that purpose obstructing the laws for naturalization of foreigners; refusing to pass others to encourage their migration hither; and raising the conditions of new appropriations of lands." Yet, particularly in places where the new immigrants differed culturally or religiously from the US-born, cultural conflicts led to localized efforts to restrict immigration. It should be noted that the prerevolutionary opposition to immigration focused primarily on cultural dimensions of the relations between immigrants and natives.

## Immigration to the New United States, 1787–1840

The Revolution slowed immigration to the United States, and the defeat of the British spurred an emigration among British loyalists. With the end of the war, however, immigration resumed and the number of immigrants rapidly grew.

Although the Constitution does not address the issue of immigration, a quick review of key national leaders' opinions demonstrates that there was a consensus, at least at the elite level, supporting unlimited immigration of white Europeans. George Washington spoke of the new United States as welcoming not only the "opulent and respected stranger" but also "the oppressed and persecuted of all Nations and Religions" (quoted in Muller 1993: 19). Thomas Jefferson expressed some fears about the political assimilation of immigrants from nations ruled by absolute monarchs, but he also advocated government policies to attract immigrants who were wealthy or skilled. Further, Jefferson anticipated a problem that was to plague immigration in future years. He was concerned that if immigrants were to concentrate in one region, they would maintain their language and customs and be slower to assimilate, but this concern did not temper his support for an open immigration policy for Europeans. In sum, although they anticipated the kinds of issues that challenge national immigration policy even now, the leaders of the new United States welcomed immigrants from Europe even as they increasingly included non-Protestants and non-English speakers.

The Constitution was more explicit concerning the forced immigration of Africans into slavery. Although the statement was ambiguously worded in the document, the framers of the Constitution prohibited Congress from restricting the importation of slaves prior to 1808 (Article I,

Section 9). The guarantee that new slaves would be imported for at least twenty years was one of several compromises that ensured Southern support for the Constitution. Acting on its Constitutional authority, Congress prohibited the importation of new slaves after 1808. For the most part, though, there were few laws concerning immigration in the nation's early years, and most that were enacted until the Civil War addressed transatlantic shipping and reporting requirements for the ships bringing immigrants to the United States.

During the first decade of the country's history, this elite consensus supporting unfettered European immigration gave way to a period of anti-immigrant fervor that reached its peak with the passage of the Alien and Sedition Acts (1798). The origins of these concerns were domestic and international. Domestically, the party then in control—the Federalist Party—saw the immigrants as a potential source of support for their emerging opposition—the Jeffersonians, or Democratic Republicans. Internationally, the cause was the French Revolution and the political turbulence that it spurred throughout Europe. Political refugees from the European tumult arrived in the United States. Many in the United States feared that the ideas of these political refugees—on all sides of the ideological spectrum—would destabilize the new American republic. Not believing that it was within its jurisdiction to restrict immigration, Congress limited naturalization as a tool to reduce the desirability of immigration and to slow the political ascendance of immigrants in American politics. This concern about immigrants ended rapidly with the election of Thomas Jefferson in 1800, which then led to the repeal of the Alien and Sedition Acts in 1802.

Although there are no exact numbers, voluntary immigration in the period between the end of the Revolution and 1820, when the United States first began to record information on migrants who arrived in the country by ship, slowed from prerevolutionary levels and probably did not exceed 2,000 people per year. In part, this decline resulted from British efforts to restrict emigration (which lasted until the 1820s). Also, the wars that raged through Europe in this period increased the difficulties of securing transport. The composition of the voluntary immigration in this era was not significantly changed from the prerevolutionary period. British and Scottish immigrants dominated the flow. Most of these British and Scottish immigrants settled in the cities of the Northeast and in newly settled territories in the Appalachian region and the upper Midwest. The first decade of the nineteenth century also saw the migration of the first non-white, non-slave population—Haitians fleeing their revolution.

Like their prerevolutionary predecessors, these early nineteenth-century immigrants experienced considerable economic opportunity. Most immigrants in this era had the option of domestic migration westward. This geographic mobility—of both immigrants and US-born populations—reduced the potential for the formation of cohesive ethnic communities and also reduced the likelihood of anti-immigrant movements by the US-born in the cities and regions where the immigrants first settled.

## The First Great Wave, 1840–1860

The slow but steady flow of immigrants that characterized the post-revolutionary period became a torrent by the 1840s and 1850s—what became known as the First Great Wave. Whereas annual immigration levels had numbered approximately 14,000 in the 1820s and 60,000 in the 1830s, the pace quickened to 171,000 yearly in the 1840s and rose to 260,000 yearly in the 1850s (US Department of Homeland Security 2012). The 2.8 million immigrants who arrived in the United States during the 1850s comprised 9.0 percent of the national population counted in the 1860 census.

Higher numbers were not the only change in this period. The national origin of the immigrants in the First Great Wave differed significantly from the immigrants who had come before. In the 1820s, Germans and Irish made up just four in ten immigrants. By the 1840s and 1850s, this proportion increased to seven in ten. In addition to the new national origins of the majority of immigrants, the Germans and Irish introduced a second element of diversity—religion. The majority of the Irish immigrants were Roman Catholic; many of the German immigrants were Jewish. Before this era, most immigrants and natives had been Protestants.

One thing did remain consistent: the Germans, Irish, and others who arrived in the 1840s and 1850s did not spread themselves evenly across the country. Instead, they concentrated in Northeastern cities; the Germans moved to New York, Philadelphia, and Boston. These immigrants joined a migration of US-born Americans from rural areas to the cities, which stimulated substantial growth in urban areas. Between 1800 and 1860, the share of the US population in urban areas grew from 6 to nearly 20 percent, with New York City as perhaps the most extreme example of this growth. It grew from a town of 60,000 in 1800 into a city of 1 million by 1860 (Seller 1988: 71–72).

The growth of the cities and the increasing volume of immigrants in urban areas created a new dynamic in the history of immigration: the character of the cities came to overlap with the character of its dominant immigrant ethnic populations. Thus, the concentration of the Irish and German immigrants (particularly German Jewish immigrants) in the cities of the Northeast, particularly in New York, shaped the future economic and social options of these populations and shaped the national perceptions of those cities. After this period, discussions of the "problems" of cities were often veiled ethnic references to immigrants and their descendants.

These immigrants challenged the dominant culture of the United States, particularly in terms of language and religion. The German immigrants of this era spoke German instead of English, whereas most previous immigrants had been English speakers. But religion was perhaps the issue of greater consequence. As previously noted, the overwhelming majority of Irish immigrants were Roman Catholic and many of the German immigrants were Jewish. Although most immigrants of this era learned English, few converted to the Protestant faith.

Despite these differences, the country absorbed ever-increasing numbers of immigrants. For the most part, the immigrants were unskilled, and their origins were rural. This is not to say that the United States attracted only unskilled immigrants. Skilled European workers seeking to take advantage of the better wages and better opportunities in the United States also immigrated during this era. Even so, the vast majority of immigrants in the First Great Wave had few skills. Although the economic opportunities available in the United States certainly guided the destination decision, privation and social change in the home countries acted as catalysts to emigration. For example, the Irish fled the Great Potato Famine, which caused a million deaths between 1845 and 1851; throughout Europe, this period was one of poor harvests and political unrest, spurring many to emigrate. Thus, the combination of push factors (food shortages, population growth, political unrest in Europe) and pull factors (the demand for unskilled labor, the expansion and decline in cost of transatlantic shipping and labor recruitment) spurred immigration to the United States.

How did the United States absorb these immigrants, most of whom were unskilled? The needs of the economy in that era were different from those of today. The level of industrialization of the mid-nineteenth century required little more than a brawny labor force with a willingness to work. The level to which they succeeded economically varied with the ups and downs of the economy. There were few social services, so survival depended on work and the charity of family members and friends.

In this era of US immigration history, although the average immigrant was, for the most part, poorer and less educated than the average US-born citizen, this gap did not cause as much conflict as it did for later generations of immigrants. First, the differences rapidly narrowed or disappeared, particularly for immigrants who left the Northeastern cities for the West. The federal government distributed land in the West to homesteaders (people who would live on, and farm, the land), and the states and territories of the West actively sought immigrants among their targeted populations. Second, the overwhelming majority of the US-born population resided in rural areas. Thus, the immigrants who stayed in the cities—as the majority did—did not challenge the economic well-being or cultural hegemony of the majority of the US-born.

However, this did not mean that there was no cultural conflict whatsoever. The American Party, the so-called Know-Nothings, emerged in the early 1850s with anti-immigrant mobilization as part of its platform. Central to its agenda was a concern about the cultural and political differences that the Know-Nothings perceived as stemming from immigration. One of the Know-Nothings' demands was for an extension of the period prior to naturalization from five years to twenty-one years (more on this in Chapter 4). The Know-Nothing Party reached its peak in the 1856 election, but it never strongly influenced national immigration policy. Its decline, however, was not necessarily a reflection of national support for immigration. Rather, the Civil War reshaped American politics and the party system. Concern over immigration policy was lost in the bigger controversies of the day, and widespread opposition to immigration disappeared for nearly thirty years (Schrag 2010).

Although the Know-Nothings reflected concern among some US-born Americans about immigration and immigrants, immigrants during the First Great Wave were generally tolerated and incorporated into the labor force. Through domestic migration, immigrants had access to an immediate social mobility that would not characterize later generations of immigrants. Even in this era, though, the culturally or religiously distinct immigrants—the Irish and the German Jews, in particular—were less likely to move beyond the cities.

## The Second Great Wave, 1870–1920

The anti-immigrant fervor of the 1850s was lost to the greater national tumult of the Civil War (Anbinder 1992). Although the immediate impact of the Civil War initially slowed immigration, the North's victory jumpstarted a period of steadily increasing immigration that was to last for fifty years. Although immigration expanded steadily throughout this period, it was also a period of increasing restriction. This wave of immigration ended with the most severe restrictions that the United States has ever imposed. Thus, this era, known as the Second Great Wave, was a period of vast immigration as well as a time of increasing selection of who could immigrate and in what numbers.

Between 1870 and 1920, more than 26 million people immigrated to the United States. Immigrants in this period alone exceeded the national population in 1850. The major markers of immigration in this period— the Statue of Liberty in New York Harbor, and Ellis Island and Angel Island as immigrant processing stations—remain symbols of immigration today. It was also during this era that the national pro-immigrant ideology was first articulated, in part to serve as a device to unify the nation during a period of unprecedented immigration.

The Second Great Wave is significant for three reasons. First, the immigrants of the Second Great Wave settled throughout the nation. Second, they began to come from Asia and the Americas as well as from Europe and Africa. Finally, this era saw the federal government assert the authority to regulate immigration.

In the period immediately after the Civil War, immigrants resembled those who had come during the First Great Wave. From the 1860s to the 1880s, Germany, the United Kingdom, and Ireland were the top three countries sending immigrants to the United States, accounting for over half of total immigration. However, beginning in the late 1880s, the composition shifted considerably. Southern and Eastern Europeans replaced the Northern and Western Europeans. These "new" immigrants came from such countries as Italy, Austria-Hungary, and Russia (the Soviet Union after 1917). Prior to 1880 these countries made up a relatively small share of immigrants, but collectively came to provide more than 40 percent of immigrants between 1890 and 1920.

It was with the growing numbers of these "new" European immigrants that anti-immigrant concerns began to rise again. In the popular imagination, the "new" immigrants came to be seen as less capable than their predecessors—less capable of working, less capable of learning American ways, and less capable of assimilating (Grant 1916). As the concerns about the new immigrants grew among the US-born population, restrictionist efforts became more active. Eventually, this concern about immigration led to severe reductions in immigration in the 1920s, including the National-Origin Restrictions (or "Quota Acts"), which we discuss later in this section.

Canadians and Mexicans also began to account for large numbers of immigrants in this era. In the 1860s, and again in the 1870s and 1910s, Canada sent the fourth largest number of immigrants. During this same period, immigration across the southern border also increased. Immigration from Mexico does not rank among the top four countries sending immigrants until the 1920s, but this could be because the records for Mexican immigration were sporadic until 1917 (Sánchez 1993; Hernández 2010).

The vast majority of the immigrants of the Second Great Wave, like their predecessors, moved to cities, particularly the cities of the East Coast and the industrial Midwest. The rapid growth in the cities of this era was driven in large part by rapid immigration. However, it is important to note that some nationalities—particularly Scandinavians, Germans, and Mexicans—migrated directly to rural areas. Many of the immigrants moved almost immediately into industrial jobs. Recruitment to these positions often began in the immigrants' countries of origin and intensified when immigrants reached a US port. Steamship companies, representing specific employers or industries seeking to expand their pool of immigrant labor, would conduct the initial stage of the labor recruitment, often using representatives in Europe. The cost of passage was often subsidized in order to attract needed labor. At the US port, additional incentives were offered by specific employers. States and cities also sought to attract immigrants, including Midwestern states that wanted to increase their populations and cities that wanted to ensure a sufficient labor supply for new industries. Some states even sought to attract immigrants by offering them easy and rapid access to the rights of citizenship and assistance with naturalization. Certainly, these patterns indicate that immigrants, due to their value as workers, were welcome in this era. The intensified recruitment of immigrants in this era partially explains the changing national origins of immigrants.

The diversification of immigrant origins in this period reflects the expansion of transportation infrastructure, the disruption of traditional labor relationships in the countries of origin, and the ever-expanding demand for labor within the United States (as well as in other parts of the Americas, particularly Argentina and Brazil). Although emigration had been restricted formally and informally in earlier periods, the late nineteenth century saw virtually no restrictions by European states. On the contrary, many governments used emigration as a tool to maintain domestic tranquility by reducing population pressures and encouraging political dissenters to migrate. Interestingly, in the late nineteenth century, the countries that sought to restrict emigration—namely, Mexico and China—were those that would later send many nationals to the United States. Mexico sought to keep peasants on the land, and China yielded to diplomatic pressure from the United States to exclude Chinese immigrants.

Throughout this period, men were more commonly in the immigrant stream than women. Many men immigrated without their wives or families, and far fewer women embarked on the journey without first having family in the United States. Throughout the late nineteenth and early twentieth centuries, US immigration law discouraged the migration of women traveling without fathers or husbands (Gardner 2005). The technological advances of the shipping industry in this era, however, made it increasingly easy for immigrants to return to their countries of origin (known as *return migration*) and for families to follow after one family member had established a beachhead in the United States. Thus, by the early twentieth century, the sex ratio of immigrants increasingly approached 1:1 (Gibson and Lennon 1999: Table 7).

Return migration was not new to this era. It was, however, possible at a previously unattainable scale. In the Spanish and French colonies of the New World, return migration was the most common pattern, particularly early in the colonial era. In the British colonies, by contrast, the vast majority of migrants did not return to Europe, nor did they plan to.

Those who did were often the most elite migrants. Some of the non-elite immigrants in the British colonies and later in the United States did, of course, return to Europe, though in small numbers. In the 1740s, Benjamin Franklin observed this phenomenon and worried that what he called the "reverse flow" would counterbalance the new immigrants. Franklin's fears were unfounded then and have continued to be since. Even in the early twentieth century, when return migration became more affordable and less arduous (and when data on rates first became available), estimates indicate that no more than 35 percent of immigrants returned to their home countries (Wyman 1993). Return migration rates varied considerably among national-origin groups in this era. As many as 90 percent of Bulgarian, Serbian, and Montenegrin immigrants returned to their countries of origin, but the Northern Italian return rate was just 11 percent. Although not from a single country, Jews had the lowest rates of return, at just 5 percent. Seasonal labor migration also occurred for the first time among immigrants from Europe. Some immigrants in this era migrated several times over a series of years.

*Sequential migration*, in which one family member would migrate to test the waters and ease the transition for other family members to migrate (or not), was not new, but it became much more common during the Second Great Wave, in the post–Civil War era. Earlier generations of immigrants had primarily come either with their families (the prerevolutionary immigrants and the more affluent or skilled in later periods) or without them (many of the convicts and the early Irish and German immigrants). The ease of family immigration and of return migration created conflicting pressures on the immigrants. With their families in the United States and their children raised here, immigrants could make their lives in the United States. This could lead to the development of social attachment and political loyalty to the United States. Whereas the potential for family immigration created an incentive to develop a permanent attachment to the United States, the ease of return migration offered an incentive to maintain ties to the country of origin. Clearly, these twin attachments—to the United States and to the home country—are not mutually exclusive. Immigrants in this era began a process that continues today (Foner 2000: Chapter 6). The process of becoming American is by no means immediate but rather occurs for many immigrants steadily over time, though the presence of family in the United States certainly speeds up this process for many immigrants.

In the period after the Civil War, immigrants experienced a new incentive to develop an attachment to the United States. The cities to which most immigrated, at least initially, were under the control of urban political machines. In most cities, these machines were themselves controlled by first- and second-generation immigrants, that is, the children of people who had immigrated in the early part of the nineteenth century or by people who themselves had immigrated to the United States after the Civil War. These machines played several important roles for immigrants. They provided a crude social welfare system, at least for the co-nationals and political supporters of the machine leaders. The machine also provided jobs for some new arrivals, and food or other emergency needs in times of crisis. As the national and state governments provided no such assistance, this assistance was often crucial to immigrant survival. These political machines also acted as intermediaries between immigrants and non-immigrants. Crude though it was, their assistance was often the immigrants' first contact with American life. These political machines served a final role for some immigrants—assistance with socialization, naturalization, and voting. In return, it was immigrant votes that allowed the machines to remain in power throughout the late nineteenth and early twentieth centuries (Erie 1988).

Machine outreach to recent immigrants aside, immigrant life in the cities of the Northeast and Midwest in this period was quite dismal (Ziegelman 2010). Housing conditions were poor; work opportunities were exploitative and often dangerous; and crime and disease were rife. Women and children worked in the factories, with no added protections and less pay than adult men (Foner 2000). Formal education lasted no more than four years for most children.

Nationalistic rivalries from Europe carried over to the New World and were often inflamed by political leaders seeking to control immigrant populations. Life for many immigrants involved few who were not co-nationals, even in the workforce, which tended to be segregated by national-origin group. Thus, many immigrants did not assimilate linguistically or geographically. Although opportunities for internal migration within the United States continued to exist, the availability of land in the West that had characterized the early years of the nineteenth century had diminished, particularly for those with limited resources. Thus, immigrants in the Second Great Wave, or at least those who immigrated to urban areas, did not experience the rapid upward social mobility or assimilation of the previous immigrants. More often than not, this upward social mobility and assimilation occurred not for the immigrants themselves but instead for their children or grandchildren.

## The Roots of Immigration Restriction

With the exception of the prohibition on importing slaves after 1808, the United States had not barred immigrants from its shores during most of the nation's first century. Immigration had been taxed by local governments, but this policy was understood as a tool to generate revenues, not to restrict immigration. During the Second Great Wave, however, policymakers experimented with various restrictions. These efforts increased dramatically between 1875 and the end of the Second Great Wave in the early 1920s (Hing 2004). The end of this period saw the strictest restrictions that the United States has ever placed on immigration. Equally important, the process of establishing immigration restrictions centralized control over immigration with the federal government and spurred an increased federal role in border enforcement.

We review the specific restrictions here in order to examine how the United States moved in fifty years from virtually unrestricted immigration to the most severe limits in the country's two-hundred-year history. Beyond the specific limitations discussed, it is important to note that the process of establishing constraints was accompanied by a steady centralization of immigration administration. At the start of the period, any restrictions were largely meaningless because the federal government did not have the capacity to control the actions of local government officials. By the end, to enter the country legally, immigrants had to have visas issued abroad before they could begin their journey, and federal employees were in place at ports of entry to ensure that immigrants had the proper documentation. Thus, the immigration restriction effort that culminated in the Quota Acts of 1921 and 1924 shifted responsibility for immigration policymaking to the federal government.

In 1862, Congress introduced the first restriction on voluntary immigration by individuals, prohibiting the importation of Chinese "coolies," or contract laborers, transported on American-flagged ships, with their costs of passage paid by others (12 Statutes at Large 340, enacted February 19, 1862). However, this restriction demonstrated how unsure Congress was in the breadth of its power to regulate immigration. Congress limited the law's scope because it was only confident of its authority to regulate American shipping. By 1875, Congress was more confident of its authority and passed the first federal immigration law targeting specific classes of immigration in response to growing public concern about these classes. The 1875 act prohibits criminals, prostitutes, and contract labor from Asia from immigrating to the United States (18 Statutes at Large 477, enacted March 3, 1875). The government also developed administrative mechanisms, such as the placement of federal immigration personnel at major ports of entry and oversight of the steamship companies, to exclude these specific classes of immigrants.

Non-Asians in California sought to restrict the economic power of Chinese immigrants. Thus, Congress's response specifically addressed this concern (Gyory 1998; Motomura 2006). Congressional intentions behind restrictions on convicts and prostitutes were more nebulous. The law enforcement practices of the day did not allow immigration inspectors to determine whether an individual immigrant was undesirable. And so this law responded to a generalized public concern about the character of immigrants and gave immigration inspectors a tool by which to exclude immigrants they felt were "undesirable," even if they were not, in fact, convicts or prostitutes. The anti-prostitution provisions were, for example, a tool to exclude single women from immigration (Gardner 2005). Some immigration inspectors used these provisions rigorously, others not at all. Potential immigrants faced varying treatment from port to port and from inspector to inspector, though in practice, this law deterred few immigrants.

In 1882, Congress strengthened the anti-Chinese provisions, suspending the immigration of all Chinese laborers (though permitting the return migration of Chinese laborers already in the United States). It did permit the entry of Chinese students, teachers, merchants, and those "proceeding to the United States from curiosity" (22 Statutes at Large 58, enacted May 6, 1882). The class bias in this law—excluding labor while admitting more elite Chinese—was soon applied to other nationalities as well. In that same year, Congress established the first centralized control over immigration by establishing standards for state boards of immigration, and it added to the categories excluded from immigration. Persons likely to become a "public charge" could no longer immigrate. The bar on immigrants likely to be a "public charge" has been interpreted differently over time; initially, it allowed immigration inspectors to exclude immigrants if they seemed unable to work upon arrival. Congress also enacted a federal tax of fifty cents on alien passengers to the United States (22 Statutes at Large 214, enacted August 3, 1882).

In 1885, Congress extended the Contract Labor Law to all nationalities. Henceforth, it was unlawful to import aliens to the United States to perform specific services for specific lengths of time (23 Statutes at Large 332, enacted February 26, 1885). The exclusion of contract labor sought to reverse earlier patterns of labor immigration, such as indentured servitude and contract labor, and to prevent the emergence of unfree populations of labor in the United States who might, in the popular imagination, become a new slave or slave-like population. Again, this law was weakly enforced. European contract labor continued until the enactment of the Quota Acts in the early 1920s. In the Southwest, immigration of contract labor from Mexico became national policy from 1943 to 1964 with the establishment of the Bracero Program. To this day, many visas are available for short-term agricultural contract labor, for caregivers, for workers in seasonal industries, and for workers in technology industries. Despite the erratic enforcement of the Contract Labor Law, it is important to understand that this provision in the immigration law sought to break one of the anchors of the immigrant flow—the pull of employment contracts and the expansion of labor recruitment into new areas of Europe and the world.

These piecemeal efforts at immigration control declined after 1885. Taking their place was a series of increasingly restrictive comprehensive efforts at immigration control. In 1891, Congress passed the first comprehensive immigration control bill (26 Statutes at Large 1084, enacted March 3, 1891). This bill established a Federal Bureau of Immigration to enforce immigration laws and expanded the excluded classes of immigrants to individuals suffering from contagious diseases, polygamists, felons, individuals convicted of other crimes and misdemeanors, and aliens whose passage was paid by others (another stab at controlling labor recruitment). This law also forbade the encouragement of immigration by advertisement.

The second, third, and fourth comprehensive immigration control bills in 1903, 1907, and 1917, respectively, further limited immigrant access to the United States (32 Statutes at Large 1213, enacted March 3, 1903; 34 Statutes at Large 898, enacted February 20, 1907; and 39 Statutes at Large 874, enacted February 5, 1917). As a result, newly excluded classes of immigrants included a virtual rogues' gallery of popular fears: anarchists, the illiterate, the feebleminded, those with physical or mental defects, children unaccompanied by their parents, and women coming to the United States for "immoral purposes."

In 1907, to address growing dissatisfaction from opponents of immigration, Congress created a commission to examine immigration, headed by Vermont's senator William Dillingham. The commission alleged that some nationalities—particularly those from Southern and Eastern Europe—were less assimilable than others and that those less likely to become good Americans should be excluded from immigration. Held up to today's standards for empirical research, the Dillingham Commission's methods were flawed, but in their day, they offered the intellectual justification to close America's doors to immigrants from some countries.

In 1908, Japan and the United States negotiated a "Gentlemen's Agreement" to stop emigration from Japan to the United States. Japan entered into this agreement to avoid the outright exclusion that China suffered, but in 1917, Congress passed legislation that excluded all Asians from immigration (39 Statutes at Large 874, enacted February 5, 1917). But the establishment of the literacy requirement in the 1917 bill was the most sweeping of this period's changes. In this era, literacy was not the norm, particularly in those countries sending the lion's share of immigrants to the United States. Enforcement of this new literacy requirement slowed the immigration of Southern and Eastern Europeans as well as that of immigrants from Mexico and the Americas.

In these bills, Congress also mandated the deportation of immigrants who became public charges or were found, subsequent to immigration, to have any of the characteristics or beliefs that merited exclusion at immigration. Congress identified a key enforcement tool for the assertion of federal authority regarding immigration. Prior to these laws, deportation was virtually unheard of for immigrants already residing in the United States, so once they had been admitted, their past was largely irrelevant. Even after the passage of these pieces of legislation, deportation was sparingly utilized. Between 1908 and 1910, the United States deported an average of 2,300 immigrants annually. And despite the security concerns that surrounded World War I, this number increased to just 2,800 annually during the 1910s (Department of Homeland Security 2013: Table 39). Congress's piecemeal efforts at immigration control and the more comprehensive measures that followed shared a theme: excluding less desirable aliens from residence in the United States. Efforts such as these faced a problem, however. Enforcement rested largely with local authorities, mostly at ports in Eastern cities, and they did not share the Congressional concern about immigration. Thus, the specific exclusions did not have the impact desired by Congress.

In the early 1920s, Congress crafted legislation that completed the US move away from open borders (42 Statutes at Large 5, enacted May 19, 1921; 43 Statutes at Large 153, enacted May 26, 1924). The Quota Acts of 1921 and 1924 were not as narrowly focused as the previous legislation had been. With these bills, Congress established a barricade against the national-origin populations that had increasingly dominated the immigrant flow in the early twentieth century. The Quota Acts established a national annual limit on immigration and allocated visas within this national limit based on the presence of foreign-born persons by country as measured in the 1910 census (for the 1921 bill) and in the 1890 census (for the 1924 bill). However, these national-origin limits served only to reinforce previously dominant immigrant patterns. For example, Congress, in using the 1890 census, clearly sought to exclude Southern and Eastern Europeans, who had only begun to immigrate in large numbers after 1890.

Congress also established a preference system for allocating the limited number of visas. Parents, spouses, and unmarried children of US citizens were first in line. Perhaps most important, Congress mandated that European immigrants have visas issued by a US consulate abroad at the time of entry. Thus, Congress limited which nationalities could immigrate and developed an effective enforcement mechanism to ensure that local officials could not create their own policies. Congress also created a major exception to the quotas. Immigrants from countries in the Americas, including Mexico, could immigrate without numerical restriction so long as they could meet certain requirements, such as being literate and not being likely to become a public charge. These standards were erratically applied to immigrants from the Americas, however. The Border Patrol overlooked these standards when Mexican labor was in demand (Hernández 2010).

Unwittingly, Congress created a new category of immigrant—the unauthorized immigrant—by establishing categories of immigrants ineligible for immigration. These included immigrants residing in the United States who had entered without advance approval, who had entered despite having the characteristics or traits specifically prohibited among immigrants, or in later years, those who had entered the United States on a temporary basis and had remained beyond the authorized period. In these first years of immigration restriction, unauthorized immigration was of only minor concern to Congress. In 1929, it passed registry legislation that granted a presumption of legal status if an immigrant had been residing in the United States for eight years (45 Statutes at Large 1512, enacted March 2, 1929). This was the nation's first legalization program for unauthorized immigrants (and remains on the books today for unauthorized immigrants who entered the United States before January 1, 1972). As demand for immigration increased and the categories of potential immigrants who were excluded from immigration eligibility grew, concern about unauthorized immigration would also grow (Ngai 2004).

## Federal Versus Local Government and Private Responsibility in US Immigration

As the federal government increasingly took responsibility for stimulating and regulating immigration in this period, the role of private interests and local governments in shaping immigrant flows became diminished (Zolberg 2006). When the borders were open, the federal government's sole role was to process immigrants at the ports. Incentives to immigration were private or local in nature, such as those offered by employers, shipping companies, states in the Midwest and West seeking new populations and new workers, or immigrants already in the United States seeking to encourage relatives or friends to immigrate.

Once it began to address who could and could not immigrate, the federal government became the focus of popular concerns about immigration. Thus, employers seeking a specific type of laborer—agricultural laborers, for example—could no longer simply recruit labor abroad. Instead, they had to convince lawmakers that the country needed agricultural labor (or they had to violate the law and recruit the unauthorized). Similarly, immigrants seeking to ensure that their relatives could immigrate to the United States had to make sure that federal immigration laws respected the notion of family unification. Thus, as demand for immigration to the United States increased, Congress faced extensive pressures from diverse interests to expand immigration. Beginning in the 1960s, these demands reached fruition with the repeal of the Quota Acts. However, popular opinion often opposed immigration, or at least specific forms of immigration, like unauthorized immigration. The process of establishing federal control over the borders helped make immigration a contentious national policy issue.

States and localities, however, continued to act autonomously in some cases. During the Great Depression, for example, states and cities in the Southwest deported large numbers of Mexican nationals and some US citizens of Mexican ancestry (Balderama and Rodríguez 1995). In the contemporary era, states and cities are again attempting today to discourage immigration, particularly unauthorized immigration, by making state and local employers responsible for ascertaining the immigrant status of people seeking state services and by requiring state and local police to check for immigrant status. Overall, the federal government still effectively has responsibility over shaping immigrant flows, but who actually implements immigration legislation continues to be contested.

## Immigration Post-1965 to September 11, 2001

As we discussed briefly in Chapter 1, the United States experienced another great wave of immigration that began with the Immigration and Nationality Act of 1965, also known as the Hart-Celler Act, after its authors Philip Hart (D-MI) and Emanuel Celler (D-NY). This law eliminated the national-origin quotas and established a new principle for US immigration—family unification. The effect of this law on the immigrant numbers was immediate, steadily growing with each decade. By the 1990s and the first decade of the twenty-first century, immigration to permanent residence grew to approximately 1.1 million annually. These legal immigrants were supplemented by an 300,000 to 500,000 new unauthorized immigrants who took up residence in the United States each year—at least until 2008, when their numbers began to decline in response to a slowed US economy and stricter enforcement against unauthorized immigration. Immigration at this level exceeded the peak years in the early 1900s; equally important, the period of high immigration since the 1990s has gone on for longer than the period of high immigration at the turn of the twentieth century. In addition to the dramatic increase in the number of immigrants, the 1965 act has changed the makeup of immigrants' countries of origin. The act, however, did not anticipate components of the immigrant stream that today vex policymakers, particularly unauthorized immigrants and refugees/asylees. In the years since 1965, most recently in 1996, Congress has amended the 1965 act and restricted the immigration opportunities of some who were eligible to immigrate under the original act. These piecemeal changes, however, have failed to alter the 1965 act's liberal provisions for immigration.

In the place of national-origin quotas, the 1965 act established two categories of immigrants who would be eligible to immigrate—family members of US citizens and permanent residents, and those with special occupational skills, abilities, or training. Family members, including spouses, children, parents, and siblings of US citizens and permanent residents, made up about 80 percent of immigrants (this level has been reduced since 1990). Immigrants with desired job skills made up the remaining 20 percent of immigrants in 1965. The 1965 act established a permeable cap of 290,000 immigrants to the United States annually, with a limit for any single country of 20,000—*permeable* because Congress exempted immediate relatives (spouses, minor children, and parents) of US citizens from these limitations (Johnson 2013).

Over the intervening three decades, the 1965 act has been amended several times to address three concerns. First, Congress has sought, largely unsuccessfully, to include the admission of refugees and asylees in the annual caps on immigration. Second, Congress has endeavored to control unauthorized immigration. Finally, Congress has reexamined and reduced the preference for family unification in the 1965 immigration act. We address each of these concerns below.

The first of the pressures on immigration unanticipated by Congress in 1965 was a need to provide for the admission of refugees and asylees. Refugee and asylee admissions cannot be anticipated in advance; they emerge during periods of political strife. As a result, immigration laws give the executive branch the power to award refugee status. However, the executive branch's exercise of the power to admit or deny refugees often conflicts with foreign policy objectives. Immigration law seeks a regulated and predictable flow of immigrants with predefined traits or characteristics so that the immigrants do not come into conflict with US-born populations; foreign policy seeks to strengthen the United States relative to its foes. Generally, when the two laws come into conflict, the executive branch usually responds in favor of foreign policy objectives, to the disadvantage of an orderly refugee and asylee program. The United States has tended to admit as refugees the nationals of states that stand in opposition to the United States, such as nationals of Communist states, and has tended to deny refugee status to those from nations the United States supports (Kerwin 2014). In the 1980s, for example, the United

States readily admitted refugees from Nicaragua while rejecting nationals of El Salvador. Similarly, the United States has rejected virtually all Mexican applications for refugee status regardless of the evidence provided by applicants. On the other hand, the massive inflows of refugees of former Communist states—Cubans in the 1960s, 1970s, and early 1980s, and Vietnamese in the mid-1970s—significantly altered the immigrant flow and created exactly the tensions with US-born populations that immigration laws seek to avoid. The rationale for this policy was to admit political but not economic refugees; however, these distinctions have been nearly impossible to maintain in reality.

Congress's efforts to restructure refugee policy have not been successful. Beginning in 1980, refugees did not count against the annual limit in immigration, so regular immigration does not have to be reduced during periods of refugee admissions (94 Statutes at Large 102, enacted March 17, 1980). Congress has been unwilling to bar the admission of all refugees, but it has sought to cap the annual number of refugee admissions. However, these efforts conflict with the unpredictable nature of refugee immigration. Congress has also sought, in some cases, to negate executive branch denial of refugee status based on foreign policy considerations, such as linking the fate of Haitians and Cubans in 1994. Finally, in the 1996 immigration bill, Congress narrowed the standards for awarding refugee status, required that individuals seeking asylee status apply within one year of arriving in the United States, sped up the process for administrative review of refugee and asylee applications, and expedited the removal from the United States of individuals denied asylum. In general, however, immigration reform since 1965 has not significantly reduced executive branch authority over refugees and asylees (Schrag 2000).

The second element of immigration unanticipated in the 1965 act—unauthorized immigration—has proved even more vexing for Congress. Although unauthorized immigration existed when Congress passed the 1965 immigration law, it was not taken seriously by the public or policymakers. The unauthorized immigrants of the era tended to be concentrated in the Southwest, and most were Mexican nationals working in US agriculture who had the protection of the agricultural lobby. Another explanation for the policymakers' lack of concern was a conscious effort by the Immigration and Naturalization Service (INS) to hide the problem. Using a federal government program designed to provide short-term agricultural labor—the Bracero Program—the INS periodically legalized any unauthorized immigrants from Mexico (Calavita 1992). Essentially, in the late 1950s and early 1960s, when Congress became concerned about the problem, the INS would make it literally disappear. As a result, the kind of public outrage about unauthorized immigrants that had swelled in the early 1950s was not an issue when Congress reformed immigration in 1965.

Beginning in the mid-1970s, however, policymakers and the general public grew to fear the level of unauthorized immigration. For over a decade, Congress tried to craft a response. In 1986, it passed the Immigration Reform and Control Act (IRCA), which united the needs of diverse interests but in the end did little to slow unauthorized immigration (Gimpel and Edwards 1999). As we discussed in Chapter 1, the IRCA penalized the knowing employment of the unauthorized, established a new requirement that citizenship or work eligibility be proven upon starting a new job, and gave permanent resident status to unauthorized immigrants who had resided in the United States for at least five years or had ninety days or more of work in perishable agriculture.

Although the IRCA succeeded in legalizing the status of long-term unauthorized immigrants already in the United States, it was unsuccessful in discouraging new unauthorized immigrants from immigrating (Newton 2008). It also gave rise to widespread fraud among many who were able to "legalize" their status based on false documents or claims of work in agricultural industries. In addition, employers continued knowingly to hire unauthorized immigrants. In part because of pressures from employer organizations and chambers of commerce, the government was unwilling and unable to enforce the employer sanctions provisions of the act until approximately 2005. Certainly, some employers were fined for hiring the unauthorized, but few were jailed. Congress drafted the law in such a way as to offer employers an easy excuse. As long as they had no reason to believe that the documents that new employees presented were false, they could not be prosecuted for employing the unauthorized. A plethora of false documents and employer ignorance combined to ensure that little changed after the IRCA was passed.

In the early 1990s, Congress and the executive branch vigorously pursued a new strategy for controlling unauthorized immigration: vastly increasing appropriations to the INS, particularly to the INS border control operations. For example, between 1993 and 1996, the INS budget increased by 68 percent, exceeding the Clinton administration's budget requests. In this same period, Congress appropriated funds to increase the Border Patrol by 85 percent. This increase in funding dramatically increased the number of apprehensions of unauthorized immigrants caught along the border or at work sites, but there is no evidence that it has slowed the pace of unauthorized immigration.

In 1996, Congress again revisited policy toward immigrants and, particularly, unauthorized immigration (Illegal Immigration Reform and Immigrant Responsibility Act, 110 Statutes at Large 3009). While continuing the pattern of adding to INS resources and expanding the Border Patrol, this legislation also barred subsequent legal immigration for unauthorized individuals caught in the United States. Unauthorized immigrants would not be able to receive a permanent resident visa for a minimum of three years after returning to their home country; a second apprehension would lead to a ten-year bar on legal immigration.

Congress passed a second piece of immigration legislation in 1996 focused on terrorism and criminal aliens (the Antiterrorism and Effective Death Penalty Act, 110 Statutes at Large 1214). In addition to a series of provisions on deportation of members of terrorist organizations regardless of immigration status, this legislation made it easier to deport legal immigrants who had committed crimes in the United States. Legal immigrants convicted of felonies had long been subject to deportation. This legislation expanded the list of crimes leading to deportation to include certain misdemeanors. It also sped up the deportation process for legal immigrants convicted of crimes and reduced the legal protections and appeal rights for these immigrants.

And finally, since the passage of the 1965 immigration bill, Congress has also reexamined the level and composition of annual immigration to the United States. The same legislation that sought to guarantee the admission of refugees also reduced the number of *preference immigrants*— those other than immediate family members of US citizens—admitted annually to 270,000. In 1990, Congress addressed the issue of immigrant numbers again, raising the annual target of immigrants to 675,000 (104 Statutes at Large 4978, enacted November 29, 1990). Although this may appear to be an overall increase, it more accurately reflects the level of non-preference immigration. Again, this was a permeable cap, with immediate family members of US citizens exempt from numerical limitations. The 1990 bill also reallocated the share of visas dedicated to family unification and employment-related visas, reducing visas allocated to family members to approximately 70 percent of the total and reducing employment visas to 20 percent. The remaining visas were allocated to a new program called, somewhat disingenuously, the Diversity Immigrant Visa Program. These *diversity visas*, available to nationals of countries that have not made up a large share of recent immigrants, are awarded at random through a mail-in lottery. As we mentioned in Chapter 1, the Diversity Visa program has simply created new streams for future preference and non-preference family unification immigration.

In the period leading up to the vote on the 1996 immigration bill, many analysts expected more than incremental reform. These expectations emerged because of the rise in mass interest in immigration that began with California's approval of Proposition 187—a state ballot initiative that was later found to be largely unconstitutional and was not implemented. The proposition sought to deny social welfare and education benefits to the unauthorized themselves and to the US-citizen children of the unauthorized. Its goal was to reduce the number of unauthorized migrants in California. During the year leading up to Congressional consideration of this bill, it seemed quite likely that Congress would enact legislation that would cap the number of immigrants at a level lower than average immigration in the early 1990s, and perhaps even at levels significantly below the then-current levels.

The bill that Congress passed—the Illegal Immigration Reform and Immigrant Responsibility Act of 1996—proved to fit better with the pattern of incremental reform. It included no cap on immigration to permanent residence. It focused more on enhanced border enforcement than on immigration to permanent residence. One section of the bill, however, changed the composition of immigration. The bill tightened requirements for immigrant "sponsors," that is, the US citizens, permanent residents, or companies that petition for the immigration of foreign nationals and promise to take financial responsibility for the immigrants. Prior to the passage of the 1996 law, this promise meant little and only applied during the first three to five years of an immigrant's residence.

The 1996 bill changed these responsibilities in three ways. First, Congress established a minimum income level for the sponsor—125 percent of the poverty level for the sponsor, the sponsor's family, and the immigrant being sponsored (including the size of the immigrant's family if the petition is for an entire family). In addition, states could take the sponsor's income into account when deciding whether the immigrant was eligible for benefit programs. Second, it made the sponsorship legally enforceable, so the sponsor could not subsequently abandon the immigrant. Finally, it extended the duration of the sponsorship to ten years (or until the immigrant naturalizes, if that occurs before ten years).

Of these changes, the first had the most dramatic impact on who was allowed to immigrate. For example, if the petitioner has a family of four and seeks the admission of an immigrant, the combined income of the petitioner, the petitioner's family, and the immigrant must exceed approximately $34,900 (at 2014 levels). A larger petitioner family or petitions that included the immigrant's family would raise the required level of income by $5,100 (in 2014 dollars) per person. These provisions added a class dynamic that was not present for family preference immigrants prior to 1996, when immigration eligibility was established through blood, skills (employment preference visas), or randomness. These changes ensured that only petitioners and immigrants of a certain income level could use this channel of authorized immigration, thus limiting the class diversity of authorized immigrants and adding to the incentives for unauthorized migration.

Congress also limited the access of immigrants to federal social welfare programs and other such government benefits (we discuss the relationship of the state to immigrants in greater depth in Chapter 3). Again, this appears to limit authorized migration to immigrants of a certain class status, but it is unclear whether this would act as a significant disincentive to immigration as a whole.

## Immigration Post-9/11

Immigration policy and patterns since 9/11 are similar to those of the previous era, though with a few key differences. The similarities include the openness of immigration to all nationalities and races, the continued emphasis on family- and skill-based immigration, and efforts to reduce unauthorized migration. The changes consist of defining immigration as a national security issue and creating a new federal apparatus to address immigration in accordance with this definition. This approach reflects a fear that terrorists are exploiting liberal immigration laws to threaten national well-being.

In 2003, Congress created the Department of Homeland Security (DHS) to act as the principal civilian agency to protect the United States within, at, and outside its borders. The responsibilities of DHS include preventing and responding to domestic emergencies, particularly terrorism. On March 1, 2003, DHS replaced the Immigration and Naturalization Service and created two new and separate agencies to carry out its mandate—the Immigration and Customs Enforcement (ICE) Agency and the Citizenship and Immigration Services (CIS) Agency. Additionally, functions of the INS, the US Customs Service, and the Animal and Plant Health Inspection Service were consolidated into a new DHS agency, the US Customs and Border Protection Agency. The creation of DHS constituted the largest government reorganization in American history: DHS incorporated twenty-two government agencies into a single organization. DHS is the third largest cabinet department, with more than 200,000 employees; only the Departments of Defense and Veterans Affairs are larger.

The title, structure, and responsibilities of DHS indicate a major shift in immigration policy. The emphasis now is on securing the border and other points of entry as well as enforcing US immigration law in the nation's interior. This has included militarizing the border by deploying large numbers of federal agents, erecting fences, using high-tech surveillance to prevent illegal entry, and identifying immigrants without legal status in the nation's interior at unprecedented levels (Isacson and Meyer 2012).

Presidents George W. Bush and Barack Obama have followed this "enforcement first" strategy to move the nation toward comprehensive immigration reform. Each president increased spending on border security. The border fence does not cover the entire Southern border but instead provides a barrier where most unauthorized immigrants enter the United States—it now extends 651 miles along the US-Mexico border. Extending the fence across the entire Southern border would cost approximately $22.4 billion (Preston 2011). Each president also expanded DHS staffing, particularly focusing on Border Patrol personnel (see Table 2.4).

However, as policymakers increasingly realized that border enforcement alone was insufficient to discourage unauthorized migration, President Bush, and later President Obama, focused a higher share of enforcement efforts on the nation's interior. Under the Bush administration, ICE increasingly focused its energies on pinpointing and raiding large workplaces deemed likely to employ unauthorized migrants. This led to some highly publicized raids at large employers, but they were not particularly effective due to the high numbers of ICE personnel required

TABLE 2.4. US Border Patrol Staffing Levels, by Fiscal Year, 1992–2013

| Fiscal Year | Agents |
|---|---|
| 1992 | 4,139 |
| 1993 | 4,028 |
| 1994 | 4,287 |
| 1995 | 4,945 |
| 1996 | 5,942 |
| 1997 | 6,895 |
| 1998 | 7,982 |
| 1999 | 8,351 |
| 2000 | 9,212 |
| 2001 | 9,821 |
| 2002 | 10,045 |
| 2003 | 10,717 |
| 2004 | 10,819 |
| 2005 | 11,264 |
| 2006 | 12,349 |
| 2007 | 14,923 |
| 2008 | 17,499 |
| 2009 | 20,119 |
| 2010 | 20,558 |
| 2011 | 21,444 |
| 2012 | 21,394 |
| 2013 | 21,391 |

*Note:* These data reflect filled positions, not positions authorized by Congress. In many years, the Immigration and Naturalization Service/US Customs and Border Protection has not been able to fill all positions authorized by Congress.

*Source:* US Customs and Border Protection (2014).

for the raids and the difficulty of processing so many potential deportees at one time. Such raids also often violated the civil rights of workers
legally in the United States (as either permanent residents or US citizens).
And probably as important, employers also complained that the raids dis-
rupted work sites and that the fear of raids caused workers to disappear to
many nearby businesses (Camayd-Freixas 2013).

Responding to these criticisms, the Obama administration shifted
away from targeting work sites, instead focusing ICE's energies on unauthorized immigrants who had broken criminal laws, recently crossed the
border, repeatedly entered the United States, or were fugitives from previous deportation orders. Whatever the specific strategy, the post-9/11
period has seen a considerable increase in the removal of inadmissible
and deportable immigrants (see Table 2.5). This increase—to an average of 400,000 annually since 2009—is all the more surprising considering that new unauthorized migration has declined considerably with
the post-2008 US and global recession and the increase in US immigration enforcement. In 2012, the Pew Hispanic Center estimated that net
migration (the sum of new immigrants minus those who returned to
their country of origin, voluntarily or involuntarily) from Mexico to the
United States had stopped and had even possibly reversed (Passel, Cohn,
and Gonzalez-Barrera 2012).

This DHS approach to immigration control is likely to continue for
the foreseeable future. As both Presidents Bush and Obama have recognized, support for comprehensive immigration reform will remain low
until a national consensus emerges that unauthorized immigration can
be controlled. To date, this "enforcement first" strategy has not opened
the door to a legislative compromise on immigration. It has, however,
prompted one change in immigration policy in the post-9/11 era. The
Obama administration has recognized that Congress as it is presently
composed is unlikely to engage in a serious debate about comprehensive
immigration reform. As a result, Obama has used his executive powers to
provide temporary protections for some unauthorized immigrants. The
subset of unauthorized immigrants who received these protections under
the Obama policies were young adults who had immigrated with their
parents as children and were enrolled in, or had completed, high school—
the DREAMers and parents of US citizens and permanent residents.

The Obama administration's focus on criminal aliens reduced but didn't
eliminate the chance that potential DREAMers would be swept up in the

Table 2.5. Aliens Apprehended, Removed, and Returned, 1970, 1980, 1990, and 2000–2012

| Year | Alien Apprehensions[1] | Removals[2] | Returns[3] |
|------|------------------------|-------------|------------|
| 1970 | 345,353 | 17,469 | 303,348 |
| 1980 | 910,361 | 18,013 | 719,211 |
| 1990 | 1,169,939 | 30,039 | 1,022,533 |
| 2000 | 1,814,729 | 188,467 | 1,675,876 |
| 2001 | 1,387,486 | 189,026 | 1,349,371 |
| 2002 | 1,062,270 | 165,168 | 1,012,116 |
| 2003 | 1,046,422 | 211,098 | 945,294 |
| 2004 | 1,264,232 | 240,665 | 1,166,576 |
| 2005 | 1,291,065 | 246,431 | 1,096,920 |
| 2006 | 1,206,417 | 280,974 | 1,043,381 |
| 2007 | 960,772 | 319,382 | 891,390 |
| 2008 | 1,043,863 | 359,795 | 811,263 |
| 2009 | 869,857 | 393,457 | 584,436 |
| 2010 | 752,329 | 385,100 | 475,613 |
| 2011 | 641,633 | 391,953 | 323,542 |
| 2012 | 643,474 | 419,384 | 229,968 |

*Source:* US Department of Homeland Security (2013: Tables 33 and 39).

[1] Not all apprehensions result in removals or returns and not all removals and returns occur in the same year as the apprehension, so the sum of removals and returns does not sum to the apprehensions in any year.

[2] Compulsory movement of an inadmissible or deportable immigrant outside of the country based on an order of removal.

[3] Movement of an inadmissible or deportable immigrant outside of the country.

raids. Reviews of pending deportations were conducted to see if young adults who might be eligible for the DREAM Act were facing immediate deportation. As part of this review, the deportation cases against many young adults were put on hold. Despite the fact that some deportation cases were suspended, there was no guarantee that the deportation proceedings would not be resumed at some point, and the suspension did not guarantee any new rights, such as the ability to work in the United States.

In 2012, President Obama announced a new program, Deferred Action for Childhood Arrivals (DACA), which provided two years of residence and work eligibility to those who qualified. To be eligible, applicants had to (1) have migrated to the United States before they turned sixteen; (2) have resided continuously in the United States for the five years prior to their application; (3) be currently enrolled in school, have graduated from high school, obtained a GED, or be honorably discharged from the military; (4) have not been convicted of a felony or significant misdemeanor; and (5) be younger than thirty. Application levels were low in comparison to the number of those eligible. This is in part due to the difficulty in collecting the evidence of continuous residence, the cost of applying, and fears in the young adult unauthorized immigrant community that the program could be terminated by President Obama's successor (Bahrampour 2012). In 2014, President Obama extended the program for an additional two years and extended it to older applicants and parents of US citizens and permanent residents.

## Who Are We Today? Composition of Contemporary Immigration

The composition of contemporary immigration is driven by the 1965 immigration act. The act establishes an immigration system that guarantees steadily increasing levels of immigration. It concentrates access to immigration on nationals of those countries that have recently sent immigrants to the United States. Finally, the 1965 act limits immigration for many who desire access to the United States while simultaneously still allowing large numbers to immigrate, thus incentivizing unauthorized immigration and creating large legal immigrant communities into which unauthorized immigrants can merge and, in many cases, disappear.

Between 1965 and 2013, 36.5 million people immigrated to the United States as permanent residents. The period of high annual levels of immigration in the current wave of immigration is much longer than the years of highest immigration during the Second Great Wave. However, though these levels are high by historical standards, today's immigrants enter a United States that is much larger than it was at the turn of the century. Today, 1.1 million immigrants would constitute less than four-tenths of 1 percent of the national population. The same 1.1 million immigrants would have added 1.2 percent to the nation's 92 million residents in 1910. Thus, depending on the measure, immigration can be seen as being at a record high or at just moderately high levels. But as we have seen in other eras of US immigration history, raw numbers are not necessarily the factors that generate concern about immigration among the US-born population. Instead, concerns arise from perceptions of economic or cultural challenges resulting from immigration and from fears that immigrants are not adapting adequately to life in the United States.

These immigrants are not randomly selected from throughout the world. Although the 1965 act and its successors reversed the racist elements of the Quota Acts, they did not ensure unfettered immigration to the United States. Instead, the immigration law rewards foreign nationals who have immediate relatives in the United States, as well as those with desirable job skills. The consequence of the family preference bias in immigration law is that some nationalities dominate the contemporary immigrant flow (see Table 2.6). Over the last several decades, immigrants from Asia and Latin America have made up more than 75 percent of legal immigrants and an even higher share of unauthorized migrants. At any given period, a few countries have always dominated the immigration flow. Today, however, this phenomenon is a by-product of the law and not a function of private initiatives or the availability of transportation, as it was in the earlier periods of immigration. Unless the law is changed, the countries that have dominated the flow in recent years will continue to dominate as long as there is demand for immigrant visas in those countries.

Just as today's immigrants do not immigrate evenly from throughout the world, they do not settle evenly throughout the United States. As they have from the nation's first days, immigrants disproportionately settle in cities. Even among cities, the most likely destinations are those near borders and those with the most extensive international air links—cities such as Los Angeles, New York, Miami, Houston, and Chicago are home to more immigrants than Kansas City, Minneapolis, or Seattle. In 2012, for

TABLE 2.6.  Regions and Countries of Origin of Permanent Resident
Immigrants, 1950–2009[1]

| Regions/ Countries | 1950–1959 | 1960–1969 | 1970–1979 | 1980–1989 | 1990–1999 | 2000–2009 |
|---|---|---|---|---|---|---|
| TOTAL | 2,499,268 | 3,213,749 | 4,248,203 | 6,244,379 | 9,775,398 | 10,299,430 |
| Region | | | | | | |
| Europe | 1,404,973 | 1,133,443 | 825,590 | 668,866 | 1,348,612 | 1,348,904 |
| Latin America and the Caribbean | 921,610 | 1,674,174 | 1,904,355 | 2,695,329 | 5,137,743 | 4,442,226 |
| Asia | 135,844 | 358,605 | 1,406,544 | 2,391,356 | 2,859,899 | 3,470,835 |
| Africa | 13,016 | 23,780 | 71,408 | 141,990 | 346,416 | 759,742 |
| Oceania | 11,353 | 23,630 | 39,980 | 41,432 | 56,800 | 65,793 |
| Country, Sorted by Region | | | | | | |
| Mexico | 273,847 | 441,172 | 621,218 | 1,009,586 | 2,757,418 | 1,704,166 |
| Cuba | 73,221 | 202,030 | 256,497 | 132,552 | 159,037 | 271,742 |
| Dominican Republic | 10,219 | 83,552 | 139,249 | 221,552 | 359,818 | 291,492 |
| El Salvador | 5,094 | 14,405 | 29,428 | 137,418 | 273,017 | 251,237 |
| Guatemala | 4,197 | 14,357 | 23,837 | 58,847 | 126,043 | 156,992 |
| Argentina | 16,346 | 49,384 | 30,303 | 23,442 | 30,065 | 47,955 |
| Colombia | 15,567 | 68,371 | 71,265 | 105,494 | 137,985 | 236,570 |
| Ecuador | 8,574 | 34,107 | 47,464 | 48,015 | 81,358 | 107,977 |
| China and Hong Kong[2] | 22,167 | 81,107 | 134,977 | 283,029 | 458,952 | 649,294 |
| India | 13,781 | 67,047 | 117,350 | 112,132 | 116,894 | 590,464 |
| Korea | 4,845 | 27,048 | 241,192 | 322,708 | 179,770 | 209,758 |
| Philippines | 17,245 | 70,660 | 337,726 | 502,056 | 534,338 | 545,463 |

Source: Authors' compilations based on US Department of Homeland Security (2013:
Table 2).

---

[1] Recipients of legalization under the Immigration Reform and Control Act of 1986
appear as legal immigrants in the year in which they obtained legal permanent resident status. For most IRCA recipients this occurred between 1989 and 1993.

[2] After 1957, data for China include Taiwan. Until the 1980s, Hong Kong sent more
emigrants to the United States than did China.

example, more than 25 percent of new immigrants to permanent residence intended to reside in just two cities—New York and Los Angeles—and just 1.3 percent of immigrants reported that they would reside in rural areas.

The diversity of today's immigrants who become permanent residents makes it difficult to generalize about their economic and social opportunities. Because of their educational and occupational resources, many immigrants live, at least initially, around other immigrants from the same region of the world (or in many cases, the same country of origin). These residential patterns and the types of jobs that many immigrants take when they initially move to the United States slow their assimilation into the broader population. In addition, the factory jobs that allowed the immigrants of the Second Great Wave and their children and grandchildren to move up in society have largely disappeared. In their place are service sector and other low-skill jobs that do not offer extensive opportunities for economic advancement. The nature of employment and the range of opportunities have changed considerably since the last period of high levels of immigration, disadvantaging both immigrants and US-born citizens with low levels of education or job skills. Previous immigrants were able to become successful and contributing members of the economy, but given the current economic circumstances, it is tough to say the same of most of today's immigrants. Immigrant households, however, often try to overcome these limitations by having multiple wage earners who often hold multiple jobs. In addition to these high levels of labor force participation, immigrant households have higher savings rates than comparably situated US-born households.

One opportunity available to immigrant households that has improved since the turn of the century is public education. The ethos of opportunity that drives immigrants to hold multiple jobs appears to extend to their children. However, language difficulties as well as the decline in urban public education raise the question whether immigrant children, no matter how motivated, can take full advantage of educational opportunities.

As we stated earlier, the diversity of today's immigrants means we cannot paint their experiences with a single brush. The United States also attracts many highly skilled immigrants who seek better wages or living conditions than are available in their countries of origin. For example, many immigrants from India arrive with medical degrees and many from the Philippines are registered nurses. Other nations send large numbers of professionals each year. This heterogeneity in the skills and resources of contemporary immigrants is often lost in discussions of immigrant contributions to US society.

Some immigrants, and even immigrant communities, have achieved great economic success and social prestige in the United States. In some cases, this is simply due to the wealth individual immigrants brought with them when they immigrated. For example, Rupert Murdoch, the president of News World Communications, became a naturalized citizen at least in part so that he could purchase US television stations. He is hardly an American success story, though he has certainly prospered here. A more interesting case is the immigrant populations that have formed self-reinforcing economic identities, or *enclaves*, that allow the immigrant ethnic community as a whole to prosper. In these enclaves, which have appeared in the Cuban, Chinese, and Korean immigrant communities of some cities, immigrants work for coethnic immigrant-owned businesses, patronize stores owned by coethnics, and generally live in an economic world revolving around coethnics. Thus, resources stay within the immigrant ethnic population and help to build the community. These businesses employ new coethnic immigrants and offer them opportunities disproportionate to those they would encounter outside of the ethnic community. Enclaves do not form automatically. Discrimination by the dominant society is a key initial incentive for entrepreneurs to look within the ethnic community economically. And the enclave is no guarantee of success. Communities without any resources would not be advantaged by looking only within, yet they offer a tool for immigrant communities to grow economically despite changes in the national economy and in public education.

So far, this discussion of the composition of contemporary immigration has neglected a key component—unauthorized immigration. According to the best estimates, approximately 11.7 million unauthorized immigrants resided in the United States in 2012. As these are people who do not wish to be counted, this figure can only be an estimate, subject to a great deal of controversy. Like the permanent resident population, the unauthorized are unevenly distributed nationally. The one concrete state-level estimate suggests that 22 percent of the unauthorized immigrants who resided in the United States in 2012 lived in California (Passel, Cohn, and Gonzalez-Barrera 2013). Table 2.7 offers the most recent (2011) comprehensive assessment of the states of residence and the national origins

TABLE 2.7. Unauthorized Immigrant Population, by Country of Origin and by State, 2011

| Country of Origin | Population |
| --- | --- |
| Mexico | 6,800,000 |
| El Salvador | 660,000 |
| Guatemala | 520,000 |
| Honduras | 380,000 |
| China | 280,000 |
| Philippines | 270,000 |
| India | 240,000 |
| Korea | 230,000 |
| Ecuador | 210,000 |
| Vietnam | 170,000 |
| Other countries | 1,750,000 |
| TOTAL | 11,510,000 |
| **State** | |
| California | 2,830,000 |
| Texas | 1,790,000 |
| Florida | 740,000 |
| New York | 630,000 |
| Illinois | 550,000 |
| Georgia | 440,000 |
| New Jersey | 420,000 |
| North Carolina | 400,000 |
| Arizona | 360,000 |
| Washington | 260,000 |
| Other | 3,100,000 |
| TOTAL | 11,510,000 |

*Source:* Based on Hoefer et al. (2012: Tables 3 and 4).

of the US unauthorized immigrant population. States with more than 500,000 unauthorized immigrants include California, New York, Texas, Florida, and Illinois. The national origins of these unauthorized immigrants are slightly more diverse than their states of residence. Mexico provides the largest number, though the share of unauthorized immigrants from Mexico is steadily declining.

The economic and social opportunities available to the unauthorized are less known than those available to permanent residents. As late as the 1960s, most unauthorized immigrants worked in agriculture. Increasingly, the unauthorized population has moved into urban areas. Although the research is not comprehensive, the labor market opportunities include day labor, construction, light industry, textiles, and service sector work. As risks exist for employing the unauthorized, they are more likely to be employed by smaller than larger firms, and these smaller firms are less likely to offer benefits and worker protections. Because of their status, unauthorized immigrants also face a greater likelihood of working for employers who violate US labor laws, particularly minimum wage and overtime laws. Increasingly, there is also evidence of employers who imprison unauthorized immigrants and create conditions reminiscent of slavery.

Finally, despite the way they are discussed in the media and political debates, the unauthorized do not comprise a distinct population separate from the permanent residents. Many immigrant households include both permanent residents and unauthorized immigrants. The unauthorized in these households are waiting for permanent resident visas, although the wait may be one of many years—and in reality, those visas will never come. There are many fewer unauthorized immigrants than there are permanent residents—no more than one unauthorized immigrant for every two non-naturalized permanent residents. In the public mind, however, most immigrants are unauthorized immigrants (see Chapter 3).

Not surprisingly, the areas of high immigrant concentration coincide with those that experience the greatest conflict between immigrants and the US-born. The roots of the English-Only movement (an effort to promote English as the "official" language of the jurisdiction) were in Miami, where Cuban immigrants and US-born whites were in conflict over culture and language. California, which has received more immigrants than any other state, spurred the national consideration of immigration restriction with its approval of Proposition 187. Popular support for this proposition suggested two important lessons about the contemporary concern over immigration. First, the proposition received its highest levels of support from parts of California with few immigrants. Thus, like the support for the American (Know-Nothing) Party in the 1850s, opposition to immigrants does not come from those who have direct contact with them. Instead, it comes from those more removed from immigrant populations but who perceive that the quality of their lives is worsened because of immigration. Second, the engine of the concern about immigration is not labor—California has long sought the labor of the unauthorized. Instead, the impetus came from the government's provision of services, particularly education and health care. Thus, the unauthorized immigrants were an easy target for those who sought to change the relationship between the government and the people, a topic we return to in Chapter 3.

## Conclusion

The fundamental dilemma in US immigration policy—oscillating between welcoming immigrants and promoting anti-immigrant sentiment—has not been resolved and probably never will be. Instead, each generation will decide how many immigrants should be admitted and what characteristics they should have. The trend through the twentieth and early twenty-first centuries has been to admit ever more immigrants but to be selective about what traits these immigrants should have, with immediate or blood relationship to a US citizen or permanent resident being of greatest value after 1965. Although the public today supports reducing the overall number of immigrants, this popular consensus will come into conflict with the economy's demand for immigrant labor. If history is a model, it will take years of popular opposition to immigration before Congress acts. Although Washington has centralized control over immigration, it has never been in a position to dominate the economy's demand for immigrant labor. Moreover, concern about immigration has never overcome reverence for immigrants in this country—as has been true throughout the history of immigration in the United States.

Since the centralization of immigration policy in the federal government during the twentieth century, it is now a given that the federal government both shapes and implements policy in terms of the path from immigration to permanent residence. Although these policies often conflict with other federal objectives, the states are not given the opportunity to take an active role in this area. Instead, federal immigration policy is often subordinated to other federal programs. However, in terms of unauthorized immigration, some states are following the lead of Arizona and S.B. 1070 in seeking to discourage unauthorized immigration. In this regard, the states are filling a void that has been left open by the federal government's unsuccessful policies.

# 3

. . . . . . . . . . . . . . . . . . . . . . . . . . . . . . . . . . . . . . . . . . . . . . . . . . . . . . . . . . . . .

# *Immigrants and Natives: Rights, Responsibilities, and Interaction*

OUR DISCUSSION OF IMMIGRATION IN THE PREVIOUS CHAPTER primarily focused on the question of immigration from the perspective of the government. Clearly, however, that is only the beginning of the story. For immigration to be successful, immigrants must adapt to their new country of residence. Equally important, the native population must come to tolerate, if not welcome, the newcomers. In this chapter, we examine the legal and social relationships between immigrant and US-born populations. This legal relationship is distinct from the formal process of incorporation through naturalization that is examined in Chapter 4. We look at the policy areas where the needs of immigrants may conflict with those of the US-born and examine how federal and state governments resolve these conflicts. In particular, questions of the rights, responsibilities, and opportunities of unauthorized migrants cause the deepest tensions between natives and immigrants. These tensions—especially over demands to create a path to legal status for many of today's unauthorized immigrants—complicate legislative efforts to craft the foundation of US immigration policies for the twenty-first century.

We look at the social and institutional interactions between immigrants and natives in the United States in three ways. First, to highlight the fundamental contradiction between concerns over high levels of immigration and respect for what immigrants contribute to US society, we examine attitudes of native populations toward immigrants and immigration policies. Second, looking at both federal and state policymaking, we analyze the rights, privileges, and responsibilities that noncitizens have in US society to see what opportunities and restrictions immigrants face. Finally, we consider how policies designed to assist other groups within US society, particularly minority populations, affect immigrants and shape contemporary immigrant incorporation. Throughout this discussion, we also look at the governmental resources available to immigrants today for *settlement*, that is, the transition from new arrival to full and equally participating member of US society. Many of the policies that benefit immigrants in the United States were not, in fact, designed with immigrants in mind. Rather, they were authored by Congress for other populations, particularly US-born minorities. As a result, these policies do not necessarily meet the needs of immigrants. They may serve to shape the immigrant experience in ways that will lead to greater demand for government programs to remedy past discrimination, or what we call *remedial programs.*

The unauthorized population has grown in recent years and has experienced ever-longer average periods of residence in the United States (resulting in part from significant increases in border enforcement, which makes return migration and reentry into the United States more difficult). With narrow exceptions, however, federal and state policies to facilitate immigrant incorporation exclude unauthorized immigrants from access to government services. As a result, more of today's immigrants than ever before have only limited access to state resources to facilitate their incorporation into American society, and they face the ongoing threat of deportation. This in-between status cannot survive indefinitely, but it is one of the core dilemmas that Congress must address as it seeks a comprehensive reform of US immigration policy. The nation will have to decide either to create a path for many or all unauthorized immigrants to join US society, as the majority of the US Senate and President Obama have proposed, or to deport them. As we show, popular attitudes toward immigration policy and immigration reform are shaped by divisions in the general public over which of these approaches the United States should follow.

## Public Attitudes Toward Immigrants and Immigration Policies

Columnist Ben Wattenberg noted, "I'm convinced that when the second boatload of pilgrims landed in Massachusetts, those on the *Mayflower* said, 'There goes the neighborhood'" (quoted in Espenshade and Belanger 1997). From early in the nation's history, though perhaps not quite as early as Wattenberg pithily observes, the United States has had a contradictory approach to the engine of its own population growth. Immigrants are revered, whereas the aggregation of the immigrant experience—immigration—is treated with much more caution and often outright opposition. When we introduced this contradiction at the beginning of Chapter 2, we indicated that the course of US policy has been to facilitate large-scale immigration through most of the nation's history. The exceptions, however, have been stark. Periods of mass mobilization in opposition to immigration have led to significant, if in some cases short-term, changes in policy.

Congress has to grapple with this contradiction as it debates comprehensive immigration reform. In the current period of debate over immigration policy, the American public is much more likely to support a reduction in the current level of immigrants, or maintaining immigration at current levels, than to endorse an increase in immigration. A 2014 Gallup poll, for example, found that 41 percent of adults nationally think that immigration should be decreased, 33 percent think that it should be maintained at current levels, and 22 percent think that it should be increased (Saad 2014). These percentages have remained in these ranges throughout the period of contemporary debate over comprehensive immigration reform. In annual polls conducted from 1999 to 2014, Gallup found that between 35 percent and 50 percent of adults polled supported a decrease in immigration and between 32 percent and 42 percent supported maintaining it at current levels. The share of the American public advocating an increase in immigration levels has steadily increased from 10 percent in 1999 to a high of 23 percent in 2013, but the share of the American public advocating an increase has always remained well below those advocating a decrease or maintenance of the status quo. These findings are confirmed by a variety of survey organizations (see Pew Research Center 2013).

This cautious attitude toward the levels of immigration to the United States is balanced by a generally positive evaluation of the overall contribution of immigrants to the nation. Gallup polls since 2001 have consistently found that a majority of American adults evaluate immigration as a "good thing" for the nation as a whole (Saad 2014). The percentage of those taking this position has varied from a low of 52 percent in 2002 (soon after the September 11, 2001, attacks on the World Trade Center and Pentagon) to a high of 72 percent in 2013. Between 25 percent and 42 percent of adults see immigration as a "bad thing" for the United States today. In part, the perception of immigration as a "good thing" is driven by a sense that immigrants generally take jobs that the native-born don't want and are willing to work for less money than native workers (Gallup 2014). However, 52 percent express the concern that immigrants are a burden to US society because they take jobs from native workers and use housing and health care services disproportionate to their contributions; just 41 percent feel that immigrants strengthen US society with their hard work (The Opportunity Agenda 2012).

The public's perceptions of immigrant status can also shape its views on immigration. The general public mistakenly believes that the majority of immigrants are undocumented—two-thirds of the respondents in a 1993 Gallup survey expressed this opinion. However, scholarly consensus is that unauthorized immigrants account for approximately 25 percent of immigrants resident in the United States (approximately 33 percent of non-naturalized immigrants) (Pew Research Hispanic Trends Project 2013). Regardless of the actual numbers, this perception of an uncontrolled border negatively shapes popular views about immigration. The public's views are also influenced by short-term crises in immigration, particularly when they reinforce perceptions that the United States is not in control of its immigration system or the border. For example, in 2014, when a large number of Central American migrants, particularly children, appeared at the Southern border and sought asylum, popular attitudes toward immigration increasingly trended toward enforcement and more rapid deportation of unauthorized immigrants (Pew Research Center 2014b). While Americans are broadly opposed to the current levels of immigration, they do have some sense that not all immigrants are the same (as the scholarly evidence that we have presented demonstrates). This recognition of the complexity of immigration offers a foundation for policymakers and immigrant advocates to temper popular misunderstandings and build a consensus that large-scale immigration—and the compromise necessary for comprehensive immigration reform—are necessary and desirable for the nation's future.

Popular concern about the volume of contemporary immigration has not altered a basic respect for the immigrants themselves. The polling data cannot tell us how individuals reconcile these contradictory feelings—in reality, most individuals never have to actively do so. Instead, government institutions establish balance by creating and enforcing restrictions on immigration while facilitating the entrance of immigrants with popularly respected and needed traits. This process appears from the first restrictions on immigration in the late nineteenth century, which controlled the admittance of immigrants with unsavory behavioral and ideological traits, to today's efforts to facilitate the immigration of family members, professionals, and those with needed labor skills. However, as mass and elite attitudes toward immigration policy often diverge, maintaining the balance between these conflicting positions on immigration and immigrants is quite difficult. Whereas the mass interests have long shown opposition to immigration, as demonstrated by the data presented in this chapter, the history of US immigration policy reveals that these restrictionist impulses have rarely been dominant in American policy.

If popular opposition to immigration persists, why has US policy so continuously favored large-scale immigration and naturalization opportunities for some or all immigrants? First, average Americans may oppose immigration in general, but their attitude toward individual immigrants is more positive. Second, immigration is only intermittently a salient issue for the American public as a whole. Immigration policy is important for some groups in US society, but not for the majority. Instead, issues such as economics, crime, and social issues are much more likely to be identified as the most important issue facing the nation or one's community (CNN/ORC Poll 2014). Tea Party organizations voice concerns about legalization policies ("amnesty" in their lexicon) and the border, but generally focus more on economic issues and the scope of federal government policies. Latinos and Asian Americans are generally more concerned about immigration policies than (non-Hispanic) whites, but even in these ethnic communities, which have grown rapidly over the past forty years, in part due to immigration, economic issues and education policy often dominate the political agenda, particularly for Latino and Asian American citizens.

A third factor that facilitates the continuing openness of the United States to immigration and naturalization is that elite consensus consistently supports immigration. In part, this elite consensus is driven by organized interests in the society, such as manufacturers and the agricultural industry, that benefit from a large immigrant workforce. These sectors of the economy typically do not require a high level of skill, and immigrants provide person power while also accepting low wages for their work. Manufacturing and agriculture are not alone in their interest in immigration. Universities benefit from the immigrant flow to fill graduate classrooms and laboratories that the US-born population cannot fill, and some high-tech industries also depend on immigrant labor. Although this list of sectors that depend on immigration is not exhaustive, it does suggest the ongoing demand for immigration by elites within the society. As a result, their concerns are more often met than those of the general population, who may regard immigration negatively but without being overly concerned about it most of the time.

With these contradictory attitudes and interests toward immigration and immigrants in US society, it should come as little surprise that the American public does not speak with a single voice on the components of comprehensive immigration reform. However, there is an increasing sense that change is needed. A 2014 survey found that 61 percent of the American public felt that it was "important" to pass "significant" immigration legislation (Pew Research Center 2014b). A higher share of American adults felt that immigration—more than the tax system, education, health care, Medicare, Social Security, or homeland security—needed to be "completely rebuilt" (Pew Research Center 2013).

What Americans feel this rebuilt immigration system should look like, however, is less clear and is highly susceptible to the way the question is phrased. Consistently, polls show that the majority of adults in the United States support an "earned path" to legal status for unauthorized immigrants even as they oppose "amnesty." At their core, these policies are similar. The notion of an "earned path" for unauthorized immigrants who seek legal status speaks to the numerous requirements that Congress would undoubtedly impose on them, such as fines and back taxes, an English-language requirement, and a long period of temporary residence prior to permanent residence. But the end result is that the unauthorized immigrant is forgiven for having violated US law—arguably a form of "amnesty."

With this caution in mind, polls do offer a sense of how the US public would balance the treatment of individuals and the creation of new barriers to unauthorized migration as part of an immigration reform. A 2013 poll found that 88 percent of Americans would allow unauthorized immigrants to naturalize as part of comprehensive immigration reform, 84 percent would require business owners to check the legal status of potential workers as part of the hiring process, 83 percent would add to security at US borders, and 76 percent would expand the number of short-term immigration visas for skilled workers (Dugan 2013). Just 55 percent would allow employers to hire immigrants if they could prove that they could not find native workers for the position. Slightly more than half (53 percent) would adjust the number of lower-skilled immigrants allowed to enter the country when the US economy is weak (Newport and Wilke 2013). Despite this seeming willingness to accept some form of legalization as part of comprehensive immigration reform (or perhaps acquiescence in the face of the likely direction of policymaking), more than one-third of adults (37 percent) say that giving unauthorized immigrants legal status is rewarding them for doing something wrong (Pew Research Center 2013).

The American public goes back and forth on the question of what the US government should do with unauthorized immigrants. In 2010 and 2011, when the economy was performing poorly, and in 2014, when large numbers of children from Central America were presenting themselves at US border stations seeking asylum, the majority of the American public indicated that the government should stop the flow of unauthorized immigrants and deport those already in the United States as its top priority. In 2012 and 2013, on the other hand, in response to the same question, most said that the United States should create a system so that unauthorized immigrants could become legal residents (CNN/ORC 2014). The public is evenly divided on the issue of increased deportations of unauthorized immigrants—45 percent said that it was a "good thing" and 45 percent said it was a "bad thing" in a 2014 poll (Pew Research Center 2014a).

The internal contradictions and fluidity of public opinion on immigration policy are certainly not new in the current era (Masuoka and Junn 2013). What is new, however, is the growing sense that immigration policy needs reform more than other areas of policy. However, vacillating public opinion makes it difficult for Congress to identify and sell the compromises that will be necessary to craft legislation to address the nation's immigration needs in the twenty-first century. This has proven particularly vexing for the US House of Representatives, which represents smaller districts that are often relatively homogeneous. Many of these districts, particularly in rural areas, have few immigrants or racial/ethnic minorities to advocate on behalf of comprehensive immigration reform (DeSipio 2011).

## Noncitizen Rights, Privileges, and Responsibilities

Noncitizens have many of the same responsibilities to the state as citizens. Noncitizens must obey the laws of the land and are subject to all forms of taxation, including taxes for the Social Security program (the Federal

Insurance Contributions Act, or FICA). Noncitizen males must register for the draft and are then subject to the draft on an equal basis. Noncitizens may not serve on juries, but they are subject to the same criminal and civil law as citizens—in a sense, they can never be judged by a jury of their peers. These responsibilities extend to unauthorized migrants as well (Institute on Taxation and Economic Policy 2013; Lee 2014).

Permanent residents also have responsibilities that citizens are not subjected to. For example, from 1940 through 1981, noncitizens had to report their residence addresses to the government annually (95 Statutes at Large 1611, enacted December 20, 1981). In addition, noncitizens are subjected to additional restrictions and rules, and violations of these restrictions can lead to a change in status. Immigration law limits the amount of time permanent residents can spend outside of the country, and extended absences can result in the loss of permanent resident status. Non-naturalized immigrants who retire abroad, but who have worked for long enough in the United States to be eligible for Social Security, receive lower benefits. Permanent residents convicted of crimes can be deported. Finally, permanent residents also face the danger, though slight, that immigration laws could be changed to alter their status, putting them at risk of losing any or all rights, privileges, and responsibilities that they enjoy in the United States.

Rights and privileges are often confused. *Rights* refers to fundamental guarantees provided in the Constitution, such as equal protection. Although rights can be reversed by legislatures, that would require an amendment to the Constitution. *Privileges* are the statutory implementations of rights. So, although the Constitution guarantees equal protection under the law, Congress can establish (and the courts can review) differential treatment of groups in US society. Not all discrimination—differential treatment—is unlawful. Immigrants, for example, have long been subject to differential treatment under US law. According to judicial rulings, legislatures can lawfully discriminate, depending upon the type of discrimination and what public interest is at stake. Thus Congress allows employers to select US citizen job applicants over equally qualified (non-naturalized) immigrant job applicants without the risk of being charged with employment discrimination. The denial of certain privileges and program benefits to immigrants is one of the most actively debated issues in Congress and in state legislatures today.

Below, we examine three areas of rights and privileges where there are substantive differences between immigrants and natives: (1) electoral rights, (2) employment rights and privileges, and (3) eligibility for participation in federal social welfare programs.

## Electoral Rights

With a few exceptions, noncitizens cannot participate in electoral politics (Hayduk 2006). They are barred from voting in all federal and state elections and most local races. This pattern of exclusion extends equally to the documented and undocumented. A few jurisdictions—Cambridge, Massachusetts, and Takoma Park, Maryland, for example—grant the *franchise*, the right to vote, to noncitizens in municipal elections.

This has not always been the case. As recently as the turn of the twentieth century, more than one-half of the states had granted long-term noncitizens the vote or had done so in the recent past (Rosberg 1977). Most states extended the franchise to immigrants after they had filed their *first papers*—a formal statement of intention to naturalize—after a minimum of three years of US residence. The federal government had also permitted noncitizen voting in some of the territorial governments. These states and territories with noncitizen voting, primarily in the Midwest and West, were not necessarily acting out of a sense of altruism or to promote a rigorous conception of democracy. Instead, they saw the franchise as a lure for immigrants to settle in their states. As national support for immigration declined in the first decades of this century, the number of states granting the franchise to noncitizens also declined, ending with the removal of the franchise privilege in Arkansas in 1926.

Many immigrant advocates assert that extending the franchise to immigrants offers a valuable, largely untapped tool that would simultaneously empower immigrant communities and connect them further to American society (Hayduk 2006: Chapter 6). In their argument for this proposition, they tap into the American creed—noting that immigrants pay taxes, yet have no say in their representation. This claim of "taxation without representation" means that in cities with large immigrant concentrations, local officials have no electoral connection to the majority of their constituents. Thus, they may not represent the needs of these non-enfranchised constituents. By extending the franchise to noncitizens, then, jurisdictions could ensure better representation, arguably the goal of democratic government. Within immigrant populations, the noncitizen vote would offer a tool for mobilization and might serve to maintain community cohesion.

Proposals to grant the franchise to noncitizens have not received extensive support beyond that of immigrant community leaders. As a result, there has been no coordinated opposition or a single set of arguments shared by all who oppose the idea (Horowitz 2012). The general notion that links all opposition to noncitizen voting, and the position of most jurisdictions nationwide, is the idea that voting is a privilege that is reserved for citizens. Only citizens have an appropriate stake in the country or the government to make the sorts of decisions that would be in the nation's best interests.

As few governments have seriously considered adopting noncitizen voting, there has been little analysis of its potential impact, whether on immigrant populations or on local, state, or national governments. Arguably, the impact of an energized noncitizen electorate could be great in local elections in cities such as Los Angeles, Houston, Miami, and Chicago, with their sizeable noncitizen populations. If there were a close election in which the noncitizen population was cohesive and the citizen population divided, this impact could extend to statewide elections in immigrant-receiving states such as California, Texas, Florida, and New York. Much less likely is the influence of noncitizens in national politics, even if noncitizens were to be granted the vote in all fifty states. However, it must be noted that the only "national" race—the presidency—is in fact just fifty state races (plus the District of Columbia) in which the popular-vote winner in a given state takes all of that state's electoral votes (Nebraska and Maine are exceptions in allowing splitting of their electoral votes). Thus, in a very close presidential race that is determined by the votes of the larger states (most of which are immigrant-receiving states), an empowered noncitizen electorate could swing the election.

Advocates of noncitizen voting have not been, and have not had to be, very specific about their proposals. It is not clear, for example, whether advocates of noncitizen voting seek to extend the right to all offices at all levels of government or to local races only. Nor has there been any discussion about when noncitizens should be eligible to vote should they be given the privilege. Advocates of noncitizen voting cannot simply rely on arguing that it once existed in some states and territories. Instead, they need to determine the specifics of what they are calling for and how this form of voting would interact with contemporary voting law and practice.

Regardless of one's philosophical attitudes toward noncitizen voting, it has a serious flaw in the contemporary political environment: relatively few noncitizens would use the right. Most noncitizens have the same characteristics as those who generally do not participate in electoral politics in our society (de la Garza and DeSipio 1993, 2006; see also Chapter 5 of this volume). Immigrants are younger, less educated, and poorer than the average citizen. Regardless of race or ethnicity, young adults vote less than older adults; the poor vote less than the middle class or the rich; and the less educated vote less than the more educated. In addition to these demographic factors that influence all potential electorates, many noncitizens face linguistic barriers as well. Many immigrants do not speak English, or speak it poorly. Although the Voting Rights Act (VRA) requires that registration and voting materials be available to Asians and Spanish speakers in their native languages in areas where their density or numbers are great, candidate and campaign information is only primarily available in English.

These concerns about the utility of noncitizen voting are substantiated by observations of noncitizen participation in those few areas that permit it today. There is little evidence that noncitizens exercise their right in great numbers, even in local school council elections that presumably have direct importance to noncitizen parents. Thus, at the individual level, we believe that few noncitizens would take advantage of the franchise.

Two populations suffer if noncitizens do not receive the franchise: the undocumented, and permanent residents with less than five years of legal residence. In the current political environment, it is unlikely that states or localities would consider extending the undocumented the franchise. At a more conceptual level, their undocumented status raises the question of what the franchise means. Is it a *quid pro quo*—something received for something given—in this case a privilege received for paying taxes, for example, or for residing geographically within a nation's territory? Or is it an act of trust extended to those who have a long-term stake in the society? The way people answer these questions likely shapes their view on whether the undocumented should receive the franchise.

A more problematic dilemma relates to the rights of the recently arrived permanent resident. Although these new arrivals will attain citizenship eligibility and, if they naturalize, voting eligibility in the future, the process takes five years. Furthermore, permanent residents potentially have a long-term stake in the society, so their claim on the vote is stronger than that of undocumented immigrants. In our work, we have suggested, and continue to believe, that a case can be made for extending the franchise to permanent residents not yet eligible to naturalize, limited to the period before their statutory eligibility to apply for naturalization (de la Garza and DeSipio 1993, 2006). Although we believe that few would take advantage of this limited noncitizen voting, we think that those who were to vote regularly would be demonstrating the sort of good citizenship that the naturalization exam seeks to ascertain through its knowledge-based measure (history, civics, and English-language knowledge). For those immigrants who were to vote regularly during this five-year period of citizenship ineligibility, we would grant citizenship automatically upon application.

We disagree on the sorts of elections that short-term permanent residents should be eligible to vote in. Because of concerns about their ability to shape national policy, particularly policy toward their sending countries, de la Garza would extend this limited noncitizen voting only to state and local elections. DeSipio, however, objects to the administrative burdens placed on local election officials, who would have to create two sets of voting lists and two ballots to allow permanent residents to vote in all elections—federal, state, and local—during the first five years of residence. Again, it is important to note that neither of us thinks that noncitizens would vote in large numbers under this proposal.

The issue of the rights of noncitizens to electoral access raises fundamental questions about the link between the polity and its residents. The question of who should participate in US politics has been an active topic of debate from the nation's first days and will likely never be conclusively resolved. Initially a privilege of white male citizen landholders, it slowly expanded to all white male citizens, to all male citizens regardless of race, to women, and to those of ages eighteen through twenty. Each of these formal expansions of the electorate accompanied a new sense of who should have a stake in the nation. Thus, the meaning of citizenship expanded as the franchise expanded. Noncitizen voting raises a question unanswered in the modern era: Can voting be detached from citizenship?

### Employment and Occupational Privileges

A second area in which the government restricts privileges of noncitizens is occupational access. These restrictions appear at both the federal and state levels and apply differently to permanent residents and the undocumented. Permanent residents have extensive employment privileges in the private sector, but they face heavy restrictions on most public sector employment. Below, we look at four types of employment restrictions: (1) restrictions on undocumented workers, (2) limitations faced by permanent residents in the public sector, (3) restrictions in professions that require licensing, and (4) employment restrictions in the private sector for permanent residents.

**Restrictions on Employment of the Undocumented.** The undocumented face the most severe restrictions. Beginning in 1986, as part of the Immigration Reform and Control Act (IRCA), it became illegal to employ an undocumented immigrant. The goal of this legislation was to discourage potential undocumented immigrants from migrating in the first place by removing the incentive of employment. The complete and perfect enforcement of these "employer sanctions" would deny employers the right to employ the undocumented, and as a result almost all undocumented immigrants would lose their jobs. In practice, enforcement of employer sanctions is erratic. Estimates suggest that approximately 11.5 million undocumented immigrants resided in the United States in 2011 and that undocumented adults have higher labor force participation rates than the US-born. For many years after the passage of the IRCA, the government did little to restrict employers' practices. In response to public outrage over this lack of enforcement, the George W. Bush administration did orchestrate some large and very public raids on work sites. These generated lots of public attention and arguably mass violations of worker rights. Although some employers did temporarily lose their labor forces, these raids did little to threaten employers generally (Camayd-Freixas 2013).

The Obama administration shifted the focus of enforcement to requirements that employers with large labor forces electronically check the work eligibility of their employees and request appropriate documentation from workers whose names and Social Security numbers do not match those in government databases. Workers who could not prove their work eligibility, or prove an error in the government database, were to be fired. As this was part of an ongoing program with greater accountability, many large employers took seriously the possibility that they would be held accountable and be subject to fines, or even criminal prosecution. Despite this increase in enforcement and greater consistency in federal attentiveness, the quantity of false identity documents and the depth of immigrant networks ensure that most unauthorized immigrants seeking work are able to find employment.

The Obama administration implemented a second set of policy changes that expanded opportunities for some unauthorized immigrants to work in the United States. In 2012, Obama implemented the Deferred Action for Childhood Arrivals (DACA) Program, which established a temporary (two-year) period of work eligibility for young adults aged thirty or younger who met all the requirements (see Chapter 2). In 2014, the Obama administration extended this program and allowed applicants who had completed their initial two-year period of work eligibility to apply for an additional two years. Approximately 600,000 young adult unauthorized immigrants received DACA status in the program's first two years (US Citizenship and Immigration Services 2014). There is no firm estimate of the number of potential DACA applicants, but it is safe to say that the cost and the concern about making one's status (and one's family's status) known to the government discouraged many potential applicants, perhaps as many as half, from applying for DACA protections (Singer 2013).

At this writing, the Obama administration expanded DACA to older immigrants who initially arrived as children or teens and to the parents of US citizens and permanent residents as long as they had resided in the United States for five years. These expansions enlarged the pool of unauthorized immigrants with short-term work eligibility to as many as 5 million. It also created an ongoing challenge for the executive branch because such extensions of privilege would make it all the more unlikely that the targeted populations would ever be singled out for deportation. At the same time, work eligibility under DACA remains tenuous and highly dependent on support from the president. It also adds to the pressure on Congress to craft a more permanent solution to the presence of more than 11 million unauthorized immigrants, the majority of whom have lived for ten years or more in the United States.

**Public Sector Employment of Permanent Residents.** Permanent residents face less severe restrictions on occupational access than undocumented immigrants, but the restrictions they do face are more severe in the public sector than in the private sector. Permanent residents with specialized professional skills are also more restricted in their employment opportunities than US citizen workers.

The federal government reserves most of its jobs for US citizens. States and localities vary in their employment practices, but most restrict public safety positions—police and fire—and education positions, including teaching in the public schools, to US citizens. Some of these restrictions emerged from turn-of-the-twentieth-century Progressive-era reforms, whereas others, including the restrictions placed on federal employment, were implemented during the period of low immigration (but rapid growth in the federal government) between the 1930s and early 1960s. The Progressive reformers sought to restrict the power of the urban machines by restricting the machine leaders' abilities to reward their supporters (or their coethnics) with municipal employment. This was achieved in part through new civil service requirements that potential employees demonstrate the skills necessary to hold their jobs, and by protecting civil employees from losing their jobs just because the government's elected leadership had changed. But the reforms were more directly apparent in the erection of absolute barriers to the employment of noncitizens.

Since the decline of the political machines, the justifications for public sector restrictions on noncitizen employment have shifted to concerns about national security and political loyalty. These related concerns increased dramatically during the anti-Communist Red Scares of the 1940s and 1950s. All Americans were suspect, especially those with ties to Europe, particularly Southern and Eastern Europe. During this period, federal agencies and many states increasingly expanded barriers to noncitizen employment. With certain exceptions that include employment abroad, skilled positions that cannot be filled with citizen workers, national security positions, and the military, all federal agencies have denied permanent residents federal jobs since the 1960s (5 CFR Sec. 338.101).

**Restrictions on Professional Licensing.** Governmental restrictions on employment take a second form: restrictions on professional licensing. As most licensing in the United States is under the jurisdiction of state and local governments, this form of occupational control is felt mostly at those levels. These restrictions extend from professions requiring extensive training (e.g., in the legal, medical, and dental fields) to those requiring licenses but much less training (e.g., beautician, barber, or mortician's assistant). These restrictions vary from state to state and tend to be stronger in states with large immigrant populations. US citizens in these professions lobby, through their professional associations, to restrict noncitizen access to these licenses. These restrictions are often justified by citing concerns that training abroad is not functionally equivalent to that offered in the United States and that professional standards in other countries are lower. Professional regulators and members of professional associations also express concerns that immigrants do not speak English well enough. Either of these sets of concerns could be addressed through testing requirements—to assess knowledge, experience, or language skills—but subtle anti-immigrant messages and the power of the professions in state legislatures often prove sufficient to deny immigrants outright the opportunity to receive licenses for these professions.

The impact of limiting opportunities in professions requiring licensing is not equal for all immigrants. These sorts of restrictions on international occupational mobility have a greater effect on those with more education and more skilled job experience and those who migrate from nations with an extensively developed professional class. Cuban immigrants, for example, faced extensive restrictions on access to the professions in Florida in the 1960s and 1970s. Similar restrictions have been applied to Asian immigrants in California over the past one hundred years.

However, the United States does not seek to limit the migration of all skilled immigrants. Instead, it selectively encourages the immigration of certain professionals. As we indicated in Chapter 2, approximately one-third of immigrant visas are allocated to immigrants based on labor skills and not on family unification ideals. This employment-related share of the pool of visas has been steadily growing over the past twenty-five years. Immigration law often specifies the skills being sought, and tends to reward those professions with a widespread perception of popular need and those representing more narrow interests. Since World War II, for example, immigration law has always contained special provisions for the immigration of doctors. In the early 1950s, more narrow interests appeared in the allocation of almost 1,00 visas to sheepherders (66 Statutes at Large 50, enacted April 9, 1952). Thus, public sector exclusion of permanent resident employment and access of permanent residents to the professions are tempered by the presence of a small pool of immigrants with needed job skills.

**Private Sector Employment of Permanent Residents.** The law does not allow the private sector anything near the latitude it does to the public sector to restrict employment opportunities of permanent residents. In fact, most private sector jobs are open to permanent residents. Federal law offers contradictory protections and limitations in terms of private sector employment. The first principle is the right to equal protection, or *nondiscrimination*. For the most part, private sector employers cannot discriminate based on citizenship status—that is, they cannot exclude permanent residents from employment simply because of their status. However, in 1986 Congress modified this principle of nondiscrimination with a form of legally sanctioned discrimination in federal law. Beginning that year, private sector employers who have equally qualified job candidates, one of whom is a citizen and one of whom is a permanent resident, may select the citizen without fear of losing a discrimination suit (100 Statutes at Large 3359, enacted November 6, 1986). Although this may seem to be a minor restriction on the job opportunities of permanent residents, it is notable as it is one of very few US laws that explicitly sanctions discrimination against a named population.

In addition to this sanctioning of discrimination against permanent residents, Congress has recognized a special category of private sector jobs that can exclude noncitizens. This category includes employment with contractors doing work for the government in areas related to national security. This includes several million jobs, including those engaged in by contractors for the Department of Defense and Department of Homeland Security. The justification for the exclusion of noncitizens from these jobs is similar to the rationale used to exclude them from government employment—their loyalty is in doubt and, as a result, they cannot be offered these jobs.

In sum, employment and professional opportunities for immigrants vary considerably, based both on immigrant status and on the type of employment. The nation bars the undocumented from all employment, though it fails to enforce the prohibition rigorously. Permanent residents are barred from many public sector jobs, though by contrast, they face few formal restrictions on private sector employment. However, permanent residents can face legal discrimination when competing against a US citizen. In addition, many permanent residents with professional skills that require licensing are denied the opportunity to earn these licenses based on their citizenship status.

## Programmatic Privileges in Federal Government Programs

Increasingly, the United States has determined that non-naturalized permanent residents can receive levels of benefits from social welfare programs different from those provided to US citizens. We refer to the ability to participate in federal and state programs designed to meet the needs of the population as *programmatic privileges*. The most debated social welfare programs in terms of immigrant programmatic privileges include the Supplemental Nutritional Assistance Program (assistance to purchase food in households with children), Temporary Aid to Needy Families (cash and services provided to low-income households with children), Medicaid (health insurance for low-income households), CHIP (health insurance subsidies for households with children), and Supplemental Security Income (a cash assistance program for low-income elderly persons). These programs are mandated by the federal government and paid for by federal and state taxes to provide a safety net for the economically disadvantaged. The differential levels of access for immigrants versus natives are often dictated by fiscal concerns rather than consideration of what level of investment is needed to ensure immigrants' speedy adaptation to US society.

The debate over immigrant access to programmatic privileges is distinct from both voting and employment rights and privileges. Voting privileges have long been a part of the national discussion on immigrant settlement, as many states granted the franchise to immigrants around the turn of the twentieth century. In that same era, immigrants were employed by municipal governments—the major form of public sector employment during that time, as the federal government was quite small. The national debate over immigrant programmatic privileges began after social welfare programs were created under the New Deal in the 1930s and then during the Great Society era in the 1960s.

The creation and expansion of federal and state guarantees to food and to such services as health care and housing came during a period of relatively low immigration. During the initial establishment of the social safety net in the 1930s, few immigrated to the United States and some previous immigrants were deported—justified in part as a response to the cost of providing social relief. In the 1930s, when the federal government created the first national social insurance programs, such as Social Security, the needs of immigrants were not part of the debate. Similarly in the 1960s, with Great Society programs such as the expansion of Aid to Families with Dependent Children (AFDC) and the creation of Medicaid, immigration was low and so the cost of providing immigrant eligibility for these programs was also low.

The increase in the cost of the social safety net, however, spurred a steady growth in restrictions on immigrant access to these programs.

These limitations on immigrant access are particularly felt in programs that are *needs-tested*, in which eligibility is determined by income, as a measure of need. Restrictions are fewer on immigrant privileges in *contributory programs*, in which benefits are related to the previous contributions made by the beneficiary to programs such as Medicare or Social Security.

Advocates of denying permanent residents eligibility for federal social welfare programs use three main points to advance their argument. The first is cost. Since the 1980s, Congress has sought to cut the cost of *entitlement programs*—programs in which spending is determined by the total demand from people who meet the low-income threshold and thus are entitled to benefits. Thus, in order to cut the cost of the program, Congress must change the eligibility criteria. If costs have to be cut, some argue that the government has a greater responsibility to citizens than to noncitizens, and so the pain of cost-cutting for citizens can be lessened by denying benefits to noncitizens. Half of the $55 billion in savings in the 1996 Welfare Reform Bill was achieved simply by making cuts in services to noncitizens. From a political perspective, this strategy of budget cutting has a second advantage to Congress. Noncitizens are not voters, so electoral backlash is less likely if noncitizen benefits are cut.

A second argument offered by supporters of benefit restrictions is that access to social welfare programs may actually slow rather than facilitate the process of immigrant adaptation and acculturation. They offer as examples some recent groups of refugees, such as the Hmong and Cambodians from Southeast Asia, arguing that although Congress granted these refugees social safety net program eligibility as well as special refugee assistance programs, these groups remained in poverty and have become disproportionately dependent on public aid. Thus, some critics of government social welfare spending on immigrants argue that denying benefits is actually beneficial to the immigrants' long-term advancement. This position, though frequently argued by the political right, also taps into the rhetoric used by immigrant advocates—that no immigrant comes to the United States to receive assistance and, in fact, simply wants the opportunity to succeed. The denial of benefits, then, is not a problem.

A third argument to restrict the federal benefits paid to immigrants is that the responsibility for caring for the immigrant should be on the person who petitioned for the admission of the immigrant and not on the federal government—after all, the sponsor promises to support the immigrant during the immigrant's period of transition to citizenship. Prior to the 1996 reforms, the sponsor's income was added to the immigrant's to determine whether the immigrant was eligible for federal social welfare programs for the first three to five years after immigration. However, the sponsor's promise was not legally enforceable. Under the 1996 amendments to the Immigration and Welfare Reform Bills, the sponsor's responsibility was made a legally binding commitment, and extended to covering the first ten years of the immigrant's permanent residence.

Those who oppose limitations on immigrants' programmatic privileges have not developed a comprehensive response to these three arguments. Instead, they base their support on humanitarian grounds and on the empirical observation that few immigrants use these programs. The humanitarian argument is straightforward—Congress designed these programs to address the needs of the poor in society. If the permanent resident's level of poverty is sufficiently severe, then he or she should be eligible for these programs. The argument for this eligibility is particularly strong when the cause of the poverty is something that happened post-immigration, such as illness, disability, or inability to find employment due to the kinds of occupational restrictions discussed above. However, with the exception of emergency medical services, few extend this argument to addressing the social welfare needs of the undocumented.

Studies indicate that the more generous system of social welfare program eligibility available before 1996 did not spur social welfare dependence among permanent residents—in fact, social welfare utilization rates are lower for permanent residents than for the population as a whole. However, these studies did find one exception: elderly immigrants had high utilization rates for Supplemental Security Income (SSI), Medicaid, and Medicare. Although elderly immigrants lost access to SSI in 1996, Congress restored their benefits in 1997. States have also selectively restored some of these benefits for recent arrivals at their own expense. Although these state efforts certainly facilitate new immigrant adaptation to the United States (and send a more welcoming message to potential immigrants than states that did not make such provisions), some of these states have reversed their policies during periods of poor state budgets or when control of the state governments shifted from one party to the other.

Although this has not been discussed in Congressional debates so far, there is a final argument against linking social welfare benefits to citizenship. Such a linkage would create an instrumental motivation to naturalize—that is, if naturalization were the only way that immigrants could ensure that they would be protected in times of poverty, then they would be much more likely to become citizens as soon as they became eligible. This goal may be laudable, but the reasons behind this goal may strike some as less than laudable. As we discuss in Chapter 4, naturalization has sought to measure political attachment to the United States through a knowledge-based test. Although the formal standards are minimal, the citizen population has largely welcomed the voluntary citizens. However, if citizens were to come to perceive immigrants as seeking naturalization simply to become eligible for federal benefits, the support for the nation's voluntary citizens could dissolve.

Interestingly, when Congress implemented the health care subsidies provided in the Affordable Care Act, it included permanent residents, regardless of their length of residence, among the eligible. Like citizens, permanent residents are required under the law to have health insurance or pay a fine. The unauthorized are ineligible for health insurance subsidies under the Affordable Care Act.

## Conclusions on Immigrant Rights, Privileges, and Responsibilities at the Federal Level

As a nation of immigrants, the United States must continually reassess what rights, privileges, and responsibilities it chooses to extend to immigrants and what immigrants have to do to earn these rights and privileges. At present, US society has developed a three-tiered system for immigrant civic participation: naturalized citizens, legal permanent residents, and undocumented immigrants all have different rights and privileges. At one extreme, full membership is offered. At the other end of the spectrum, most rights, privileges, and government services (with the exception of education) are denied.

Exclusion from full integration into the civil society based on citizenship status has evolved for different reasons in each of the three policy areas discussed above. Exclusion from voting rights has been justified through a determination that immigrants do not have enough of a stake in the society to merit a say in its future. Exclusion from employment rights and privileges, however, developed in response to fears of the potential disloyalty and corrupting influences of immigrants. Finally, financial considerations in times of increasing concern about the costs of social welfare programs justified immigrants' exclusion from programmatic benefits. Essentially, US society has developed three reasons to keep immigrants in a secondary status: membership, loyalty, and cost.

After five years, permanent residents become eligible for full membership, and they can overcome these barriers through naturalization, an act that proves their membership, their loyalty, and their value to the society. Unless they can regularize their status, undocumented immigrants are consigned permanently to the excluded category (though erratic enforcement ensures that this exclusion is not complete). In between are non-naturalized permanent residents who have access to many of the rights, privileges, and responsibilities of citizens but who have explicitly been excluded from most electoral rights and some employment and programmatic privileges.

What is asked in return from the immigrant? From the naturalized citizens, the society asks for political loyalty and civic knowledge. The naturalization exam tests knowledge of the United States, its history, and its governmental system. The oath of naturalization requires immigrants to swear (or affirm) loyalty to the United States and to renounce their loyalty to the former sovereign states. Although the debate over immigration is often phrased in cultural terms, it is important to notice that this full membership does not require cultural loyalty. The nation requires most naturalizing citizens to know English, but this knowledge is not expected to replace their native languages. Cultural change undoubtedly occurs when immigrants come into contact with natives, but formal political membership and full rights are not determined by culture.

Permanent residents attain many rights and privileges at immigration. These rights and privileges are awarded by meeting the standards of US immigration law. This immigration law does include both political considerations (immigrants may not be anarchists or former officials of the Communist or Nazi Party) and some cultural characteristics (the law is now more likely to award some visas to English speakers). For the most part, however, these considerations are minor relative to the complexities of US immigration policy, which focuses more on family and employment than on politics and culture. Thus, the rights and privileges extended to permanent residents are a result of, and are tied to, their residential status in the United States. For the undocumented, therefore, residence does not guarantee rights or privileges, although it should be noted that they are accorded fundamental constitutional guarantees, including due process guarantees (although local officials often violate these guarantees).

# The States, Immigration Reform, and Immigrant Settlement

In the modern era, the federal government has had primary policymaking responsibility for immigrant incorporation by setting the standards for immigration and naturalization and by determining social welfare program eligibility. However, with the ongoing failure of Congress to craft a framework for immigration policy in the twenty-first century, the states are increasingly demanding to influence the immigration debate with their own state policies (Hessick and Chin 2014).

We should acknowledge at the beginning that states do not speak with a single voice and that states can change their policies over time. In the early twenty-first century, several states have drawn national attention for their efforts to criminalize unauthorized status and push unauthorized immigrants even further into the shadows, with the ultimate goal of making their continued residence in the state, if not the United States, untenable. The harshest of these efforts have largely been blocked by the federal courts, which recognize that immigration policy falls within the scope of the enumerated Constitutional powers of the federal government (*Arizona v. United States*, 567 U.S. ___ [2012]). What is less noticed is that in this same period, many states have also acted to provide a more inclusionary path for unauthorized immigrants.

Although we cannot explore the specific policies of each state in depth here, we suggest a partial explanation for both restrictive and inclusionary efforts by the states in general. The more restrictive policies include limiting unauthorized immigrant access to state benefits and enforcing immigration laws at all levels. The more inclusionary policies include providing services to unauthorized immigrants that the states are not otherwise required to perform under federal law. On the one hand, these state interventions speak to state-level concerns, fears, and hopes, but they also seek to influence the shape of an eventual national, comprehensive reform. Ultimately, just as Congress must reach a compromise, these different views from the states must be balanced. Until Congress acts, however, it is highly likely that states will continue to seek to be active in shaping US immigration policy.

## *Who Pays for Undocumented Immigrants?*

In the late 1990s, several states sued the federal government to recoup the costs of providing services to undocumented immigrants. These states—including California, Florida, and Texas—argued that because the federal government is responsible for the protection of the borders, it should also be responsible for the costs of its failures. The suits sought reimbursement for a variety of costs. The largest among these was the cost of providing education to undocumented children and the states' shares of federal social welfare programs for benefits provided to the US citizen children of unauthorized immigrants. Some states have also sought reimbursement for emergency medical services in public hospitals and the costs of incarceration of undocumented immigrants. All such efforts were rebuffed by the federal courts—judicial outcomes that ultimately added to the anger already felt by many in states with large unauthorized immigrant populations.

The goals of the states have been varied and must, in part, be seen as fiscal opportunism. When the attorney general of Texas filed suit, for example, he noted that he was taking no position on undocumented immigration. Instead, he stated that he would be derelict if he failed to pursue such a lucrative opportunity for Texas, given that other states might benefit if they were to win suits against the federal government but that Texas might not, if it failed to file suit.

Failure in the courts has not meant that these efforts have been without impact. Congress has appropriated funds to partially offset the states' costs in providing services to the undocumented. These funds account for a small percentage of the billions sought by the states. Yet, their appropriation reflects the fact that Congress recognized the legitimacy of state demands or, at least, the resonance of these claims with voters.

## Public Education and Undocumented Immigrants

As we have mentioned above, the undocumented are barred from almost all federal social welfare benefits. This prohibition extends to contributory programs, such as unemployment compensation (90 Statutes at Large 2706, enacted October 20, 1976). The cost, however, of undocumented immigrants is felt more at the state and local levels and, particularly, in the provision of primary and secondary education.

In *Plyler v. Doe* (457 U.S. 202 [1982]), the US Supreme Court held that undocumented immigrant children have a constitutional right to education, as long as it is being offered to others and as long as Congress has not asserted responsibility in this area. However, the nature of the Supreme

Court majority in this decision—a series of loosely related concurring opinions, the convoluted argument for this right, and the failure of Texas (the state being sued in the case) to assert that there was a compelling state interest in denying education to undocumented immigrant children—has led many observers to think that the Supreme Court would be open to a renewed effort to deny education to undocumented children. Whether or not the Supreme Court does revisit its ruling in *Plyler*, denying education to undocumented children would have long-term consequences—and not just for the state denying benefits.

### The States and Immigration Enforcement

As popular concern with unauthorized migration grew in the late twentieth and early twenty-first centuries, several states sought to step into the debate by passing their own restrictionist legislation. For the most part, these efforts have been blocked by federal judges. They should not simply be dismissed as nativism or political grandstanding, however. The public debate surrounding these state efforts leads to the hardening of popular positions on immigration reform, thus making it more difficult for Congress to negotiate the compromises necessary to shape an immigration framework for the twenty-first century.

In the contemporary era, the first of these state-level restrictionist efforts was California's Proposition 187 (1994). Proposition 187 restricted the access of unauthorized immigrants to state services and would have required state employees to identify unauthorized immigrants, including schoolchildren, to federal immigration authorities (Ono and Sloop 2002). Proposition 187 passed with nearly 60 percent of the vote. Although the federal courts quickly held most of the proposition to be unconstitutional, it spurred a series of efforts to restrict the rights of immigrants and of racial and ethnic minorities in California and other states. It also emboldened national leaders, such as commentator and presidential candidate Pat Buchanan, to voice restrictionist messages.

In 2010, the Arizona legislature passed Senate Bill 1070 (S.B. 1070), the Support Our Law Enforcement and Safe Neighborhoods Act (Magaña and Lee 2013). The bill required immigrants in Arizona to have evidence of their legal status (as required by federal law) and made it a violation of state law to violate this federal requirement. State law enforcement officers were required to determine an individual's immigration status during a "lawful stop, detention or arrest" or during a "lawful contact" when there is reasonable suspicion that the individual is an unauthorized immigrant. S.B. 1070 barred state or local officials or agencies from restricting enforcement of federal immigration laws, and imposed penalties on those "sheltering, hiring and transporting" unauthorized immigrants. Again, the federal courts (including the Supreme Court) held much of the law to be unconstitutional, though they allowed some provisions that focused on the activities of state police forces to remain in place.

Approximately twenty states followed Arizona's lead and considered legislation along the same lines, though it passed in few of the states. Alabama did pass legislation more restrictive than Arizona's law. The federal courts held this law to be unconstitutional as well, though not before enough immigrants in Alabama left the state to prevent some crops from being harvested. The other states along the US-Mexico border did not follow Arizona's lead, reflecting in part the strength of Latino electoral constituencies in these states.

Restrictive legislation along the lines of California's Proposition 187 or Arizona's S.B. 1070 has galvanized restrictionist voices in the states and, somewhat more tentatively, immigrant advocates. To date, the federal courts have limited the implementation of these policies, adding to the popular sense of stalemate or inaction for advocates of restriction and a sense of unwelcome for immigrants and their supporters.

In the contemporary era, a wider range of states and localities have engaged in a different form of immigration restriction. As the federal government increased immigration law enforcement during the George W. Bush administration, the Immigration and Customs Enforcement (ICE) Agency of the Department of Homeland Security engaged in "cooperative agreements" with state and local law enforcement agencies to empower the local law enforcement agencies to enforce immigration law and to deputize local officers to hold unauthorized immigrants charged in other crimes with immigration law violations. This cooperation was authorized under Section 287(g) of the Immigration and Nationality Act. At its peak, ICE had agreements with thirty-five law enforcement agencies in eighteen states and has trained and certified over 1,500 local officers as adjunct immigration agents. States that have not pursued highly controversial efforts such as Proposition 187 or S.B. 1070 have willingly worked with ICE, though some have subsequently sought to end the cooperation agreements. These agreements are often little debated at the local level.

## The States and Selective Incorporation of Unauthorized Immigrants

State policies in the contemporary era should not be seen simply as further restricting the rights of the unauthorized. In the same period that has seen state legislation like S.B. 1070 or enhanced cooperation between ICE and local police under Section 287(g), some states have sought to provide targeted resources for some unauthorized immigrants. These have focused most on two dimensions of state policymaking: college tuitions and driver's licenses. At least in their earliest incarnations—providing in-state tuition at public colleges and universities for unauthorized immigrants who graduated from high school in that state—these state policies could be seen as anticipating a quick national resolution to the immigration reform debate that would include a large-scale legalization. Later efforts—such as the provision of state-issued driver's licenses to unauthorized immigrants—seek to prevent unauthorized immigrants from running afoul of the law over minor issues that might ultimately prevent their legalization. For the most part, these policies have appeared in states that have large and organized Latino and Asian American electoral constituencies.

Eighteen states allow unauthorized immigrants who graduate from state high schools to attend state colleges and universities at in-state rates (two by the authority of boards of regents, the rest by legislative action). Three states—Arizona, Georgia, and Indiana—bar unauthorized immigrants from receiving in-state tuition, whereas South Carolina bars unauthorized immigrants from enrolling in state colleges. Texas and California were the first states to provide in-state tuition for the unauthorized in 2001; in the mid-2010s, California established the opportunity for unauthorized university students to receive some state financial aid. Federal rules preclude federal financial aid eligibility for unauthorized students. Eleven states allow or are planning to allow unauthorized immigrants to get state driver's licenses (National Conference of State Legislatures 2014). Under federal rules, these must be distinct from driver's licenses issued to citizens and permanent residents, but they do ensure that unauthorized immigrants cannot be charged with a crime for simply driving, or face the loss of their cars if they are stopped by police.

Although these two policy areas offer only modest state support for unauthorized immigrants, they do suggest a changing political environment in which some of the states seek to ensure that there are legal protections for at least some in the unauthorized immigrant community. The number of states offering these targeted protections is growing and, over time, it is likely that immigrant advocates will identify other state policies that can be made more inclusive, at least in those states that are taking the lead in addressing immigrant, and particularly unauthorized immigrant, rights.

The large number of immigrants—both documented and undocumented—raises questions about what rights, privileges, and responsibilities US society chooses to offer. The federal government denies certain, but limited, electoral, employment, and programmatic rights and privileges to noncitizens. For the most part, it has restricted state and private sector efforts to do the same. It is at the state and local levels, however, that the day-to-day process of settlement occurs. As these governments have been asked to share a greater burden of settlement, they have begun to ask for greater responsibility in deciding what rights and responsibilities immigrants in their states should have. To date, calls for a shift in the balance between the federal government and state governments have focused primarily on undocumented immigrants. Regardless of who is the focus, however, these new efforts by states to enter the debate over settlement potentially represent a major change in the direction of future settlement policies in the United States.

## Settlement and the Interaction Between Immigrants and Minorities

Immigration to, and settlement in, the United States do not occur in a vacuum. From their first days in the United States, immigrants interact with other immigrants and with US-born populations, and reshape what it means to be American for all involved. The impact of immigrants is particularly strong among one segment of US society—minorities. We use the term *minorities* to mean US-born racial and ethnic minorities but also the US-born coethnics of contemporary immigrants.

There are tangible foundations for immigrant and minority interaction in US society—namely, geography, ethnicity, and class. Overwhelmingly, immigration since 1965 has been an urban phenomenon. Within cities, immigrants often live in specific neighborhoods, ones that tend to already be dominated by US-born minorities. Geographically, most immigrant populations often come into immediate contact with minority populations before they have sustained contact with nonminority natives. For example, an immigrant from Mexico will likely live around and work with both US-born citizens of Mexican ancestry and other Mexican immigrants. Finally, class dictates that immigrants and minorities interact. The majority of immigrants are at the lower end of the economic spectrum. Again, this puts them into contact with US-born minorities, particularly in the urban environment.

This contact is not just interpersonal. This interaction between immigrants and minorities offers insights into the way US society tries to address the public policy needs of disadvantaged groups. Immigrants' class position dictates that they can benefit from policies designed to assist poorer US-born populations. As there is little explicit assistance from the society with settlement, these public policies become a de facto settlement policy. And similarly, though the needs of US-born minorities and immigrants are different, the public policies developed for immigrant populations often follow those developed for minorities. Society has not recognized the difference between minorities and immigrants; instead, it has extended to immigrants programs that were designed to assist minorities and to remedy past discrimination against minorities. Undeniably, immigrants have benefited from these programs in the short term, whereas the cost to minorities has not been great. Nevertheless, it does both populations a disservice: programs for minorities are diluted, and immigrant needs are not met with carefully crafted public policies.

During the same period that many social welfare programs emerged, the United States also developed group-based programs targeting groups that had experienced discrimination in the past. Initially designed to remedy past discrimination against African Americans, these programs—civil rights and voting rights protections, and affirmative action programs—were soon expanded to other minority populations that had also experienced discrimination in the past, including Latinos, Asian Americans, and Native Americans. These remedial programs are the exception in American political history, where policy had explicitly or, more often, implicitly benefited society's dominant population. These remedial programs have been highly controversial and, at this writing, are being attacked in the courts and in legislatures.

Immigrants have come to benefit from these programs since their inception. An example is the Voting Rights Act of 1965 (VRA). In its initial form, the VRA sought to remove barriers to registration and voting experienced by African Americans. Ten years later, Congress extended these same provisions to other US populations that had experienced discrimination: Latinos, Asians, Native Americans, and Alaskan Natives. Congress mandated new electoral resources to combat the discrimination they had experienced and provided bilingual registration and election materials (de la Garza and DeSipio 1993). Congress further amended the VRA in 1982 so that minority communities not only had protections against electoral exclusion but also received a guarantee that their votes could not be diluted by districting strategies. The practical consequence of this guarantee was that in areas where minority populations are concentrated, officeholder districts must be drawn with majority-minority populations to increase the likelihood of a minority officeholder. All districts drawn after the 1990 census were influenced by these requirements.

Since the passage of the VRA, the African American population has expanded only modestly through immigration. Latino and Asian populations, however, have seen considerable immigration. Thus, it is clear that immigrants have benefited from the protection of the VRA, even though they were not discriminated against before the passage of the VRA because they did not yet live in the United States. This same pattern of immigrant beneficiaries appears in affirmative action programs designed to improve minority access to employment, education, and government contracting. Some of today's beneficiaries include immigrants who could not have experienced the discrimination Congress designed these programs to remedy.

Immigrant access to programs designed to remedy past discrimination against minorities raises questions for the polity, among them questions of equity, effectiveness, and backlash. First, in terms of equity, minority communities could well resent the dilution of these programs. In an era of limited resources, affirmative action programs may end up rewarding well-trained immigrants over their US-born coethnics or African Americans who have experienced discrimination in the United States—the intended beneficiaries of the program. Such equity, or fairness, issues may also be raised by nonminority populations that may (or may not) grudgingly accept the VRA, affirmative action, and other such programs but that are opposed to the extension of these remedial programs to immigrants.

A second question that must be asked about the extension of programs designed for minorities to immigrants concerns effectiveness. We have indicated that the nation offers little in terms of a formal settlement policy for immigrants; instead, it offers opportunities to individual immigrants through naturalization. Remedial programs have come to be seen by some immigrant leaders as a substitute in the absence of a well-developed settlement policy. Congress did not, however, design such remedial programs with the intent of addressing immigrant needs. If immigrant leaders or policymakers argue that a set of policies specifically designed to speed or ease the transition of immigrants into equal citizens is needed, they need to design and implement such policies, rather than simply relying on expedient borrowing from minority programs.

The final concern—backlash—is implicit in the first two issues. Opponents of remedial programs have used the expansion of the program's beneficiaries as a tool to undermine popular and policymaker support for these programs. Again, the VRA is an excellent example of this. The act was designed to remedy voting discrimination practices against US-born African Americans. However, Congress also mandated bilingual election materials as a tool to remedy discrimination (particularly educational discrimination) against immigrant Latinos and Asian Americans. Today, however, many interpret these ballots as a tool of immigrant empowerment. If these concerns are used to undermine the VRA, then concerns about immigrants will take away a hard-won program that benefits minorities. Similar concerns are being raised about immigrant beneficiaries of affirmative action programs.

The "mission creep" of public policies originally designed for minority populations but now serving immigrant communities as well has a more insidious side. It puts these two populations in competition both for public resources and for public sympathy. The needs of minority populations have become partially lost in the growing debate over immigration. As vitriolic as some of the rhetoric has been about immigrants, the society continues to regard them favorably as compared to minorities, particularly African Americans. Reasoned debate about the public policy needs of each population has been lost. The absence, then, of a US settlement policy may soon be matched by the absence of a US policy to assist US-born minority populations.

Finally, by not distinguishing immigrants from minorities, the United States runs the risk of encouraging immigrants to behave and view themselves as minorities rather than as part of the dominant society. This *minoritization* has not characterized previous waves of immigrants.

Efforts to deny education to the children of the undocumented (regardless of the child's citizenship status) offer disturbing evidence of this minoritization. It was the denial of education that characterized the discrimination against African Americans, Mexican Americans, Chinese Americans, and Puerto Ricans, which then spurred the remedial programs of the 1960s and beyond. If immigrants came to perceive that their denial of access to opportunities in the society was based on their membership in the immigrant group, they could well decide to organize around this identity to demand specific rights and privileges for the group, which could have long-term effects on our society as a whole.

Although immigrants may benefit in the short term from affirmative action and other such programs, the programs do not provide specifically for immigrant needs. They might ameliorate some of the class characteristics of immigrants but they do not necessarily ensure that immigrants move toward citizenship and full political rights. Clearly, policies such as these might be part of a thoughtful settlement policy, but they do not replace the core need of immigrants to attain full civic rights.

A related tension in the settlement of immigrants emerges from the group-based nature of immigration. It is easy to view immigrants as members of a group—in fact, we do that in this book by examining the characteristics of immigration in the aggregate. We speak of national-origin groups making up a period's immigration, we speak of waves of immigration, and we speak of immigrant ethnic populations in cities or regions. Equally important, American society awards basic rights to groups. The undocumented, as a group, earn basic constitutional guarantees simply by being physically present in the United States. Permanent residents earn certain statutory privileges, again based on group membership. Full membership, however, is individual (or familial for minor children). The individual must petition the government for membership and demonstrate individual qualifications to be a member.

The individual nature of gaining full rights and privileges in the society suggests the direction the US government would need to take in adopting a settlement policy, should it choose to do so. Individuals, and not groups, must be empowered to develop political attachments to the United States and to be able to meet the bureaucratic requirements of naturalization. This is a difficult prospect for many immigrants. At a minimum, immigrants require additional resources for education, particularly civic education and English-language training. In addition, many immigrants need assistance with the bureaucratic requirements. These educational services are in short supply, and assistance with bureaucratic requirements is largely provided by overtaxed community groups, not by the government. And there are few similar programs that were originally constructed to benefit US-born minorities that immigrants can "borrow." Many permanent residents do not see the benefits of citizenship. As full membership requires individual and not group action, the government must promote the idea of citizenship and develop immigrant-specific resources in order to empower individuals to assert their membership.

The US government has another option, one that it has never followed at the national level—group-based incorporation. Other immigrant-receiving societies use such policies in part to incorporate immigrants through their ethnic group identity. Canada, for example, sponsors organizations to maintain the cultures of immigrant ethnic populations such as Italian Canadians. These government-sponsored ethnic organizations are given the responsibility to distribute some government resources to fellow ethnics. Such governmental multicultural policies maintain ethnic group membership and the cultural connection of the group membership as a way to allocate government resources to encourage membership while building, it is hoped, new bridges to Canada. Although this is an option for the United States, it would represent a complete reversal of the direction that settlement policy has taken in the past in the United States.

## Conclusion

Public opinion on immigration is characterized by a contradiction between popular reverence for immigrants and opposition to immigration. The process of settlement shapes which of these aspects the mass of the citizenry pays attention to when it considers the process of bringing new people into the United States. When settlement is successful, reverence appears. When it is unsuccessful, the citizenry reacts with concern. For many in American society today, particularly for those who oppose legalization as part of comprehensive immigration reform, we are in such a period of concern.

By successfully crafting settlement policy, however, the government can shift attention to the value of immigrants. However, for the most part, the government has left the process of immigrant settlement to private institutions. This privatized response has become more difficult as society has expanded its responsibilities to all residents. Selectively, the United States has chosen to exclude non-naturalized immigrants from some (permanent residents) or all (the undocumented) of these benefits. It has not supplemented this selective exclusion, however, with a conscious policy of settlement, so that immigrants can develop an interest in membership in the United States and acquire the skills to accomplish this end. Nor has the government established a path for the unauthorized to move into legal status.

In the past, the nation has incorporated immigrants as individuals. Rather than develop immigrant-specific programs that could help with settlement and inclusion, the government has allowed immigrants to rely upon programs that were developed for minorities to remedy past discriminations. This has diminished minorities' access to these resources, created an increasingly negative view of such programs by the general public, and caused the minoritization of immigrants, by which immigrants could come to believe that they are being excluded as a group from the dominant society. They may, then, decide to make demands as a group for rights or for political inclusion. It is likely that US society would react quite negatively to such group-based demands. Such demands, however legitimate, would increase concerns about immigration and diminish the fondness for immigrants within US society.

# 4

. . . . . . . . . . . . . . . . . . . . . . . . . . . . . . . . . . . . . . . . . . . . . . . . . . . . . .

# *From Immigrant to Citizen: US Naturalization Policy*

THROUGHOUT THE NATION'S HISTORY, WAVE AFTER WAVE OF immigrants have populated the land, diversified the population, and kindled the economy. With their presence, immigrants have challenged the nation to meet its commitment to democracy and equal opportunity by incorporating their voices into the nation's politics. With notable (and sorry) exceptions, immigrants' desires for incorporation have been met over the past 225 years of American constitutional history. Throughout the nation's history, immigrants (and, more recently, legal immigrants only) have been eligible to naturalize as US citizens and acquire a legal status virtually indistinguishable from that of the US-born. The only limitations on naturalized citizens are that they may not serve as either president or vice president and that they are subject to the loss of citizenship through judicial denaturalization if it can be proved that the applicant lied on his or her immigration or naturalization application. In practice, however, naturalized citizens rarely face denaturalization (and, even more rarely, are in a position to seek the presidency).

Today, the nation is adding a record number of new citizens through naturalization (see Table 4.1). Over the past two decades, naturalization has added approximately 13 million people to the pool of US citizens. To put this number of new citizens in context, the other major path to citizenship in this period—births in the United States and births to US citizens abroad—created about 80 million new US citizens. So, naturalization is the source of approximately 14 percent of new citizens. The share will likely grow in coming years, as US birthrates in general are declining, but the number of immigrants remains high and will grow without significant changes in immigration policy.

TABLE 4.1. Number of New Naturalized Citizens, 1907–2013

| Date | New Naturalized Citizens[1] |
|------|------------------------------|
| 1907–1910 | 111,738 |
| 1911–1920 | 1,128,972 |
| 1921–1930 | 1,773,185 |
| 1931–1940 | 1,518,464 |
| 1941–1950 | 1,987,028 |
| 1951–1960 | 1,189,946 |
| 1961–1970 | 1,120,263 |
| 1971–1980 | 1,458,494 |
| 1981–1990 | 2,165,883 |
| 1991–2000 | 5,597,105 |
| 2001–2010 | 6,556,004 |
| 2011 | 694,193 |
| 2012 | 757,434 |
| 2013 | 779,929 |

Source: US Department of Homeland Security (2014).

---

[1] The US government did not collect naturalization data before 1907. There are no comprehensive data on the number of naturalizing citizens between 1787 and 1906. Records for individuals who naturalized prior to 1907 are sometimes available from the states and cities where they naturalized.

These steadily increasing numbers of naturalizing citizens reflect the steady growth in immigration in the period since the passage of the 1965 immigration law. Immigrants are sometimes slow to naturalize, some never do, and some leave the United States permanently without naturalizing. In only two decades of the twentieth century (the 1930s and 1940s) did naturalization exceed immigration.

This gap between immigration and naturalization creates potential challenges and tensions for the polity as well as for the immigrant. Policymakers have had to confront three policy questions: (1) Who should be eligible to naturalize? (2) Which characteristics should naturalization candidates have? and (3) Which level of government should administer the transition from noncitizen to citizen? We examine each of these conflicts in turn in this chapter.

Naturalization also involves an individual decision made by all immigrants, specifically to pledge loyalty or attachment to the United States. Throughout US history, most immigrants have developed loyalty to the United States and many have thereupon sought citizenship, a pattern that continues today. Still, attainment of citizenship varies among different nationalities. In this chapter, we also examine the individual and group determinants of naturalization.

Traditionally, the United States has offered little encouragement to immigrants to naturalize, but has willingly accepted those who have sought to join the polity and accepted them with fewer expectations than many other countries. In this voluntary system, some groups of immigrants have been more likely to seek membership than others. If this is due to the varied levels of individual desire for citizenship, the state faces a challenge only if a distinct immigrant population rejects American political values, yet stays in the United States. There is no contemporary or historical evidence to suggest that definable groups of immigrants have rejected the American political system in this way. However, if the differential rates of citizenship attainment reflect varying impediments faced by immigrants based on nationality or some other trait, then these differential rates of nationalization raise a serious challenge for the polity.

Policymakers have responded differently in different eras to the challenges of determining whom the nation should admit as citizens and on what terms. As with immigration policy, the challenges surrounding US naturalization policy have not been conclusively resolved, nor will they be as long as the United States remains a nation of immigrants. In fact, we can reasonably expect that these challenges will grow rather than diminish in the future.

## Naturalization as a National Policy

Among the few powers explicitly reserved in the Constitution for the federal government is that of naturalization. Despite the absence of an explicit conception of national (as opposed to state) citizenship at the time of the nation's founding, the founding fathers ensured that the national government would retain control of naturalization. Article I, Section 8 of the Constitution grants Congress the power "to establish a uniform rule of naturalization."

The Constitutional mandate to vest naturalization powers with the national government may be seen as part of a broad effort to guarantee that the federal government would be able to ensure continued national population and economic growth. Had naturalization powers rested with the states, states not wishing to receive immigrants could have developed restrictive naturalization rules. Further, states might have used naturalization powers to entice or dissuade immigrant settlement, which offered more tangible benefits at the time of the drafting of the Constitution. Either of these outcomes could have slowed the potential for attracting immigrants and, ultimately, the growth of the United States.

The roots of these concerns about the consequences of restrictive naturalization policies can be found in the immediate prerevolutionary period. Among the charges against King George III included in the Declaration of Independence was this: "He has endeavored to prevent the population of these states; for that purpose obstructing the laws for naturalization of foreigners; refusing to pass others to encourage their migrations hither, and raising the conditions of new appropriations of lands." The first Congress quickly acted on this concern in 1790 and developed an outline for naturalization requirements that has survived since. With the benefit of hindsight, we see that the Constitutional provision of national control over naturalization has had the desired impact. With a brief four-year exception early in the nation's history, most immigrants have been assured of the opportunity for a relatively quick transition to citizenship. In the twentieth century, Congress has added to the minimal requirements established in 1790—specifically, individual skill and knowledge requirements. Although we recognize that these additional twentieth-century stipulations do make naturalization more challenging for many immigrants, we will argue that these have been relatively minimal and do not offer insurmountable impediments for most immigrants seeking citizenship. Thus, despite periodic local passions against immigration, the United States has consistently provided immigrants with a path to citizenship. So, the question of whether or not immigrants should have access to citizenship has really never been the focus of policymakers.

US naturalization law has examined the question of who should be offered US citizenship in two ways. The first involves the categories of immigrants to be offered US citizenship (the "who" question). The second concerns the characteristics and abilities that individuals within these categories need to have to be eligible for naturalization (the "which characteristics" question). For the first 160 years of naturalization history, the "who" issue was Congress's primary concern. At the turn of the twentieth century, however, the "which characteristics" issue began to increase in prominence. Today, it eclipses the first as the key determinant of naturalization. Thus, for the categories of immigrants eligible for US citizenship, the nation has always been quite willing to welcome as citizens those individuals it has admitted as immigrants (in the twentieth century, those admitted as permanent residents). In the following section, we review the statutory history of US naturalization law. (See Table 4.2 for a summary of this legislative history.)

## Establishing the Foundations for US Naturalization Law

In one of its first acts, the first Congress established the framework for US naturalization. The 1790 Naturalization Act addressed both the question of categories and individual qualifications. Congress extended the privilege of naturalization to all "free white persons." Among white immigrants, individuals had to have resided in the United States for two years, and in the state of application for one year. Aside from length-of-residence requirements, the first citizenship law required that applicants be of "good character" and, upon award of citizenship, take an oath or affirmation to support the Constitution. Children of the newly naturalized themselves became citizens through the parent's application (1 Statutes at Large 103, enacted March 26, 1790). Although not stated explicitly in the law, the privilege of applying for citizenship was limited to men. The citizenship status of immigrant women followed that of their husbands (Bredbenner 1998; Gardner 2005). In sum, the first naturalization law demanded little of individual applicants and thus encouraged naturalization among the "free white persons" (men and their families). Although simple in many ways, the outline established in this first citizenship law offered a skeleton for subsequent amendments. It defined an eligible class of immigrants and established individual qualifications for their admission as citizens.

The first amendment to US naturalization law came just five years later. In 1795, Congress extended the minimum period of US residence to five years and added two requirements. In addition to swearing allegiance to the Constitution, new applicants had to renounce their former allegiance by name (1 Statutes at Large 414, enacted January 29, 1795). In other words, an immigrant from England had to renounce allegiance to the king

TABLE 4.2. Major Naturalization Laws, 1787–2012[1]

| Year | Categories of Immigrants Eligible for or Excluded from US Citizenship | Characteristics or Abilities Required |
|---|---|---|
| 1790 | Free white persons [men] are eligible | • Resident in United States for two years<br>• Good moral character<br>• Willingness to take an oath or affirmation to support the Constitution |
| 1795 | | • Resident in the United States for five years<br>• Willingness to renounce former allegiance<br>• File a declaration of intention to naturalize three years before naturalization |
| 1798 | Nationals of countries with which the United States is at war are excluded from naturalization (repealed 1802) | • Resident in the United States for fourteen years<br>• File the declaration of intention with the US attorney general |
| 1802 | | • Standards returned to 1795 law |
| 1868 | Citizenship extended to children born in the United States, regardless of the immigration status of the parent | |
| 1870 | Aliens of African nativity eligible | |
| 1882 | Chinese excluded from naturalization (other Asian nationalities also barred over next forty years) | |

of England. Aliens also had to renounce any hereditary titles to nobility, a requirement that remains today as a question on the naturalization application (along with other statuses that preclude naturalization, such as service in the Nazi or Axis government or military during World War II).

Congress amended naturalization law once more in the eighteenth century. In 1798 as part of the Alien and Sedition Acts, it extended the period of residence required for naturalization to fourteen years. This change was part of the anti-immigrant fervor in the new United States that reflected tensions in Europe over the French Revolution and a political battle in

TABLE 4.2. *(continued)*

| | | |
|---|---|---|
| 1906 | Anarchists and polygamists excluded from naturalization | • Speaking knowledge of English<br>• State an intention to reside permanently in the United States<br>• Provide two witnesses to five-year residence and good moral character |
| 1912 | Deserters and immigrants who left the United States to avoid the draft excluded from naturalization | |
| 1922 | Women, regardless of marital status or citizenship status of husband, eligible for naturalization | |
| 1943 | Chinese eligible for naturalization | |
| 1950 | Communists or those who teach that the US government should be overthrown excluded from citizenship | • Reading and writing knowledge of English<br>• Knowledge and understanding of the fundamentals and principles of the forms of American government |
| 1952 | Naturalization extended to all races | |

*Source:* Compiled by the authors.

---

[1] Congress has passed naturalization legislation since 1952. Relative to the legislation mentioned here, however, these recent laws have been primarily procedural. Although the foundations of today's statutory naturalization requirements can be found in these pre-1952 laws, the *implementation* of these laws—the administration of naturalization—has changed considerably in recent years.

the United States resulting from the emergence of political parties. As part of its efforts to limit access to US citizenship, Congress excluded from eligibility citizens of countries with which the United States was at war. Congress also attempted to centralize control over naturalization in the federal government. The law required clerks of the local courts that administered naturalization to send the US secretary of state the names and applications of immigrants stating an intention to become citizens (1 Statutes at Large 566, enacted June 18, 1798). By 1802, legislative concern about the loyalty of immigrants had declined and Congress returned naturalization requirements to those established in 1795. The election of 1800 had placed Thomas Jefferson in the presidency and his allies (the Democratic Republicans) in control of Congress, in part on the votes of naturalized US citizens who were angered by the anti-immigrant policies of President John Adams and the Federalists, who had led the effort to add to naturalization requirements in 1798 (Muller 1993).

Since 1802, the requirement of five years of residence prior to naturalization has not been changed for most immigrants (2 Statutes at Large 153, enacted April 14, 1802).[1] The brief effort to centralize control over naturalization also disappeared. For the next century, local officials applied the loose federal guidelines and determined who could join the polity with virtually no federal oversight.

### Naturalization Law in the Nineteenth Century: Few Requirements, Slow Expansion of Eligibility

After these several changes in the nation's first decade, Congress largely ignored naturalization through the nineteenth century. The five-year residence requirement, good character, the oath or affirmation of loyalty to the Constitution, the renunciation of former allegiance, and the declaration of intention prior to the application remained the only requirements for immigrants seeking citizenship.

Congress did, however, return several times in the nineteenth century to reconfigure the *categories* of immigrants eligible for naturalization; each change was incidental to other broader changes in public policy. In 1870, Congress extended naturalization eligibility to aliens of African nativity (16 Statutes at Law 254, enacted July 14, 1870). This change initially applied to very few people, mostly to African-ancestry migrants from the Caribbean who had little ability or incentive to migrate prior to 1865. This amendment was not the beginning of a general expansion of naturalization eligibility, but rather part of the Radical Republican efforts to legislate equal rights for blacks in one of the few policy areas controlled exclusively by the federal government. At a symbolic level, however, this change cannot be dismissed; it was the first time that naturalization extended beyond the 1790 standard of "free white persons."

Congressional action did not extend to all nonwhites, however. In 1882, among other provisions, the Chinese Exclusion Act barred the Chinese from naturalization (22 Statutes at Large 58, enacted May 6, 1882). The primary goal of this provision was to bar new Chinese immigration. In this, the law largely succeeded. It did not, however, prevent having US citizens of Chinese ancestry; the children of pre-1882 Chinese immigrants acquired US citizenship at birth, a status that the federal courts ruled could not be taken away by legislation (*United States v. Wong Kim Ark*, 169 U.S. 649 [1898]). Without new immigration, however, naturalization became irrelevant. Symbolically, however, the naturalization provisions of the Chinese Exclusion Act reinforced the statement of unwelcome found in the ban on Chinese immigration. Over the next forty years, Congress and the courts extended the prohibition on naturalization to other Asians, including nationals of India, and to South and West Asians more generally (Haney Lopez 1996).

Perhaps unintentionally, Congress appeared to settle what could have become a major naturalization issue in the late nineteenth and twentieth centuries with a Constitutional amendment ratified just after the Civil War that concerned whether the US-born children of noncitizens would be citizens by birth, or whether they would need to naturalize to become US citizens (or have their status be dependent on parental naturalization). The Fourteenth Amendment to the Constitution granted immigrants' children citizenship based on their birth. Section 1 provides that

> all persons born or naturalized in the United States, and subject to the jurisdiction thereof, are citizens of the United States and of the State wherein they reside. No State shall make or enforce any law which shall abridge the privileges or immunities of citizens of the United States; nor shall any State deprive any person of life, liberty, or property, without due process of law; nor deny any person within its jurisdiction the equal protection of the laws.

When Congress proposed this amendment, and the states ratified it in 1868, the citizenship status of the children of immigrants was not actually the issue. Instead, Congress sought to grant citizenship to the newly freed slaves (whose citizenship had been taken away by the Supreme Court's ruling in *Dred Scott v. Sandford*) and to mandate equal protection rights of the recently freed slaves.[2] With the Fourteenth Amendment, however, Congress settled a conflict between the states. Some states had granted children born in the United States citizenship and others had not (Schuck and Smith 1985). Because there was no centralized control over the implementation of naturalization, these discrepancies between state decisions about who was a citizen went unaddressed until the passage of the Fourteenth Amendment.

The Constitutional guarantee of *jus soli*, or birthright citizenship, created little debate at the time because there were relatively few immigrants and their eventual receipt of US citizenship was assumed. More important, as we indicated in Chapter 2, there was no notion of unauthorized immigration in this era. Only later did the status of immigrant children—and debate over the meaning of the clause "and subject to the jurisdiction thereof"—become a topic of Congressional and popular concern. In a sense, however, Congress's action in this area is representative of its approach to naturalization in the nineteenth century— a topic of little concern that was addressed indirectly when it was addressed at all. For white immigrants in this era, requirements remained few, and the door to US citizenship stayed wide open.

### Naturalization in the Twentieth Century: Expanding Eligibility and Increasing Requirements

The steady expansion of immigration after the Civil War raised concerns about naturalization as well as immigration. This concern manifested itself in an increase in the requirements for those immigrants seeking to become US citizens. Ending over a century without new individual-level naturalization requirements, Congress mandated in 1906 that citizenship applicants must have a speaking knowledge of English, state an intention to reside permanently in the United States, and provide two "credible" US citizen witnesses who would provide affidavits stating that the naturalization applicant was of good moral character and had resided in the United States for five years (34 Statutes at Large 596, enacted June 29, 1906). Congress addressed the classes of immigrants eligible for naturalization, excluding anarchists and polygamists. It also enacted a series of procedural reforms in the administration of naturalization that we discuss later in this chapter.

In sheer volume, the 1906 legislation was Congress's most extensive effort to date regarding naturalization. More important, perhaps, the English-speaking knowledge and the procedural reforms presaged Congress's approach to naturalization since then. Congress has slowly expanded knowledge requirements for individuals seeking to naturalize and has tried—unsuccessfully—to standardize the procedures for reviewing applicants and for granting naturalization. The exclusion of polygamists and anarchists also began a pattern of statutory exclusions of small categories of immigrants with beliefs or behaviors outside the mainstream of American society. In 1912, Congress excluded deserters or immigrants who left the United States to avoid the draft (37 Statutes at Large 356, enacted August 12, 1912).

The 1920s saw repeated efforts to streamline and eliminate inconsistencies in naturalization law. In contrast to the narrowing that was occurring in immigration policy in this era, this period reflected a steady liberalization in naturalization policy. The most notable of these changes reversed sexist aspects of naturalization law. Beginning in 1922, women (whether married or single) could apply for and be naturalized on their own (42 Statutes at Large 1021–1022, enacted September 22, 1922). This ended the previous practice that provided that foreign-born women were naturalized upon marriage to US citizens or upon the naturalization of their husbands. Also, after 1931, female US citizens no longer lost their citizenship upon marriage to foreign males (Bredbenner 1998; Gardner 2005).

After the late 1920s, Congress did not revisit naturalization law until wartime pressures forced an acknowledgment that the provisions of the Chinese Exclusion Act (and subsequent legislation excluding other Asian nationalities from naturalization) were incompatible with wartime alliances. Thus, in 1943 Congress repealed the Chinese Exclusion Act and added Chinese to the populations eligible to immigrate and naturalize (57 Statutes at Large 600, enacted December 17, 1943). Then, in 1952, Congress extended access to naturalization to all Asians and explicitly to all races (66 Statutes at Large 163, enacted June 27, 1952). Although there were few immigrant Chinese and other Asian immigrants to take advantage of these liberalized naturalization provisions in the 1950s, this change is of great symbolic importance. It represents the elimination of the final national-origin, racial, or ethnic group exclusions from access to US citizenship (although some groups united by belief or behavior continued to face exclusion).

While Congress was expanding the categories of immigrants eligible for US citizenship, it was adding to the requirements with which individual immigrants seeking citizenship had to comply. Beginning in 1950, naturalization applicants had to demonstrate a knowledge and understanding of the fundamentals of the history and principles of the forms of the American government (64 Statutes at Large 1024, enacted September 23, 1950). Congress also expanded the language requirements enacted in 1906. Henceforth, applicants had to read, write, and speak "words in ordinary usage in the English language." This language requirement was not designed to be onerous for the applicant. Congress exempted applicants over fifty years old who had been residing in the United States for more than twenty years. Further, the law stated that the requirement was met if "applicant[s] can read or write simple words and phrases . . . and that no extraordinary or unreasonable conditions shall be imposed upon the applicant." The administrative regulations that guide the implementation of this law require that the naturalization examiner take into account the education level of the applicant.

The 1950 law also created more classes of immigrants ineligible for naturalization based on beliefs. Joining polygamists, anarchists, and draft evaders were members of Communist organizations, immigrants who had served in the Nazi or Axis government or military, and those who advocated or taught that the US government should be overthrown. The changes are virtually the last legislative efforts to define who is eligible for naturalization and what skills they must have.

Today, the first policy question is largely resolved—no group is excluded on social, ethnic, or religious grounds. Instead, most adult immigrants to legal permanent residence who have resided in the United States for five years, are of good moral character, are willing to renounce loyalty to the country of origin, and are willing to swear (or affirm) loyalty to the Constitution and laws of the United States are eligible to become US citizens (see Box 4.1). These requirements largely date from the beginning of the republic. Few immigrants who meet these standards are denied naturalization. Those ineligible for US citizenship include self-admitted polygamists, anarchists, Communists, and those who served in the Nazi regime. Also excluded from citizenship are immigrants who have committed certain crimes (felonies or multiple misdemeanors) while permanent residents and thus are deemed not to be of "good moral character," as well as those who have received needs-based social welfare benefits for at least half of the five-year period before applying for naturalization and thus are deemed to be a "public charge."

The second policy question—which traits the successful citizenship applicant should have—is not as settled as the first. Since 1906, Congress has steadily increased the range of knowledge an applicant must have, and it may do so again in the future. Applicants must read, write, and speak English (with some exceptions for elderly immigrants who have lived

---

**BOX 4.1. OATH OF ALLEGIANCE FOR NEWLY
NATURALIZING CITIZENS**

I hereby declare, on oath, that I absolutely and entirely renounce and abjure all allegiance and fidelity to support any foreign prince, potentate, state or sovereignty, of whom or which I have heretofore been a subject or citizen; that I will support and defend the Constitution and laws of the United States of America against all enemies, foreign and domestic; that I will bear true faith and allegiance to the same; that I will bear arms on behalf of the United States when required by the law; that I will provide non-combatant service in the armed forces of the United States when required by the law; that I will perform work of national importance under civilian direction when required by law; and that I take this obligation freely without any mental reservation or purpose of evasion; so help me God.

---

in the United States for long periods). Also, they must demonstrate an understanding of American history and government. Although unstated as a formal requirement, the increasing complexity of the application and the examination process requires that naturalizing citizens demonstrate a bureaucratic and technological competence or the willingness to hire a professional to assist with the application.

## Who Should Administer the Award of Citizenship?

For its first century, US naturalization policy was characterized by local administration. States and localities implemented the minimal federal standards and decided who could join the polity with almost no federal oversight. As has been suggested, the federal laws that these local governments administered were more concerned with the question of what types of people were eligible for US citizenship than with the skills and knowledge that individual immigrants possessed. The nature of local administration, however, was that whatever federal standards did exist were only loosely administered. As a result, the opportunities for immigrants to naturalize varied considerably from place to place and local authorities frequently disregarded legal requirements for naturalization.

Beginning in the early 1900s, the federal government centralized administration of the naturalization program. This centralization eliminated the excesses created by local administration, but created a system that has continued to be characterized by inconsistent administration. This inconsistency adds to the confusion that many applicants feel about how to proceed with their desires to naturalize as US citizens. The failure to ensure standardized administration reflects a problem in the delivery of many government services (Lipsky 2010). These questions notwithstanding, however, the United States has designed a relatively inclusive system of naturalization that offers the prospect of membership to those categories of legal immigrants being welcomed.

## Local Administration, 1790–1907

The debate over the Alien and Sedition Acts signed into law by President John Adams in 1798 identified a problem that was to plague the administration of naturalization for the next century. The local governments that administered naturalization had virtual carte blanche to evaluate whether naturalization applicants met the minimal federal standards and then to provide documentation to demonstrate that the immigrants were US citizens. By contemporary standards, the Alien and Sedition Acts' mandate that jurisdictions awarding naturalization provide the US secretary of state with the names of applicants so that the federal government could evaluate whether they were subjects of an enemy sovereign may seem minimal. Yet even that requirement fell in 1802, and federal review of individuals seeking naturalization was not to be resurrected for over one hundred years. The legacy of local administration remains today. As there was no reporting requirement, we have no idea how many immigrants earned US citizenship through naturalization prior to 1907, and it is virtually impossible in many cases to determine if a specific immigrant naturalized in this era.

The excesses of local administration have been well documented. Urban machines relied on the lax federal administration to build their cadre of supporters. At the extreme, some immigrants were naturalized on the day of their arrival in the United States in open violation of the statutory requirement of a previous five-year residence in the United States. Before a particularly crucial election, New York's Tammany Hall political machine printed 105,000 blank naturalization applications and 69,000 certificates of naturalization. Immigrants fresh off the boat were given red tickets, allowing them to get their citizenship papers free.

Tammany paid the required court fees and provided false witnesses to testify that the immigrants had been in the country for the necessary five years (Erie 1988: 51).

What has been less documented is the impact outside of the urban machines. Without federal regulation, local governments could use their power to limit or facilitate access to naturalization. In the absence of extensive historical investigation, we can only speculate that both of these practices occurred. Many state and local governments in the late nineteenth and early twentieth centuries saw immigration as a rich pool for populating empty territory (these were the same governments that recruited immigrants in Europe and at ports of entry). Voting rights were extended to noncitizens, for example, explicitly to attract residents to states and territories needing people (Rosberg 1977).

In other areas, officials with nativistic impulses used local discretion to exclude some immigrants who were statutorily eligible from successful naturalization. Texas offers such an example. At the turn of the century, it was home to large German, Czech, and French immigrant populations that had little difficulty in naturalizing. One nationality, however, faced difficulty: Mexicans. Whereas one notable case—*In re Rodríguez* (District Court for the Western District of Texas, May 3, 1897)—established a precedent that assured Mexican nationals of the right to naturalize, local authorities discouraged and intimidated Mexicans seeking to avail themselves of this right. In the case of *In re Rodríguez*, the federal court naturalized Rodríguez based on Congress's granting of citizenship to the former subjects of Mexico in the Treaty of Guadalupe Hidalgo. The judge reasoned that the Treaty guaranteed Mexicans the right of US citizenship and that since that right was only available to white people at the time of the ratification of the Treaty, Mexicans, then, must be white or, at the very least, eligible for US citizenship (De León 1979). Texas, nevertheless, remained inhospitable to the naturalization rights of Mexicans for many years to come, although welcoming many other nationalities (Menchaca 2011). Local governments, and often the same local government, facilitated naturalization for some and hindered it for others. Such contradictory patterns coexisted before centralized naturalization administration. Although more research needs to be done on the treatment of citizenship applicants outside of the Eastern cities, the available data do indicate that many naturalized in this era. Despite the potential for local abuse and the exclusion of immigrants from citizenship, the pattern seems to have been the opposite: local discretion facilitated naturalization.

### National Administration, 1907 to the Present

Congress became concerned that political machines naturalized ineligible immigrants. To address these concerns, President Theodore Roosevelt appointed an interagency commission in 1905. This commission designed the administrative outline of today's naturalization program. Based on the commission's recommendations, Congress established the federal Bureau of Naturalization and enacted procedural reforms. Broadly, Congress's goals were to centralize administration and to ensure that applicants met the statutory requirements for naturalization. In order to accomplish this goal, Congress took the power to grant naturalization away from local courts and the power to review applicants' credentials away from local officials. After 1907, only federal courts and designated state courts (in areas without sitting federal courts) could grant naturalization. (This power later devolved in most jurisdictions to the administrative agency that reviewed naturalization applications—the Immigration and Naturalization Service [INS] and later the Bureau of Citizenship and Immigration Services [USCIS]—although the courts continue to host naturalization ceremonies.)

In addition, Congress required that investigations into applicants' eligibility, including the five-year period of residence and the English-language ability, be conducted by federal employees, taking the power away from local officials who were more likely to be beholden to the local political machines. The agency also created a single application form and a standard certificate of naturalization. Prior to this time, localities had printed their own applications and had issued their own documents to prove naturalization. Finally, Congress standardized application fees nationwide. In 1907, it cost $4 (approximately $100 in 2014 dollars) to become a US citizen (34 Statutes at Large 596, enacted June 29, 1906). This fee has subsequently increased to $595 (plus $85 for fingerprints).

These reforms did not necessarily achieve all of the reformers' goals. Authority to naturalize was concentrated at the federal level; consequently political parties and political machines saw their role in naturalization disappear. In the more than one hundred years that have elapsed since these naturalization reforms were enacted, however, there has been a recurring pattern of inconsistency and a parallel concern that inconsistency may be impeding the immigrant's path to citizenship today. Administrative inconsistencies under these reforms first appeared in the 1920s and 1930s. For example, several courts awarding naturalization interpreted the statutory requirement that applicants be "attached to" the principles of the Constitution as meaning that these courts should require a reading knowledge of English. Other courts mandated that applicants demonstrate knowledge of civics—years before Congress mandated such knowledge. Although these inconsistencies have diminished over the last two decades, some still remain.

Congress became sufficiently concerned about this variation in administration to appoint another investigatory commission to examine inconsistencies in the administration of naturalization. The result was legislation that further centralized the program's administration.

Beginning in 1933, the newly consolidated INS received authority to recommend applicants for award or denial by the courts. Subsequently, courts largely came to accept the INS recommendations and tended to limit their involvement to applicants who sought judicial review after having been recommended for denial by the INS. In 2002, Congress shifted responsibility for the administration of naturalization to the USCIS in the Department of Homeland Security.

In the contemporary period, variation in naturalization administration is compounded by two factors. First, the number of applications can vary considerably from year to year, making it difficult for INS/USCIS to serve its clients in a predictable manner. Naturalization applications, for example, surged in the mid-1990s and again in 2006–2007 in response to national debates over immigration and immigrant rights, and have been steadily increasing in recent years. After each of these application surges, the delay in review of applications grew considerably, losing many applicants in the period between application and administrative review. Second, to process the large number of applications received annually, even in low application years, INS/USCIS has increasingly turned to technologies, particularly the Internet, that are beyond the skill set of many immigrants. Applicants face a confusing bureaucracy that discourages many from pursuing their quest for US citizenship. Individualized assistance is difficult to obtain, which is a particular problem for applicants who do not want to provide information to USCIS that could make them subject to deportation. Although the risk of this is small, many applicants are wary of the risk and fear that a small mistake could have serious consequences.

In an effort to process the steadily growing numbers of applications quickly, INS and USCIS have increasingly required that applicants get information electronically and submit their applications to remote processing centers. For immigrants who do follow up on their naturalization application, the USCIS system is often difficult to penetrate and leaves many applicants unsure of where they stand, or what exactly is needed from them if they are asked to submit additional information—a frequent occurrence as applicants are asked to account for major events in their lives between immigration and the application for naturalization. The time it takes to review applications varies considerably from application to application as well as from one year to the next, in part because USCIS must rely on other federal agencies to run background checks on applicants. As late as the 1990s, treatment of applicants varied considerably in different INS offices (DeSipio et al. 2001). The development of a common pool of questions from which the civics exam is taken and the centralization of application review have diminished this problem (see Box 4.2). During periods of peak demand, USCIS often loses track of applicants who move while their applications are pending, requiring the applicants to restart the process and, in some cases, pay an additional application fee.

Congress's efforts at reform have done little to remedy the situation and, in fact, may have further entrenched decentralization. Responding to ongoing concerns about delays in processing citizenship applications, Congress granted the INS the authority to award naturalization without judicial review in 1990. For successful applicants, this speeds up the process by giving applicants the option of not waiting for a judge to administer the naturalization oath. Unsuccessful applicants would continue to have recourse via judicial review in the courts, though this review is *de novo*, or without the benefit of the record of the INS/USCIS application. This is a much more difficult process than the former procedure and lessens the likelihood that applicants facing denial will seek a court hearing. Thus, though the new procedure addressed one problem—administrative delays—it may well have worsened the problem of inconsistency.

The new INS/USCIS jurisdiction has also increased the number of applicants whose applications are formally denied. In the 1980s—the decade before the INS received authority to award naturalization— slightly less than 2 percent of applications resulted in denials (although considerably more were administratively denied by INS). In the 1990s, this rate surged to nearly 9 percent and to 17 percent in the first decade of the 2000s. These changes in denial rates do not appear to reflect a

**BOX 4.2. SAMPLE NATURALIZATION EXAM QUESTIONS**

1. What is the supreme law of the land?
   *Answer: The Constitution*
2. What do we call the first ten amendments to the Constitution?
   *Answer: The Bill of Rights*
3. What is <u>one</u> right or freedom from the First Amendment?
   *Answer: Speech / Religion / Assembly / Press / Petition the government*
4. What is freedom of religion?
   *Answer: You are free to practice any religion, or to not practice a religion.*
5. What stops <u>one</u> branch of government from becoming too powerful?
   *Answer: Checks and balances / Separation of powers*
6. Who is <u>one</u> of your state's US senators now?
   *Answers will vary. [District of Columbia residents and residents of US territories should answer that DC or the territory where the applicant lives has no US senators.]*
7. What does the judicial branch do?
   *Answer: Reviews laws / Explains laws / Resolves disputes / Decides if a law is unconstitutional*
8. What is <u>one</u> promise you make when you become a United States citizen?
   *Answer: Give up loyalty to other countries / Defend the Constitution and laws of the United States / Obey the laws of the United States / Serve in the US military (if needed) / Serve (do important work for) the nation (if needed) / Be loyal to the United States*
9. Name <u>one</u> problem that led to the Civil War.
   *Answer: Slavery / Economic reasons / States' rights*
10. Name <u>one</u> of the two longest rivers in the United States.
    *Answer: Missouri River / Mississippi River*

*Note:* The full 100 questions from which naturalization examiners must select 10 for each naturalization exam can be found at http://www.uscis.gov /sites/default/files/USCIS/Office%20of%20Citizenship/Citizenship%20 Resource%20Center%20Site/Publications/100q.pdf. The questions are also available as an audio file and translated into Spanish or Chinese.
*Source:* US Citizenship and Immigration Services (2009).

change in the degree of qualification of immigrants for naturalization, but instead a change in the way unsuccessful applications are recorded in administrative records.

USCIS, however, does not disaggregate why applicants are denied, so it is not possible to analyze whether this results from complexities in the application process (see ICF International 2011 for an initial effort to look at comparative pass rates for different sections of the naturalization exam).

Considering these ongoing problems with consistency of the administrative treatment of applicants, the increasing numbers of applicants, and the overall importance of naturalization in a nation that receives 1.1 million immigrants to permanent residence annually, the absence of discussion of naturalization as part of the recent Congressional debates on comprehensive immigration reform is quite interesting. Several members did introduce legislation that would have shaped naturalization, including reducing the residence requirement to four years for some high-skill immigrants or for immigrants who had transitioned from unauthorized status to legal permanent residence, limiting the opportunities for the establishment of dual citizenship for some naturalized US citizens, and speeding up naturalization for members of the military. Relative to the volume and intensity of proposed reforms to immigration, these proposals were few and far between, and were left completely out of the public and Congressional debates from 2005 to 2014 (see Kandel 2014 for an effort to establish a basis for Congressional debates over any potential changes to naturalization law or policies).

In sum, although Congress has steadily centralized naturalization administration—first at the federal level and then in the INS/USCIS—it has not been able to create a program that presents a common face to applicants across the country, nor has it been able to mesh its administrative need to process large numbers of applicants with the skill sets of many immigrants to the United States. Perhaps of greater significance is that it has never been national policy to encourage or stimulate naturalization, as is the case in Canada, for example, where naturalization rates are much higher (Bloemraad 2006; Mahler and Siemiatycki 2011).

In the next section, we look at who chooses to naturalize and who does not. This examination expands upon our discussion of the administration of naturalization, allowing us to assess whether immigrants want to become citizens and what impedes those who do from naturalizing. Naturalization administration will likely long face the problem of needing to process applications from hundreds of thousands of applicants annually, many of whom lack the bureaucratic competency to meet the increasing technological standards imposed by USCIS. To the degree that the United States seeks to live up to its self-imposed standard of being a nation of immigrants, it needs to treat this question of whether it is adequately incorporating immigrants with the same urgency that it treats questions of who should be able to immigrate in the first place.

## Who Chooses to Naturalize and Who Does Not?

So far in this chapter we have examined the question, to whom should the nation offer citizenship? We already know that, for the most part, formal naturalization requirements have remained few and that despite administrative inconsistencies and an increasing, but unstated, expectation that naturalizing citizens be bureaucratically and technologically competent, a steadily increasing number of immigrants who seek to naturalize are able to make the transition to US citizenship. However, these discussions have been quite general and have not differentiated among immigrants seeking citizenship. In this section, we will examine how different national-origin groups and various classes of immigrants engage the naturalization process in the current era.

### Attachment to the United States and Interest in Naturalization

Throughout this discussion, there has been a largely unstated assumption that immigrants, particularly those with the five-year residency necessary to naturalize, want to stay in the United States and are interested in naturalization. This assumption defies the counter-hypothesis present in many studies of US immigration that many immigrants want to return to the sending country or to maintain political ties to the country of origin and stay in the United States only to earn capital to take home. This hypothesis posits that many immigrants are "sojourners" instead of settlers and future citizens (Renshon 2005).

However, the evidence refutes the sojourner view of immigrants. Although the question of the permanence of immigration has only been examined empirically in a few studies (most of which have focused on immigrants from Latin America and the Spanish-speaking Caribbean), the evidence is strong that immigrants intend to stay in the United States and want to naturalize. One study, the 1988 National Latino Immigrant

Survey (NLIS), found that in terms of both attitudes and behaviors, Latino immigrants planned to stay in the United States and desired citizenship. At the simplest level, almost all Latino permanent resident immigrants with the five years of residence necessary to naturalize plan to reside in the United States for the rest of their lives. Even though the majority of respondents were not US citizens, strong pluralities (approximately 40 percent) identified more with the United States than with their countries of origin. Two-thirds believed that it is very important to become a US citizen, and an equal number had done something concrete to initiate the naturalization process, such as taking classes to prepare for the exam or obtaining the naturalization application (Pachon and DeSipio 1994). Respondents to the NLIS clearly wanted to become part of American society and only a small minority—particularly recent arrivals to the United States—could be characterized as sojourners.

A more recent survey of Latinos—the 2006 Latino National Survey (LNS)—shows similar levels of connection between long-term immigrants and American society (see Fraga et al. 2008). Approximately 39 percent of LNS respondents who were born abroad and had lived in the United States for at least five years (and who did not report that they were in the United States in an unauthorized status) had naturalized by the time of the survey. Slightly more than 10 percent of non-naturalized LNS respondents with five or more years of legal residence were applying for naturalization when they completed the survey. An additional 55 percent anticipated that they would apply for US citizenship in the future.

Approximately one-third of naturalization-eligible Latinos did not have plans to naturalize at the time of the LNS. A quick examination of the reasons offered by these citizenship-disinterested Latino immigrants offers some important insights into both the overall attachment of Latino immigrants to the United States and the structural barriers to naturalization in the current naturalization procedures and requirements. Just 4 percent of naturalization-eligible Latino immigrants from the 2006 survey who had no plans to naturalize reported that they either planned to return to their country of origin or that their affection for their home country was too strong to naturalize as a US citizen. Most respondents who had no plans to naturalize, on the other hand, reported that some aspect of the naturalization application process deterred them. Nearly 22 percent reported that they did not have the language skills to naturalize, whereas more than 16 percent reported that they did not know how to naturalize. An additional 16 percent indicated their reason for not applying was that naturalization took too long, and nearly 15 percent reported that naturalization cost too much.

In sum, these survey data on Latino immigrant naturalization behaviors and attitudes in the 1980s and the early 2000s tell a similar story, as does a 2012 study that closely examines the case of non-naturalized Mexican immigrants, who make up a large share of US Latino immigrants (Gonzalez-Barrera et al. 2013). There is little evidence of a large pool of Latino sojourners. On the contrary, a majority of citizenship-eligible Latinos have either naturalized or are in the process of naturalizing. The majority of those who are eligible but who have not applied for naturalization plan to do so. Among those with no plans to naturalize, lack of knowledge about how to pursue naturalization, or concerns over meeting the statutory or bureaucratic requirements of naturalization, dominate the explanations offered for not applying.

A 2008 national study of Asian Americans (Wong et al 2011: Appendix E) offers indications that similar barriers exist to naturalization in Asian American communities. Asian immigrants with more years in the United States and greater English-language competence are more likely to have naturalized than more recent immigrants whose English-language abilities are weak. Asian Americans who reside in areas with few Asian Americans or who are educated abroad are also less likely to have naturalized. This survey has somewhat fewer data than the Latino National Survey on non-naturalized immigrants' interest in eventual naturalization.

In our judgment, the weight of the attachment to the United States among Latino immigrants and the high levels of naturalization among other immigrant populations (discussed later in this chapter) refute sojourner notions of US immigration. Instead, permanent resident immigrants are here to stay, and they desire political inclusion through naturalization. Despite this attachment, we find that the immigrant propensity to naturalize varies and some eligible immigrants who seek citizenship are unsuccessful.

## Propensity to Naturalize by National Origin

When academics and policymakers first examined naturalization, they asked a relatively simple question: Are some nationalities or types of immigrants more likely to naturalize than others? Although the question is simple, its answer potentially raises a problem for the polity. If the country were to admit large numbers of immigrants who had no interest in naturalization, it could create a pool of politically disengaged residents. These politically disengaged immigrants could become resentful of the decisions made for them by citizens. In a more extreme case, the admission of immigrants who oppose the politics of the host country and remain loyal to their sending country could come to act as a fifth column for the interests of their homeland, challenging the national sovereignty of their host country from within. Although there has been almost no evidence that the United States has faced these kinds of politically destabilizing challenges from immigrants, policymakers and voters have feared this outcome at various points in US history (the 1790s, the 1840s–1850s, and the 1910s–1920s) and today (Huntington 2004; Spiro 2008). As a result, the simple question of who is likely to naturalize and who is not has taken on serious political implications.

Concerns about the loyalty of immigrants fueled two political crises in the nation's early years. The Alien and Sedition Acts resulted from both nationalistic and partisan fears. The governing Federalists feared not only that the loyalties of immigrants might drag the United States into the Napoleonic Wars among European powers but also that, once they were naturalized, many of these immigrants might vote for the Federalists' political opposition, the Jeffersonian Democratic Republicans. As a result, the naturalization law was changed to lengthen the necessary period of residence prior to naturalization and to test the loyalty of naturalization applicants. With the election of the Jeffersonians in the 1800 elections (in part based on the votes of naturalized citizens for Jefferson), the Alien and Sedition Acts were quickly repealed. The next burst of anti-immigrant fervor followed the first great expansion in immigration in the late 1840s and 1850s. The American, or Know-Nothing, Party unsuccessfully called for the statutory period of residence for naturalization to increase to twenty-one years and for prohibiting naturalized citizens from holding public office. Each of these demands spoke to twin fears that have characterized periods of anti-immigrant fervor in the United States. First was the concern that the immigrants of the era were not Americanizing and that they could destabilize the polity. Second was the fear that they would be able to use the democratic process to supplant the political power of US-born citizens and change the polity.

The first major national public policy debate about naturalization in the twentieth century had at its root a concern about different propensities to Americanize and, consequently, to naturalize. As we suggested in

Chapter 2, the effort to restrict immigration in the early decades of the twentieth century sought to reduce severely the overall levels of immigration. Those few who would be allowed to immigrate would come from the countries that had provided the bulk of immigrants prior to 1880. The justification for this policy was research that demonstrated that immigrants from the areas that had provided immigrants prior to 1880—mostly Northern and Western Europe—had much higher naturalization rates than those who came from the countries that had provided most of the immigrants after 1880, that is, mostly Southern and Eastern European countries. This finding, based on the results of a study by a presidentially appointed Immigration Commission, offered the intellectual justification for making American immigration law more restrictive and using immigration to reduce cultural conflict.

The finding was not so much wrong as incomplete. Even by the more limited analytical standards of the turn of the twentieth century, the Immigration Commission's approach was sloppy. It created a naturalization rate for each country of origin by examining the percentage of the total number of immigrants who had naturalized. This raw naturalization rate tells little. It compares nations that sent the majority of their emigrants in the 1870s with those that sent the majority of their emigrants in the few years immediately before the Immigration Commission conducted its study. Subsequent analysis that compared immigrants with similar lengths of residence found that there were few consistent nationality-based variations in rate of naturalization (Gavit 1971 [1922]; Guest 1980). Although these studies enriched academics' knowledge of the naturalization process, the post–Immigration Commission findings came too late to change policy. As we mentioned in Chapter 2, US immigration policy between 1921 and 1965 favored immigrants from Northern and Western European countries.

The lesson of this early scholarly examination of propensity to naturalize should not be lost on today's scholars. Examine similarly situated immigrants and do not expect just one characteristic—in this case, country or region of origin—to explain why some immigrants naturalize and others do not.

An examination of the largest immigrant-sending countries today would offer a similarly confusing picture. Table 4.3, for example, presents raw naturalization rates among immigrants eligible for US citizenship in 2005 (legal permanent resident adults with five or more years of permanent residence and legal permanent resident adults with three to five years of residence, if married to a US citizen). The share of eligible immigrants who have naturalized varies considerably by country or region of origin. For example, more than three in four eligible immigrants from the Philippines are naturalized, whereas only slightly more than one in three eligible Mexican immigrants are naturalized. On average, migrants from the Middle East, Europe, and Asia have higher rates of naturalization than migrants from Latin America. Overall, 59 percent of eligible immigrants have naturalized.

These data offer another insight: specifically, that naturalization rates are somewhat lower for countries close to the United States. Mexico has the lowest naturalization rate for any of the countries listed (35 percent) and the Central American region the lowest for a cluster of countries (41 percent). The Dominican Republic and Canada also have below-average rates (54 and 57 percent, respectively). These differences by region are somewhat artificial because they reflect vastly different immigration histories. Foreign-born people in the United States who trace their ancestry to Europe are much more likely to have been in the United States for many years. Nearly 40 percent of European immigrants, for example, who lived in the United States in 2010 had resided in the United States since before 1980. The comparable figure for migrants from Latin America is 17 percent and for Africa 9 percent (US Census Bureau, American Community Survey Reports 2012: Figure 7).

Table 4.4 offers a comparison of naturalization rates by region, but also by period of migration. These data show that the variation between regions of origin remains, but that variation in naturalization rates is considerably more evident across time. Nearly all Asian migrants from the 1970s had naturalized by 2003 (89 percent), for example, but naturalization rates for subsequent cohorts of immigrants from Asia drop considerably: 73 percent for 1980s migrants and 36 percent for 1990s migrants. More than 61 percent of 1970s migrants from Latin America had naturalized by 2003 compared to 40 percent of 1980s migrants and 13 percent of 1990s migrants.[3]

Raw naturalization rates such as those presented in Table 4.4, whether among all immigrants or recent immigrants, include many who are ineligible (permanent resident immigrants who arrived within the last five years, the unauthorized, and others ineligible to naturalize). Another strategy for assessing regions or nationalities and the propensity to naturalize is to follow a specific cohort of naturalizing US citizens. Table 4.5 compares the average number of years between immigration and

**TABLE 4.3. Naturalization Rates (%) of the Citizenship Eligible, by Country, 2005**

| Region/Country | Citizenship-Eligible People Who Naturalized (%)[1] |
|---|---|
| Europe and Canada | 69 |
| Former USSR | 69 |
| Other Europe | 71 |
| Canada | 57 |
| South and East Asia | 71 |
| China | 73 |
| Philippines | 76 |
| India | 65 |
| Vietnam | 71 |
| Korea | 71 |
| Other South and East Asia | 67 |
| Middle East | 77 |
| Latin America | 46 |
| Mexico | 35 |
| Central America | 41 |
| Caribbean | 63 |
| Cuba | 67 |
| Dominican Republic | 54 |
| Jamaica | 69 |
| Other Caribbean | 61 |
| South America | 62 |
| Africa and other | 59 |
| TOTAL | 59 |

*Source:* Adapted from Passel (2007: Table 3).

[1] The pool of naturalization-eligible immigrants includes legal permanent residents who are eighteen years of age and older and who have resided in the United States for five years or more. The pool of eligible adults also includes legal permanent residents who have resided in the United States for three to five years and are married to US citizens. Although the data source used for this analysis (the Current Population Survey) does not identify immigrants' legal statuses, the analyst has excluded unauthorized immigrants from the analysis (see Passel and Clark [1998] for a more detailed explanation of the methodology employed).

TABLE 4.4. Naturalization Rates (%) by Region of Birth and Period of Entry, 2010

| Region of Birth | Period of Entry | | | |
|---|---|---|---|---|
| | Before 1980 | 1980–1989 | 1990–1999 | 2000 and later |
| Africa | 87.5 | 77.5 | 64.3 | 21.5 |
| Asia | 91.8 | 85.5 | 67.9 | 18.8 |
| Europe | 83.4 | 67.1 | 63.2 | 22.3 |
| North America | 70.7 | 49.3 | 34.5 | 9.5 |
| Latin America | 72.3 | 49.7 | 25.1 | 8.9 |
| TOTAL Foreign-born | 79.8 | 63.1 | 42.9 | 13.7 |

Source: US Census Bureau, American Community Survey Reports (2012: Figure 9).

TABLE 4.5. Average Years of Permanent Residence Prior to Naturalization, by Region of Origin, Selected Years 1965–2012[1]

| Region of Origin | 1965 | 1975 | 1985 | 1995 | 2000 | 2005 | 2010 | 2012 |
|---|---|---|---|---|---|---|---|---|
| World | 7 | 7 | 8 | 9 | 9 | 8 | 6 | 7 |
| Africa | 6 | 6 | 7 | 6 | 7 | 7 | 5 | 5 |
| Asia | 6 | 6 | 7 | 7 | 8 | 7 | 5 | 6 |
| Europe | 7 | 8 | 9 | 9 | 7 | 6 | 6 | 7 |
| North America and the Caribbean | 9 | 9 | 13 | 14 | 11 | 11 | 10 | 10 |
| South America | 7 | 10 | 8 | 10 | 10 | 8 | 5 | 6 |
| Oceania | 8 | 7 | 8 | 11 | 11 | 9 | 7 | 8 |

Source: Adapted from Lee (2013: Table 7).

---

[1] These are the average number of years between immigration and naturalization for immigrants who naturalized in selected years. Many immigrants never naturalize, however, and these long-term non-naturalizing immigrants are not evenly distributed among immigrants from different parts of the world. The regions of the world that are slower to naturalize include a higher share of the non-naturalizing immigrants. Thus, a more complete measure that included not just immigrants who naturalized in a given year, but the complete pool of immigrants from each region, including both the naturalized and immigrants who had not naturalized, would likely widen the gap between regions that generally see rapid naturalization (Africa and Asia) and regions that see slower naturalization (North America and the Caribbean).

naturalization for immigrants from different regions of the world. This table confirms some patterns that we have already seen, specifically that migrants from Asia tend to naturalize more rapidly than migrants from North America. These data, however, also show that there is variation across time. In the 1980s and 1990s, for example, migrants from North America (primarily Mexicans and Canadians) who naturalized saw considerably extended periods between immigration and naturalization. In the early 2000s, most regions of the world saw speedier naturalization among their emigrants who naturalized, confirming other research that indicates steadily higher rates of naturalization in the early years of the 2000s (Passel 2007; Lee 2013).

In sum, it is quite difficult to determine the propensity to naturalize for different nationality groups. It is important to note that although some nationalities show consistently higher patterns of naturalization, all nationalities and regions demonstrate steadily increasing levels of naturalization over time. In the next section, we indicate some factors that help distinguish between nationalities with high naturalization rates and those with lower rates, or, more accurately, between those that naturalize quickly and those who do so more slowly.

## Propensity to Naturalize by Denizen Characteristics

In 1936, new research began to examine a wide range of factors that might influence naturalization for individual immigrants. These fit broadly into two categories: status and psychological characteristics. *Status* examines the impact of socioeconomic factors, such as income, education, and occupation, on the propensity to naturalize. *Psychological characteristics* include immigration and acculturation characteristics, such as reasons for immigration visa eligibility, English-language ability, and attachment to the United States. Despite the added complexity of this contemporary research, it is still not possible to say with certainty why one immigrant will naturalize and why another will not. Instead, we may speak of some factors that seem to influence the propensity to naturalize.

The most reliable predictor of the propensity to naturalize is time; that is, the longer that immigrants are in the United States, the higher the chance that they will be US citizens. Relatedly, older immigrants are more likely to have naturalized. This impact is felt over and above the effect of length of residence. These are the only two traits that consistently have a positive impact on naturalization. Other status factors that appear to positively predict naturalization include high median income, white-collar employment, professional status, high levels of education, home owner-ship, young children in the household, naturalization status of spouse, and being female or being married (Barkan and Khokolov 1980; Portes and Mozo 1985; Jasso and Rosenzweig 1990; Yang 1994; DeSipio 1996a; Balistreri and Van Hook 2004; Van Hook, Brown, and Bean 2006).

Studies have also identified psychological factors that are positively related to immigration and acculturation, including the following: emigra-tion for political reasons, entrance as skilled laborers or refugees, origin in Asia or Africa, immigration from a country distant from the United States, changes in national or state policies that increase the instrumental value of US citizenship, changes to immigrant-sending-country policies on dual nationality, and immigration from an English-speaking country (Portes and Mozo 1985; Jasso and Rosenzweig 1987, 1990; Yang 1994; Jones-Correa 2001; Aguirre and Saenz 2002; Van Hook, Brown, and Bean 2006).

The process of acculturation proves to be a positive predictor of nat-uralization in some studies, particularly such acculturation factors as English-language abilities, social identification as an American, roots in the United States (home ownership, children born in the United States, and immediate family in the United States), residence in areas with non-coethnics, positive attitude toward life in the United States, demysti-fication of the naturalization process, increasing attachment to the United States, finding intermediaries to help with the naturalization application, and increasing proficiency with English (García 1981; Alvarez 1987; Portes and Curtis 1987; DeSipio 1996a; Yang 2002; Wong et al. 2011: Appendix E).

Why can we only discuss these factors as likely indicators of natural-ization instead of more confidently stating their individual impacts? To begin with, there are no comprehensive studies of all immigrants from all nations of the world that can disaggregate immigrants eligible for natural-ization or those who have naturalized. Instead, studies of all foreign-born individuals tend to rely on Bureau of the Census data that include unau-thorized immigrants and others ineligible to naturalize (Barkan and Khokolov 1980; Yang 1994). Data from the INS and USCIS allow analysis of legal immigrants who have naturalized, but INS/USCIS data do not include psychological or acculturation variables. INS/USCIS data cannot account for immigrants to permanent residence who subsequently emi-grated from the United States or died in the United States. So, analysis of immigration service data is limited in that it cannot be used to define the pool of the naturalization-eligible.

Several survey-based studies that control for a variety of factors shaping naturalization analyze the propensity of different nationalities to naturalize in a methodologically sophisticated manner. In a study of all 1971 immigrants, Jasso and Rosenzweig (1990) found that Mexicans were less likely than other national-origin groups to naturalize within ten years. DeSipio (1996a) found that among Latinos, Mexicans were less likely than Cubans and Dominicans to naturalize, a finding confirmed by Aguirre and Saenz (2002) using a different data source. DeSipio, Masuoka, and Stout (2008) found variation across Asian immigrant groups in naturalization propensity, with Japanese, Korean, Filipino, South Asian, and Southeast Asian immigrants less likely than Chinese to naturalize, a finding echoed in Wong et al. (2011). Yang (2002) also found variation in naturalization propensity across Asian immigrant groups, but with Vietnamese and Indian immigrants the most likely among Asian immigrants to naturalize. No comprehensive study of all nationalities and naturalization propensity exists to test these findings. Moreover, these studies do not explicitly include political motivations in their analyses. It is likely, for example, that high Cuban naturalization rates reflect the interest among Cuban immigrants to mobilize and vote in support of candidates and policies that would undermine the Communist government of Cuba.

This analytical imprecision will only be overcome through continued and more sophisticated study in the future. A national study implemented in 2003—the New Immigrant Survey (NIS)—offers a potential first step to improve our knowledge of who naturalizes and why. NIS seeks to follow a cohort of 2003 immigrants over time (see http://nis.princeton.edu /overview.html for further information on the NIS). Should the funding for this project continue, it will be possible to better measure how immigrants who naturalize differ from those who do not and to finally move beyond simple distinctions like national origin or length of residence as primary explanatory variables.

## Entering the Third Century of Naturalization in the United States

With the rapid increase in immigration since 1965, naturalization is again a focus of interest among public policymakers and average citizens alike. The history of naturalization law and practice offers a guide to one possible outcome of this interest: relatively easy access to citizenship among these immigrants, administered somewhat erratically by the federal government, with some immigrants more likely to take advantage of this opportunity than others. Of course, the historical patterns offer just one possible pattern. Whatever course the nation follows in responding to the need for formal immigrant political inclusion, it currently faces three policy issues that will shape how the naturalization process interacts with immigrants in the coming years: (1) the appropriate benefits of citizenship that distinguish citizens from noncitizens, (2) the appropriate role of government in promoting citizenship to eligible immigrants, and (3) the citizenship status of the children of immigrants born in the United States.

## The Benefits of Citizenship

Despite its importance to the polity, the nation has never comprehensively examined the rights and benefits that should be unique to citizens (and denied to noncitizens). As we have suggested, when policymakers discuss naturalization, they focus on procedural questions. Although the slowly increasing formal requirements and bureaucratic and technological competencies for individual applicants may be viewed as a sign that we as a people are demanding more of our voluntary citizens, USCIS's practice of requiring little of citizenship applicants diminishes the value of these requirements as a measure of the meaning of citizenship.

Where then can we look for this meaning? One way would be to look at the differences in the rights and privileges of citizens and noncitizens (see Chapter 3). Between citizens and legal permanent resident aliens, these differences were traditionally few, though they increased dramatically in the mid-1990s and again after the September 11, 2001, attacks on the World Trade Center and the Pentagon. The gap is wide between citizens and permanent residents, and even wider between citizens and unauthorized immigrants. Even the unauthorized, however, have significant rights in US society—they enjoy basic constitutional rights and due process guarantees as well as emergency health care. The federal courts have also ruled that unauthorized children are entitled to a K–12 education. Additionally, some states offer in-state tuition to state colleges and universities to unauthorized students who graduated from high schools in those states.

The differences that have traditionally distinguished the rights and privileges of permanent residents and citizens relate to narrowly defined job rights and programmatic benefits for recent legal and unauthorized immigrants. As we discussed in depth in Chapter 3, Congress and many of the states exclude noncitizens, including permanent residents, from employment in most federal, state, and local government jobs. As public employment has traditionally been a means for educated immigrants to gain a foothold in the United States, these limitations on employment could be seen as a serious impediment.

Until the 1980s, few federal needs-based benefit programs restricted eligibility to US citizens. Two exceptions were scholarships administered by the federal government and access to full Social Security benefits upon retirement, and the latter restriction only applied to permanent residents who retired abroad. In the 1980s, as the numbers of immigrants began to grow, the federal government enacted waiting periods, typically lasting up to five years, after which permanent resident immigrants became eligible for social welfare programs, particularly needs-based programs.

In 1996, Congress dramatically expanded the difference in programmatic eligibility between permanent residents and US citizens with the 1996 Immigration and Welfare Reform bills (see Chapter 3). As important as these changes in programmatic eligibility are, both for the lives of individual immigrants and for the broader question of the meaning of citizenship in the modern era, there was little debate in Congress about how these changes would affect immigrants and immigrant incorporation. Instead, members of Congress saw an easy source of cuts in welfare spending that they thought would be less controversial and politically risky than other budget cuts (e.g., in Medicare spending). In 1997, in what were relatively flush economic times, they responded to pressure to restore Supplemental Security Income (SSI) benefits for elderly permanent residents.

Unintentionally, Congress created a material incentive to naturalize that did not exist prior to 1996. Immigrants seeking to retain or establish eligibility for benefits increasingly naturalized not only for civic reasons but also for more instrumental objectives. The vast increase in applications for naturalization that began in the early 1990s and continued through most of the first decade of the 2000s reflects immigrants seeking to protect themselves against future economic adversity (Van Hook, Brown, and Bean 2006; Gonzalez Barrera et al. 2013: Figure 10). However, applicants who have regularly used these federal programs are potentially ineligible to naturalize, as they can be deemed public charges, which means that current beneficiaries of these programs are choosing not to naturalize so they can retain their existing benefits.

The relative status of US citizens and permanent residents further widened as the nation crafted its response to the September 11, 2001, attacks. The nation's immediate response to the heightened sense of international terror in the months after 9/11 was to increase the scrutiny on Arab Americans and Muslims in the United States, particularly on young Arab American men. The Justice Department and the INS identified and interviewed thousands of Arab Americans and Muslims, offering little evidence that they were targeting these Arab Americans and Muslims for reasons other than their ancestry or religion. Although these investigations did not disproportionately target legal permanent residents, they raised many serious concerns among Arab Americans and Muslims. Specifically, there were concerns that profiled individuals subsequently seeking citizenship would face higher hurdles to citizenship. Many also feared that the investigations would place them on newly created national lists of those under suspicion, such as the no-fly list used to review all passengers boarding airlines. More important, Congress debated legislation that would have given the executive branch much greater authority to investigate people suspected of terrorist ties and, potentially, deport them. This legislation, exemplified by the reauthorization of the Patriot Act and dubbed the Patriot Act II, made permanent resident status much more conditional and would have reduced or eliminated immigrants' abilities to challenge deportation for alleged ties to enemies of the United States.

A related, though much more focused, question appeared when Ali Saleh Kahlah al-Marri, a legal permanent resident of the United States, came under suspicion of serving as a sleeper agent of Al-Qaeda. The Bush administration asserted that al-Marri's permanent resident status did not protect him from being declared an enemy combatant of the United States who could be imprisoned indefinitely without being charged with a crime or tried before a jury. Al-Marri challenged his indefinite detention in court and, after an initial defeat at the District Court level, won a ruling from the Fourth Circuit Court of Appeals in Chicago that held that legal residents of the United States who were detained in the United States could not be held in military custody as enemy combatants. Instead, they had to be charged and tried as would be the case with a US citizen.

The Obama administration did not pursue an appeal to the US Supreme Court but instead transferred al-Marri to civilian control for trial.

Although the nation's initial fears after 9/11 did not translate to a dramatic change in the rights of legal permanent residents, the proposed legal and policy changes of the past decade raise the possibility that another attack on the United States, particularly one that can be tied in the popular imagination to a specific immigrant ethnic population, could lead to a quick diminishment of the rights and freedoms of some or all permanent residents in the United States. Despite incidents such as the failed attempt to detonate a car bomb in Times Square in 2010, the assault at Ft. Hood, Texas, by Nidal Malik Hassan in 2009, and the failed attempt by Umar Farouk Abdulmutallab to blow up a Northwest Airlines flight to Detroit in 2009 using a bomb hidden in his underwear, additional scrutiny of Arab travelers and mosque-related activities has not spurred greater restrictions on the freedoms of Arab residents, whether citizens or noncitizens. Ironically, Latino residents of Arizona and other states have experienced a greater deterioration of their civil rights with the passage of state laws such as S.B. 1070.

## *The Government and Naturalization Promotion*

Our discussion of who should administer naturalization gives rise to another important question: Is it the government's responsibility to promote naturalization? The history of the US naturalization program offers no clear answer. Instead, there are several conflicting models for government involvement in citizenship promotion. Prior to 1907, promoting citizenship, like the practical administration of naturalization, was conducted locally. In practice, this meant active encouragement in some areas and neglect in others. The political machines of the big cities offer an example of active encouragement. The presence of a machine, however, did not guarantee citizenship assistance and promotion. Irish-led machines, for example, became more selective in their offers of assistance after non-Irish immigrants came to dominate the pool of the naturalization-eligible and elections became less competitive (Erie 1988).

During the twentieth and early twenty-first centuries, the federal government has been responsible for administering naturalization. Among these administrative responsibilities, promotion has not been very important. The government's approach to naturalization promotion is best summarized by E. B. Duarte, INS's director of outreach in the early

1980s: "the Immigration and Naturalization Service does not have a policy that identifies lawful permanent residents eligible for citizenship or that encourages them to apply for naturalization. The reason is that naturalization is viewed as a voluntary act" (NALEO 1986:16).

According to Duarte, the INS only becomes involved once an immigrant (or a community-based organization) approaches it with an application or a request for assistance. This narrow role has allowed for certain educational activities. The INS, and now USCIS, is authorized to use a small share of naturalization fees to produce textbooks for use in citizenship education classes. The Department of Education allows federal adult education funds to be used by local school districts to offer citizenship classes. USCIS has produced *A Guide to Naturalization*, a web-based outline of the application procedure, what will be expected at the exam, and what documentation applicants will need (see http://www.uscis.gov/files /article/M-476.pdf).

In the early 1990s, the INS's approach began to change this long-held practice of not promoting naturalization. In November 1993, INS Commissioner Doris Meissner announced a naturalization promotion effort that included direct contact with immigrants and earmarking funds for community-based organizations to provide information to immigrants seeking citizenship (Pear 1993). As demands for naturalization grew in the mid-1990s (after California passed Proposition 187 in 1994 and the federal government reformed welfare and immigration in 1996), these efforts took on a new intensity with added commitments of agency resources and personnel. The INS called this program "Citizenship USA."

The incentives for this intensification were mixed. In part, they reflected a record number of unprocessed applications—as many as 1.5 million (beginning in 1993, the number of applications surged). Evidently, there were also political considerations, with the White House interested in processing as many of the applications as possible before the election. In its effort to review as many applications as possible, the INS approved applicants once it had waited for 120 days for FBI review of an applicant's fingerprints. This decision allowed the INS to process over 1 million naturalization applications in 1996, a record. It also spurred controversy when it became evident that as many as 5,000 new citizens with criminal records that should have barred their naturalization became US citizens (INS initiated denaturalization proceedings against the inappropriately naturalized). After several years of Congressional and Justice Department investigations of Citizenship USA, the Clinton administration and INS were held blameless. Unfortunately, however, the lesson learned from this experience was not that outreach could be an effective tool to promote naturalization among the eligible, but instead that promoting naturalization could also promote controversy. In the years since, INS and USCIS have returned to the modal pattern and refrained from promoting naturalization in immigrant communities.

In 2009, the Obama administration signaled that it wanted to promote naturalization in a limited manner. President Obama's budget request called for $10 million to support community-based citizenship preparation programs that would have served to promote naturalization, a new appropriation that was supported by the House of Representatives. The Senate, however, did not include this program in the budget it passed and the program died. The Department of Homeland Security under the Obama administration used some discretionary funding to fund naturalization service providers for purposes of outreach and client assistance, but these funds were minimal.

Not only does the federal government not actively promote naturalization, it hobbles the process by requiring that applicants pay for the cost of their own naturalization applications and also help cover the costs for asylum and refugee applicants. Congress requires that immigration programs, which include naturalization, be self-supporting. However, some programs, such as asylum and refugee applications, cannot pay for themselves, as asylees and refugees rarely have any money. As a result all other immigration programs essentially pay a tax to cover these non-fee services. Some estimates suggest that this tax accounts for as much as 14 percent of the naturalization application fee, or more than $80 per applicant (National Immigration Forum 2009). President Obama's 2009 budget request also sought funding to address this issue, but again the Senate did not appropriate any additional funds to USCIS for this purpose.

## Birthright Citizenship

The award of birthright citizenship has had a profound impact on the way both immigrants and natives think about immigrants and naturalized citizens. Regardless of whether immigrant parents naturalize, their US-born children receive US citizenship. This policy is controversial among the American public and is opposed by the majority (Rasmussen Reports 2010). Despite this controversy and popular opposition, the policy would be difficult to change, as it is enshrined in the US Constitution and would require both Congressional and state actions to change. Section 1 of the Fourteenth Amendment states that "all persons born . . . in the United States, and subject to the jurisdiction thereof, are citizens of the United States and of the State wherein they reside." Nonetheless, Republican Party leaders have publicly begun to advocate amending the Constitution to deny birthright citizenship for children of unauthorized immigrants.

Although it is not possible to unite the positions of all opponents to birthright citizenship into a single camp, we discuss several of their overarching arguments here. First, opponents have practical concerns about the impact of the current birthright citizenship guarantees. Opponents argue that the guarantee of citizenship for US-born children stimulates unauthorized migration among adults, and that unauthorized parents believe that they are less likely to be deported if they have US-born children. The second practical concern raised by opponents is the cost of birthright citizenship. States that receive large numbers of unauthorized migrants provide social services such as education and health care based on the presence of these US-born children. A simple, or perhaps simplistic, calculus suggests that if these children are denied citizenship and therefore services, states and localities would be able to spend less on said services.

Opponents of birthright citizenship also base their positions on philosophical and nationalistic concerns. They argue that nations must control their borders. Granting citizenship based on an illegal act (unauthorized migration) extends membership in the society to those who have never been invited to join (the US-born children of the unauthorized migrant) and hence transfers decisions about membership to those who have no respect for US law. They are concerned, then, that American society is losing control of its future destiny.

Supporters of birthright citizenship have not had to defend their positions as rigorously as the opponents. The seeming clarity of the Constitutional language and the absence of any serious judicial challenges or legislative efforts to amend the Constitution have limited the need to fight to maintain its guarantees. The beginning of such a challenge, however, has formed the foundation of a defense. Again, this defense has both practical and philosophical dimensions. At a practical level, advocates of birthright citizenship do not want to create a permanent intergenerational pool of noncitizens in the nation. The elimination of birthright citizenship would mean that the children or grandchildren of immigrants would remain partially outside of US society, while also having only limited ties to their parents' or grandparents' country of citizenship (and, depending on the laws of that country, not holding any citizenship in the country of origin at all). This partial exclusion could lead to the formation of an illegal, exploitable underclass among individuals who are stateless. Germany, until 2000, provided a negative example of this dilemma by permitting Turkish families who were of the second and sometimes third generation the right to stay permanently in Germany, but without access to German citizenship. These German-born children and grandchildren of immigrants remained somewhat excluded from German society, but also had limited ties to Turkey and could not easily be deported to a homeland that many of them had never visited.

Advocates of birthright citizenship also highlight an error in the argument of their opponents. Unauthorized immigrants with US citizen children do not receive any special dispensation from immigration enforcement if they are detained. The US citizen child can stay in the United States or accompany the parent back to the country of origin. Once the child turns twenty-one, she or he can petition for the immigration of the noncitizen parent, but this petition can be slowed or denied outright due to the parent's (sometimes multiple) deportations. Supporters of birthright citizenship also raise a philosophical concern. The elimination of birthright citizenship punishes the child for the action of the parent. Thus, advocates deny that a qualitative difference exists at birth between the child of an unauthorized immigrant and the child of a descendant of the first colonizers. In this case, they make a claim of equal protection before the law.

The opponents of birthright citizenship have seized the popular concern about the volume and composition of immigration to shift the debate about birthright citizenship from the academic sphere with the ultimate goal of changing either the wording or the interpretation of the Fourteenth Amendment. How are they setting out to accomplish this goal? Most directly, Republican members of Congress have introduced Constitutional amendments to delete references to "born . . . in the United States" from the qualifications for citizenship. These proposed amendments have met with little success, but the debate is becoming more salient and intense. The failure to enact legislation has generated a concerted effort to engage the courts in the debate. To date, there has been no judicial interpretation of the meaning of the clause "and subject to the jurisdiction thereof" in the Fourteenth Amendment. Birthright citizenship opponents see this clause as the Achilles' heel of the provision. The opponents vary on whether they believe that all immigrants (permanent residents and the unauthorized alike) or just unauthorized immigrants are, in fact, *not* "subject to the jurisdiction" of the US government; they assert that this provision denies birthright citizenship to many who are its beneficiaries today. These efforts to challenge birthright citizenship may be for naught because the courts may affirm the status quo or sidestep the issue entirely. The underlying debate, nevertheless, is of fundamental importance. It seeks to define who is a member of the polity and how that privilege will be passed to the next generation. Although there is some ambiguity in the debate about whether it would affect the children of all immigrants or just those of the unauthorized, it indicates a growing interest in narrowing access to US citizenship.

The controversy over birthright citizenship in the United States appears in some form in most developed countries. Birthright citizenship is on the rise among other developed countries, but it is far from universal, and often has more restrictions than in the United States. For example, children born in the United Kingdom to parents who are not "settled residents" only acquire British citizenship at age ten if they have resided in the United Kingdom for those ten years. Australia implemented similar policies in 1986. France traditionally awarded citizenship at birth, but in 1993, this law was changed to award French citizenship at adulthood to young adults born in France to noncitizens and who have lived in France for at least five years between the ages of eleven and eighteen. French citizenship can be awarded at age thirteen if the child's parents are residents in France and request that citizenship be awarded. Germany liberalized its standards for birthright citizenship in 2000 (after a long history of only awarding birthright citizenship to the children of German nationals). After 2000, Germany awarded citizenship to children born in Germany who had one parent who had been a permanent resident of Germany for at least three years and had been residing in Germany for at least eight years. Germany will also require that the children who acquire citizenship in this manner formally apply for German citizenship at age twenty-three.

## Conclusion

Throughout its history, the US Congress has used its Constitutional authority to provide immigrants access to nearly full political incorporation. Formal requirements have remained few and enforcement of these requirements has remained lax throughout much of the nation's history. Although the polity was initially narrow in the categories of immigrants to whom citizenship was offered, few immigrants to the United States in any era were ineligible to naturalize (immigrants from Asia between the 1880s and 1950 are exceptions).

The surge in immigration that followed the 1965 amendments to the immigration law has again caused the nation to assess its openness to the political incorporation of the foreign-born. Although formal requirements remain few and eligibility is no longer restricted by nationality, varying propensities to naturalize and bureaucratic inconsistencies keep many immigrants in a semipermanent state of noncitizenship.

This potentially poses a conundrum for the nation regarding both identity and practical concerns. In terms of identity, the state must decide whether it should encourage interested immigrants to naturalize (DeSipio 2011). At a more practical level, the state must question whether the narrow but widening difference in rights and responsibilities between citizens and noncitizens acts as a deterrent to naturalization. Further, the United States must assess whether it is healthy for a polity to have such a high share of its residents remain formally loyal to foreign sovereigns.

The significance of this conundrum is intensified for the polity for reasons that we discussed in greater depth in Chapter 3, namely that programs initially designed to assist minorities are now also being used by immigrants—oftentimes diluting the effectiveness of these programs for both immigrants and minorities. Increasingly, then, as policymakers evaluate policies for immigrant naturalization, settlement, and incorporation, they must consider the differences, and the overlap, between the needs of immigrants and the programs and policies that were developed with US-born minorities in mind.

## Notes

1. Beginning in the 1920s, an immigrant married to an American who had been a US citizen for three years could naturalize after three years. Immigrants who serve in the US military are eligible for naturalization after one year of honorable service in peacetime and immediately in wartime, regardless of the length of previous residence in the United States. The opportunity to naturalize with less than five years of legal residence for service members who served during wartime also extended to spouses and children. By an Executive Order issued in 2002, all service in the US armed forces after September 11, 2001, qualifies as service in wartime.

2. As our focus is naturalization, we are not concerned with blanket grants of citizenship, such as that in the Fourteenth Amendment for African Americans. In several other cases, Congress provided citizenship to groups, usually in response to peoples in territories appended to the United States. These included former Mexican subjects in the Southwest in 1848, former Russian subjects in Alaska in 1867, native Hawaiians in 1900, Puerto Ricans in 1917 (after they lost their Spanish nationality in 1900), American Indians in 1924, Virgin Islanders in 1927, and Guamanians in 1950.

3. These data include unauthorized migrants as "immigrants"; as a result, they diminish naturalization rates for regions that have higher shares of unauthorized migrants. This impact is felt particularly in the data on the 1990s and 2000s.

# 5

..................................................

# *Immigrant Civic and Political Engagement*

FROM THE PERSPECTIVE OF THE UNITED STATES, IMMIGRANT loyalty and fealty are exercised through the act of naturalization. Although naturalized US citizens cannot serve as president and can, in rare cases, be denaturalized if it can be shown that they lied in their applications for immigration or naturalization, their status is largely equal to that of the US-born. Further, the Fourteenth Amendment to the US Constitution ensures that the US-born children of immigrants are also US citizens (the foreign-born minor children of naturalizing citizens can naturalize as part of their parents' naturalization or simply begin to exercise the rights of citizenship when their parents naturalize).

The responsibilities of citizenship, however, are greater than simply loyalty and fealty. The nation expects its citizens—regardless of the source of that citizenship—to engage in the civic and political life of the polity and to contribute to its maintenance. In some cases, such as paying taxes, enrolling children in school, and serving in the military when required, these responsibilities are mandated by law. Each of these required acts of citizen engagement, interestingly, is also required of permanent residents, so naturalization does not necessarily increase an immigrant's formal responsibilities to the state. Voluntary civic and political engagement, on the other hand, is not required of any citizen, but broadly expected, and makes the nation stronger. Immigrants, regardless of naturalization status, can and do engage the civic life of the United States, and have throughout the nation's history. Naturalized citizens earn the eligibility to participate in many forms of electoral politics that are denied to non-naturalized immigrants.

In this chapter, to assess the long-term political contributions of immigrants in the contemporary United States, we explore how immigrants and, more specifically, naturalized US citizens engage in these voluntary but critical dimensions of civic and political life. We also explore their continuing civic and political connections to their countries of origin, identified in the scholarship as *transnational political engagement*. Although we explore these separately, we do not see them as being in opposition. On the contrary, as we will suggest, civic involvement in one venue often leads to similar involvement in the other (DeSipio 2006; Staton, Jackson, and Canache 2007). Instead, we look at them separately because the scholarship has largely focused on one locus of immigrant political activity or the other and because of the differences between the forms of civic engagement in the United States and those in the countries of immigrant origin.

## Immigrant Civic and Political Engagement in the United States

Native populations have often feared the political engagement of immigrants. From the nation's first days, the new voices that immigrants brought to the political world scared some native voters. In 1798, the Alien and Sedition Acts were passed by Congress, extending the wait for naturalization by a decade. The hope of the bill's advocates—legislators in the governing Federalist Party—was that the extended wait would ensure that immigrants could not quickly shape political outcomes. They rationalized their very political desire to retain their electoral control with assertions that the era's immigrants harbored views dangerous to the American polity and needed more time to learn American political values (Zolberg 2006: Chapter 3). These assertions galvanized some native-born US citizens, even though there was little evidence to support it. With the defeat of the Federalists in the 1800 election, these acts were quickly repealed. Still, this pattern of fear of new immigrant voices and organization by natives to limit their political influence has reappeared periodically throughout American history, particularly after periods of high immigration, and is again appearing nationally and in many states today.

Should native populations fear the political voices of immigrants and naturalized citizens? The simple answer is "no," and we offer evidence to substantiate this assertion throughout this chapter. Immigrants have tended to adopt values comparable to those of natives very quickly and have only rarely taken positions or acted in a manner that would destabilize the state. In these exceptional cases in which immigrants have organized to destabilize the United States, they have often acted alone or in small groups (such as the terrorists who used US airliners to attack the World Trade Center and the Pentagon on September 11, 2001). Immigrants have on a few occasions acted in the interests of their countries of origin and against US interests (such as when German and Italian immigrants organized to support the fascist leadership of their countries of origin in the period of American neutrality before World War II). However, as we discuss later in the chapter, most contemporary transnational civic and political engagement does not entail a politics that contradicts the interests of the United States (de la Garza and Lowell 2002). In fact, when the interests of the country of origin and the United States are in conflict it is much more common for immigrants to adopt positions that more closely align with those of the United States (de la Garza and DeSipio 1998; de la Garza and Pachon 2000; Schneider et al. 2012).

At a more fundamental level, however, immigrant voices do, over time, challenge and change the national political community. In the election that followed the passage of the Alien and Sedition Acts, for example, naturalized citizens were angered by the seemingly anti-immigrant positions taken by the ruling Federalists. Their anger manifested as votes for the opposition party and its candidate, Thomas Jefferson. The results in the national race were close and New York's votes proved crucial to Jefferson's victory in the Electoral College. Some estimates indicate that it was the votes of naturalized citizens that gave Jefferson a popular vote victory in New York (Mueller 1993). The votes of the naturalized citizens made up a small share of the electorate, of course, so their influence was only felt because of a shift in the candidate choice of native-born voters as well.

Whether or not naturalized voters were crucial to the outcome of the 1800 election—and it is probably not possible to say definitively after two hundred years—the lesson of the 1800 election should not be lost to contemporary politics. Immigrants bring new policy and candidate preferences into the electorate. Although these preferences are certainly broadly within the American political mainstream, their interests may not align with existing electoral majorities. The presence of naturalized citizens in the electorate will slowly change national politics, and when they are angered and enter the electorate in large numbers, they can change national politics more quickly. Arguably, the recent politics of the

United States—which has demonized some immigrant communities and challenged the political loyalty of others—has seen a period of relatively rapid growth of the naturalized citizen electorate. This has meant that the political voices of immigrants are being heard more loudly, and that the choices of naturalized citizens have helped determine some recent electoral outcomes. In the discussion that follows, we look at the civic and political behaviors of immigrants with an eye to their likely future political voice.

## Immigrant Civic Engagement

Immigrants to the United States quickly join the civic life of their communities of residence, though they may not recognize that they are making a move toward political engagement. To the contrary, many avow a desire to avoid "politics," fearing that their outsider status makes them and their activities suspect. Instead, they engage in activities that do not appear overtly "political," like working with others to address common needs around specific issues of concern, being active in their children's schools, and keeping up with the news. Recent surveys in Latino and Asian American communities show that their rates of participation are somewhat below those of their US-born coethnics in many cases, but that community involvement is part of the immigrant experience in the United States (see Tables 5.1 and 5.2). This is neither a surprising nor profound finding, as it has long been the case in the United States and in immigrant communities in other countries (Maxwell 2010). Although there are no national surveys of all immigrants in the United States, we feel confident that the patterns seen here for Latino and Asian American immigrants are repeated among immigrant populations from other parts of the world, particularly in cases where immigrants reside around other immigrants from the same country or among US-born coethnics.

The gap between immigrant civic involvement and that of their US-born coethnics might suggest that immigrants are less interested in civic life than the native-born. We would suggest an alternative explanation. People engage in civic activity when they are asked to participate and when they get the sense that the time and energy they dedicate to the activity will pay off with the desired result. Therefore, because most immigrants are newer to US society and more focused on the day-to-day need to sustain themselves and their families, they are somewhat less likely to be connected to networks that will ask for their engagement, thus

TABLE 5.1. Non-Electoral Civic Activities and Political Values/Attitudes Among Naturalized and US-born Latinos, 2006[1]

| | Mexican | Puerto Rican[2] | Cuban | Salvadoran | Dominican | Other |
|---|---|---|---|---|---|---|
| Participates in social, cultural, civic or political group (%) | | | | | | |
| Immigrant | 12.1 | 10.5 | 21.8 | 11.1 | 18.0 | 18.6 |
| US-born | 28.9 | 26.3 | 41.0 | 12.5 | 17.4 | 39.4 |
| Contacted government officials or attended a meeting to address an issue of concern (%) | | | | | | |
| Immigrant | 22.0 | 27.0 | 34.0 | 21.4 | 24.9 | 23.9 |
| US-born | 44.4 | 45.1 | 52.6 | 38.8 | 44.3 | 50.7 |
| Pays "a lot" of attention to the politics of the country of ancestry or origin (%) | | | | | | |
| Immigrant | 12.1 | 21.1 | 27.5 | 19.0 | 22.5 | 20.8 |
| US-born | 7.1 | 14.0 | 23.8 | 10.2 | 14.3 | 10.3 |
| Supports voting in home country or country of ancestry elections (%) | | | | | | |
| Immigrant | 57.6 | 59.2 | 28.2 | 55.1 | 73.0 | 60.3 |
| US-born | 36.9 | 42.8 | 30.0 | 35.4 | 46.3 | 38.2 |
| Met with a child's teacher (%) | | | | | | |
| Immigrant | 89.4 | 72.7 | 94.3 | 91.0 | 94.4 | 89.0 |
| US-born | 92.4 | 95.7 | 95.0 | 66.7 | 100 | 100 |
| Attended a PTA meeting (%) | | | | | | |
| Immigrant | 78.6 | 54.5 | 82.7 | 79.1 | 72.2 | 76.3 |
| US-born | 60.6 | 71.0 | 75.0 | 50.0 | 88.9 | 70.4 |
| Acted as a school volunteer (%) | | | | | | |
| Immigrant | 47.2 | 72.7 | 51.9 | 45.9 | 35.6 | 52.2 |
| US-born | 65.8 | 62.3 | 75.0 | 40.0 | 55.6 | 79.6 |
| Participated in a hometown club or association (%) | | | | | | |
| Immigrant | 4.2 | 9.2 | 4.4 | 5.3 | 9.8 | 8.4 |
| US-born | 3.9 | 3.9 | 9.2 | 0.0 | 6.3 | 12.9 |

*Source:* Authors' analysis of the Latino National Survey, 2006 (Fraga et al. 2008).

---

[1] The sample included relative small numbers of island-born Puerto Ricans and US-born Cubans, Salvadorans, and Dominicans, so the margin of error around these attitudes and behaviors is somewhat larger.

[2] Puerto Ricans born in Puerto Rico are US citizens by birth and not immigrants. We present data on Puerto Rican migrants for purposes of comparison.

TABLE 5.2. Non-Electoral Political Activities Among Asian Immigrants and Asian Americans, 2008

| | Chinese | Asian Indian | Filipino | Japanese | Korean | Vietnamese | Other Asian |
|---|---|---|---|---|---|---|---|
| Discussed politics with friends and family (%) | | | | | | | |
| Immigrant | 69.2 | 73.7 | 62.9 | 74.1 | 71.9 | 57.6 | 77.5 |
| US-born | 83.3 | 86.7 | 89.0 | 77.5 | 88.2 | 78.6 | 68.4 |
| Worked for a candidate, political party, or some other campaign organization (%) | | | | | | | |
| Immigrant | 2.1 | 5.2 | 4.8 | 3.6 | 2.0 | 3.3 | 4.2 |
| US-born | 8.3 | 9.2 | 4.9 | 5.9 | 17.6 | 7.1 | 10.5 |
| Contributed money to a candidate, political party, or some other campaign (%) | | | | | | | |
| Immigrant | 9.2 | 18.4 | 16.0 | 10.0 | 12.6 | 9.1 | 9.2 |
| US-born | 20.8 | 15.0 | 25.9 | 24.5 | 11.8 | 7.1 | 30.6 |
| Contacted a representative or a government official in the United States (%) | | | | | | | |
| Immigrant | 7.8 | 13.8 | 14.0 | 9.7 | 7.4 | 6.3 | 8.5 |
| US-born | 16.7 | 20.0 | 17.1 | 15.8 | 11.8 | 0 | 23.7 |
| Worked with others to solve a community problem (%) | | | | | | | |
| Immigrant | 18.2 | 32.5 | 21.2 | 16.2 | 18.0 | 17.5 | 21.4 |
| US-born | 29.2 | 30.8 | 35.4 | 20.2 | 47.1 | 42.9 | 51.4 |
| Visited an Internet site or online community to discuss a candidate or an issue (%) | | | | | | | |
| Immigrant | 9.5 | 13.9 | 10.8 | 6.1 | 15.4 | 5.3 | 13.5 |
| US-born | 31.3 | 26.7 | 20.7 | 7.9 | 29.4 | 21.4 | 21.1 |
| Attended a protest march or rally (%) | | | | | | | |
| Immigrant | 4.5 | 3.0 | 4.6 | 2.8 | 9.8 | 9.8 | 4.3 |
| US-born | 4.3 | 7.5 | 3.7 | 5.1 | 7.1 | 7.1 | 7.9 |
| Have been contacted by political party or candidate (%) | | | | | | | |
| Immigrant | 21.2 | 33.6 | 36.2 | 31.8 | 29.9 | 18.8 | 33.1 |
| US-born | 33.3 | 33.3 | 59.5 | 56.2 | 41.2 | 21.4 | 47.4 |
| Have been contacted by other organizations about a campaign (%) | | | | | | | |
| Immigrant | 10.8 | 14.7 | 23.9 | 18.8 | 17.5 | 14.8 | 19.3 |
| US-born | 17.4 | 19.0 | 28.8 | 27.5 | 25.3 | 23.1 | 21.6 |

*Source:* Authors' analysis of the National Asian American Survey, 2008 (Ramakrishnan et al. 2011).

explaining their lower civic involvement as compared with the native-born population. In the Latino community, Mexican and Cuban immigrants, and Puerto Rican migrants are less than half as likely to participate in a social, cultural, civic, or political group. School-based activities, on the other hand, see fewer differences in levels of participation based on nativity. In fact, for some of the Latino nationality groups, immigrants are more likely to have participated in the school-based activities than are their US-born coethnics. Similar patterns appear, though for different civic activities, among Asian Americans. The vast majority of Asian Americans, regardless of nativity, have participated in the most basic form of civic engagement: discussing politics in the news. As the level of commitment increases and the likelihood of payoff decreases, overall participation goes down and the gap between US-born and foreign-born Asian Americans grows. So, immigrants are generally less likely than the US-born to report that they worked with others to solve a community problem or that they contacted an elected representative or government office. Not surprisingly, immigrant Asian Americans are much less likely to report that they had been contacted by a political party, candidate, or another organization about a campaign than are US-born Asian Americans.

An exception to this pattern appears in the transnational civic behaviors that were assessed in the survey of Latinos. Perhaps not surprisingly, immigrants are more likely to report that they pay "a lot" of attention to the politics of the country of origin than are US-born Latinos to report that they pay a lot of attention to the country of ancestry. What is important to note here, however, is that the share of highly politically attentive Latinos is well lower than the share who are engaged in US-focused civic or school-focused activities.

Engagement is, of course, only part of the story. Equally important for the future of the nation are the values and attitudes that immigrants bring to the table when they do participate. Here the contemporary evidence would support the longstanding finding that immigrants come quickly to share the political values of mainstream society (Handlin 1951; de la Garza, Falcón, and García 1996) and build on beliefs and values held by many other Americans.

Data on Latino immigrants, combined with comparative data on US-born Latinos, demonstrate that, like the American people as a whole, Latino immigrants profess broad support for individual accomplishment

TABLE 5.3. Political Values and Attitudes of Latino Immigrants and US-born Latinos, 2006[1]

| | Mexican | Puerto Rican[2] | Cuban | Salvadoran | Dominican | Other |
|---|---|---|---|---|---|---|
| Agrees with statement that "government is run by a few big interests that look out for themselves" (%) | | | | | | |
| Immigrant | 56.3 | 50.6 | 52.6 | 54.0 | 53.3 | 60.3 |
| US-born | 72.4 | 70.1 | 61.5 | 81.7 | 55.6 | 72.5 |
| Agrees with statement that "people like me don't have much of a say in what government does" (%) | | | | | | |
| Immigrant | 50.7 | 51.4 | 49.8 | 49.6 | 56.7 | 50.6 |
| US-born | 52.1 | 49.3 | 45.6 | 69.3 | 66.7 | 51.8 |
| Agrees with statement that "politics and government seem so complicated that a person like me can't understand" (%) | | | | | | |
| Immigrant | 60.6 | 65.8 | 55.0 | 58.9 | 58.5 | 56.0 |
| US-born | 60.3 | 60.6 | 51.3 | 49.0 | 68.2 | 53.2 |
| Agrees with statement that "people are better off avoiding contact with government" (%) | | | | | | |
| Immigrant | 35.0 | 33.3 | 23.1 | 36.8 | 32.4 | 32.5 |
| US-born | 27.9 | 27.8 | 16.1 | 33.3 | 31.3 | 26.1 |
| Believes that government "just about always" does what is right (%) | | | | | | |
| Immigrant | 14.7 | 11.7 | 19.0 | 17.2 | 17.4 | 13.6 |
| US-born | 6.3 | 8.3 | 11.4 | 10.2 | 4.7 | 5.6 |

and political equality, and hold a suspicion of and lack of trust in government (see Table 5.3). Although there are some variations by national-origin group, Latino immigrants are somewhat more likely to be trusting of government than are their US-born coethnics. In each of these values and attitudes, Latino immigrants, and by extension immigrants from other parts of the world, fit broadly in the American mainstream. However, Latinos generally show lower levels of political efficacy—their trust in government and their sense that they can influence political outcomes—than do non-Latinos (Michelson 2000; Michelson 2002–2003).

Assuming that it is accurate to generalize from the civic behaviors, attitudes, and values of Latino and Asian American immigrants to the broader US immigrant community, these findings should offer

TABLE 5.3. *(continued)*

| Agrees with the statement that "no matter what a person's political beliefs, they are entitled to the same rights and protections" (%) | | | | | |
|---|---|---|---|---|---|
| Immigrant | 85.4 | 87.0 | 88.0 | 82.5 | 85.3 | 88.4 |
| US-born | 90.9 | 91.5 | 93.6 | 89.8 | 96.8 | 88.3 |
| Agrees with the statement that "most people who don't get ahead should not blame the system, they only have themselves to blame" (%) | | | | | |
| Immigrant | 64.9 | 65.7 | 73.5 | 60.0 | 63.2 | 65.9 |
| US-born | 71.1 | 73.2 | 67.9 | 59.2 | 74.6 | 68.3 |
| Agrees with the statement that "it's not a big problem if some people have more of a chance in life than others" (%) | | | | | |
| Immigrant | 58.2 | 55.9 | 60.0 | 62.7 | 59.9 | 58.3 |
| US-born | 45.5 | 50.8 | 46.3 | 30.6 | 52.4 | 43.7 |

*Source:* Authors' analysis of the Latino National Survey, 2006 (Fraga et al. 2008).

---

[1] The sample included relative small numbers of island-born Puerto Ricans and US-born Cubans, Salvadorans, and Dominicans, so the margin of error around these attitudes and behaviors is somewhat larger.

[2] Puerto Ricans born in Puerto Rico are US citizens by birth and not immigrants. We present data on Puerto Rican migrants for purposes of comparison.

a generalized optimism about the long-term civic health of the nation. Immigrants do participate, if at somewhat lower levels, than do their US-born coethnics, but the differences are small. Immigrants are neither isolated from the civic life of the United States nor hyper-engaged and promoting views and beliefs distinct from the native-born majority. Their levels of US-focused civic and political involvement exceed their transnational engagement.

We do not mean to offer an overly rosy vision, however. Civic life in the United States has been in decline at least since the 1950s (Putnam 2000). Immigrants are not driving this decline, but they are subject to the increasing barriers to civic engagement that have reduced overall levels of community engagement for all Americans. To more fully rebuild American civic life, immigrants will need to be one of the many targets of new strategies to promote civic involvement (Ramakrishnan and Bloemraad

TABLE 5.4. Voting by Nativity and Race/Ethnicity, 2000–2012

| Voter Turnout in Presidential Elections, 2000–2012 (%) | | | | |
|---|---|---|---|---|
| | 2000 | 2004 | 2008 | 2012 |
| TOTAL population | | | | |
| Naturalized citizen | 50.6 | 53.7 | 54.0 | 53.6 |
| US-born | 60.0 | 64.5 | 64.4 | 62.5 |
| White, non-Hispanic | | | | |
| Naturalized citizen | 55.9 | 61.8 | 56.7 | 54.1 |
| US-born | 62.0 | 67.3 | 66.4 | 62.6 |
| Black | | | | |
| Naturalized citizen | 56.8 | 54.4 | 59.4 | 62.8 |
| US-born | 56.8 | 60.4 | 65.0 | 66.5 |
| Asian/Pacific Islander | | | | |
| Naturalized citizen | 43.4 | 46.4 | 49.1 | 49.3 |
| US-born | 43.2 | 40.5 | 45.0 | 43.9 |
| Hispanic | | | | |
| Naturalized citizen | 49.6 | 52.1 | 54.2 | 53.6 |
| US-born | 43.6 | 45.5 | 48.4 | 46.1 |

2008; Schlozman, Verba, and Brady 2012; García Bedolla and Michelson 2012). The building blocks for constructing a new American civic life are similar in immigrant and native populations.

## Immigrant Electoral Engagement

Through much of US history naturalized citizens have been less likely to vote than comparably situated native-born US citizens (DeSipio 1996a; Ramakrishnan 2005). There have certainly been exceptions to this pattern in times of particular mobilization of immigrant voters, such as by the urban political machines in closely contested municipal and state elections of the late 1800s and early 1900s (Erie 1988; Sterne 2001) and in periods of particular challenges to immigrant status in the United States (Gamm 1986; Pantoja, Ramirez, and Segura 2001; Pantoja and Segura 2003). The norm, however, has been one of lower participation among the naturalized as a result of the complexity of voting. The how

TABLE 5.4. *(continued)*

| Voter Turnout in Non-Presidential National Elections, 2002–2010 (%) | | | |
|---|---|---|---|
| | 2002 | 2006 | 2010 |
| TOTAL population | | | |
| Naturalized citizen | 36.2 | 36.6 | 37.0 |
| US-born | 46.8 | 48.6 | 46.3 |
| White, non-Hispanic | | | |
| Naturalized citizen | 45.0 | 43.5 | 42.0 |
| US-born | 49.2 | 51.8 | 48.8 |
| Black | | | |
| Naturalized citizen | 40.2 | 35.1 | 41.2 |
| US-born | 42.4 | 41.4 | 43.7 |
| Asian/Pacific Islander | | | |
| Naturalized citizen | 30.5 | 33.5 | 30.9 |
| US-born | 32.3 | 30.7 | 30.6 |
| Hispanic | | | |
| Naturalized citizen | 33.4 | 34.3 | 36.6 |
| US-born | 29.5 | 31.6 | 29.2 |

*Source:* US Bureau of the Census, *Voting and Registration in the Election of November* (various years: Table 13 for all years but 2010 and 2012; Table 11 for 2010 and 2012 data).

and why of voting must be learned and naturalized citizens do not have the same civic training from an early age that most native-born US citizens have. Equally important, civic institutions that have traditionally trained citizens to participate and political parties that in previous eras actively recruited new members have diminished their mobilizing functions (DeSipio 2001; Wong 2006; Ramakrishnan and Bloemraad 2008; Michelson and García Bedolla 2014).

Although the pattern may be slowly changing, naturalized US citizens continue to vote at lower rates than the US-born do (see Table 5.4). In the 2000 election, approximately 51 percent of naturalized citizen adults turned out to vote, compared to 60 percent of US-born adults. Turnout increased for both electorates in the subsequent three elections, but the turnout gap remained: 54 percent of naturalized citizen adults turned out, compared to 65 percent of US-born adults in 2004, 64 percent in 2008, and 63 percent in 2012. These patterns repeat in off-year Congressional elections. Turnout is lower for all adults in off-year elections, regardless of the source of their citizenship, but the gap between naturalized and native-born US citizens ranges from 8 to 12 percent.

Can this naturalized-native electoral participation gap be overcome? For some communities, it already has been. As indicated in Table 5.4, in recent elections naturalized Latinos and Asian Americans have been turning out at higher rates than US-born Latinos and Asian Americans. To some degree, these higher voter turnout rates among the naturalized reflect lower levels of electoral participation in these communities overall and the failure of mobilizing institutions to reach out to Latinos and Asian Americans regardless of nativity (Wong 2006; de la Garza, DeSipio, and Leal 2010). The relatively higher rates of naturalized citizen voting in these communities also reflect the threat that Latino and Asian American immigrants have felt in US politics over the past twenty years (Pantoja, Ramírez, and Segura 2001; Ramakrishnan 2005; Chávez 2008; Ramírez 2014). Recent research demonstrates that voter mobilization strategies require resources but can help counteract the steady decline of civic organizations and political parties that have traditionally assumed the responsibility for training citizens to participate in American democracy (García Bedolla and Michelson 2012; Michelson and García Bedolla 2014). With the steady growth in naturalized US citizens (as well as young adults entering the ages of voting eligibility), this democratic training function is increasingly needed. Close elections and the increasing flow of money into American politics will ensure that some new financial and organizational resources are available to promote democratic inclusion.

Despite these slightly lower rates of participation, the surge in immigration and naturalization discussed in the previous chapters ensures that the naturalized are making up a steadily higher share of the vote nationally. In 2000 and 2004, for example, naturalized US citizens made up 4.9 and 4.5 percent of the national electorate, respectively, and in 2008 this share grew to 7.0 percent (US Bureau of the Census various years: Table 13 [2000 and 2004] and Table 11 [2012]). Although there are no comparable data for the share of statewide votes made up of naturalized US citizens, it is reasonable to assume that several of the larger states as well as several of the states that have repeatedly proved to be competitive in the Electoral College—including California, New York, Florida, and Nevada—will see 10 percent or more of their votes coming from naturalized citizens.

The direct electoral impact of these naturalized US citizen voters is somewhat difficult to measure. In recent years, the national exit poll that is conducted by major media organizations has not included a question on the source of citizenship. As a result, it is necessary to rely on more indirect measures, particularly pre-election and post-election polling. This polling tends to focus on the largest pan-ethnic populations—Latinos and Asian Americans—rather than on naturalized citizens as a whole, so it is not possible to speak with precision to the political preferences of all naturalized US citizens. A review of these polls demonstrates two important characteristics of the Latino and Asian American naturalized citizen electorates. First, the issue preferences and voting patterns of the naturalized are similar to those of the native-born in these ethnic communities. Naturalized Latinos appear to be slightly more Democratic than US-born Latinos and naturalized Asian American voters appear to be slightly less Democratic than their US-born coethnics, but both communities offer solid majorities to Democratic candidates regardless of nativity. Second, as is popularly understood, the issue and candidate preferences of Latinos and Asian Americans are distinct from those of non-Hispanic whites. In close elections, such as the 2012 presidential race, minority voters (here adding African Americans, who have a smaller share of naturalized voters) can sway the election when the non-Hispanic white vote is more evenly divided.

The 2008 and 2012 presidential races offer some insights on naturalized citizen voting preferences and influence. In 2012, naturalized Latino voters shared the policy preferences of their US-born coethnics (see Table 5.5). The most important issues for Latino voters, regardless of nativity, were the economy, immigration reform, education reform, and health care. Naturalized citizen voters were slightly more concerned about each of these issues, particularly with immigration reform. Both US-born and naturalized citizen Latinos supported President Obama's reelection by a large margin. Naturalized Latinos were about 10 percent more likely than the US-born to vote for Obama and were twice as likely as non-Hispanic whites to vote for the president. Regardless of nativity, Latinos were less likely than blacks to vote for President Obama's reelection.

There are no data that distinguish the candidate or issue preferences of Asian American voters by nativity in 2012. Overall, Asian Americans were about as likely as US-born Latinos to support Obama's reelection (Asian American Justice Center et al. 2013). The best estimate is that approximately two-thirds of Asian American voters in presidential races

TABLE 5.5. Candidate and Issue Preferences, by Race, Ethnicity, and
Source of US Citizenship, 2012[1]

| Candidate Preference (%) | | | | | |
| --- | --- | --- | --- | --- | --- |
| | Non-Hispanic White | Black | US-born Latino | Naturalized Latino | Asian American |
| Obama | 39 | 93 | 71 | 80 | 68 |
| Romney | 59 | 6 | 27 | 18 | 31 |
| Other | 2 | 1 | 2 | 2 | 1 |
| **Most Important Issue Facing the Latino/Asian American Community (%)** | | | | | |
| Create jobs/fix economy | | | 51 | 56 | 86 |
| Immigration reform/DREAM Act | | | 32 | 39 | 43 |
| Education reform/schools | | | 18 | 22 | 81 |
| Health care | | | 13 | 15 | 80 |
| Social Security | | | | | 71 |
| National security | | | | | 72 |
| Environment | | | | | 59 |
| Race relations/discrimination | | | 3 | 4 | 54 |
| Taxes | | | 3 | 4 | |
| Energy prices | | | 2 | 2 | |
| Housing/mortgages | | | 2 | 1 | |
| Foreign policy | | | 2 | 1 | |
| Global warming | | | 1 | | |
| Something else | | | 10 | 7 | |
| Don't know | | | 8 | 4 | |

*Sources:* Non-Hispanic Whites and Blacks: CNN (2012); Latinos: Latino Decisions (2012); and Asian Americans: Asian American Justice Center et al. (2013).

[1] Non-Hispanic white and black data are reported from exit polls. The Latino data are from the final Latino Decisions pre-election poll (conducted immediately before the election). The Asian American data are from a post-election survey conducted in November 2012. The results are not directly comparable. The Asian American data include both US-born and naturalized Asian Americans. Approximately two-thirds of Asian American voters are naturalized US citizens.

are naturalized citizens, so this high share of Asian American support for the Democratic candidate is driven by naturalized voters. The issue preferences of 2012 Asian American voters are comparable to those of Latinos, with several additional issues added to the list. In addition to the economy, immigration reform, education, and health care, Asian American voters identified Social Security, national security, the environment, and race relations/discrimination as being critical issues facing Asian Americans. Asian Americans were somewhat less likely than Latinos to identify immigration reform as a critical issue.

Although no data distinguish 2012 Asian American candidate preferences by nativity, data from 2008 show that Asian American voters preferred Barack Obama to John McCain regardless of nativity. Unlike Latinos, however, naturalized Asian American voters were somewhat more likely than native Asian American voters to prefer the Republican candidate. This finding is partially muddled by the fact that the data were collected before the election, rather than after, and indicate voting intentions rather than actual votes, but they do suggest that naturalized citizen Asian American voters supported Obama by a 60 to 40 margin and US-born Asian American voters supported Obama by a 73 to 27 margin (authors' analysis of Ramakrishnan et al. 2012). For the foreseeable future, these data on the 2008 and 2012 political influence of the naturalized, at least in national elections, are tied to the broader influence of their racial and ethnic communities in US politics. Considering that candidate preferences and issue salience are comparable across ethnic groups regardless of nativity, this body of shared interests allows for potentially greater influence in close elections.

When this influence will be felt is idiosyncratic to the dynamics of each election. Close races are certainly necessary, as is division in the non-Hispanic white electorate. In 2012, for example, nine "battleground" states were the primary focus of the national campaigns. Of these, three most likely had higher than average shares of naturalized citizen voters (Florida, Nevada, and Virginia). One other battleground state had a higher than average share of Latino voters—Colorado—though most were US-born. The remaining five battleground states—Ohio, North Carolina, New Hampshire, Wisconsin, and Iowa—had relatively small naturalized citizen electorates. With this electoral geography, it is hard to argue that naturalized voters determined the outcome. Their votes did, however, join with the votes of US-born minority voters to ensure a narrow popular vote victory for President Obama (approximately 4 percent out of 127 million votes cast) and a much wider Electoral College margin (332 to 206).

Should future national elections be as close or closer in the popular vote, the electoral voice of the naturalized will be more likely to be heard (most likely in conjunction with their US-born coethnics). The size of the naturalized citizen vote will grow for the foreseeable future. Equally important, campaigns have reinvigorated what was traditionally a role of US political parties—voter education and mobilization—at least in states and localities with contested elections. Consequently, we are entering an era of US politics that will likely see an increasing opportunity for naturalized citizens—and, more broadly, racial and ethnic voters—to become critical elements of winning electoral coalitions.

## Emigrant–Home Country Relations and Transnational Engagement

As a nation of immigrants, the United States has long served as the launching pad for emigrant efforts to engage home country politics, including major reforms and revolutions. In the nineteenth century, José Martí's organizing efforts in Florida were crucial to the success of Cuba's independence fight from Spain. A principal call to arms of the Mexican Revolution, the Plan of San Luis Potosí, was written in San Antonio, Texas. Opposition to Britain because of its anti–Irish independence policies led Irish Americans to support neutrality rather than the Allies during World War I. In the 1980s, Polish immigrants mobilized in support of Lech Walesa and the Solidarity Movement, and in 1995, Bosnia and Herzegovina, Croatia, and the Federal Republic of Yugoslavia met in Ohio, home to a large Eastern European settlement, and signed the Dayton Agreement, which ended the war in Bosnia and Herzegovina.

Although they seldom do, immigrant-sending states may also act against emigrant-critics in the United States. When they do, it can lead to severe US retaliation that can result in destabilizing or overthrowing the offending government. The United States retaliated against Rafael Trujillo, a 1960s-era dictator of the Dominican Republic, for example. As Latin America's most hated and feared dictator, Trujillo represented the kind of regime that the John F. Kennedy administration was committed to replacing with democratically elected governments (Derby 2009). Trujillo's ruthlessness made him an easy example to highlight the new policies of the Kennedy administration. In 1956, on Trujillo's orders, Jesús de Galíndez, a prominent Dominican opponent, was kidnapped in New York City, taken to the Dominican Republic, and allegedly executed in Trujillo's presence. Three years later Trujillo attempted to have Rómulo Betancourt, Venezuela's democratically elected president, assassinated. Thus, when Kennedy took office in 1961, Trujillo became a target for retaliation and removal. With the assistance of the Central Intelligence Agency, Dominican revolutionaries ambushed and killed Trujillo on May 30, 1961. It must be noted that this extreme response is partially explained by the Kennedy administration's commitment to promote democracy in the Americas (Lake 2010).

US officials responded quite differently to the assassination of Orlando Letelier, perhaps the most prominent member of Chilean President Salvador Allende's cabinet, even though, as was essentially true in the Galíndez case, Letelier had been assassinated in the United States by a foreign head of state. In Chile, General Augusto Pinochet (who had replaced Allende in a military coup) had imprisoned Letelier for twenty months. Thanks to international pressures, Letelier was released in 1974 and eventually became a resident of Washington, DC, where he remained a severe critic of Pinochet. This led to his assassination in 1976 in the American capital city. The Letelier assassination did not significantly affect US-Chilean relations because US policy, led by Secretary of State Henry Kissinger, strongly supported the Pinochet regime and tolerated its violent excesses (National Security Archive 2006).

As the assassination of Jesús de Galíndez illustrates, states may also act against their emigrant-critics. This is evident in the unique case of Cuba. Cuba is one of few states to have an ongoing, conflictual relationship with most of its emigrants: most Cubans in the United States are refugees opposed to the Fidel Castro regime. Moreover, unlike refugees who are satisfied in escaping an oppressive regime, the Cuban emigrants actively support and participate in efforts aimed at overthrowing the Castro regime. As a group, they were part of the failed Bay of Pigs invasion in 1961 (Triay 2001). They were also responsible for blowing up a Cuban airliner that resulted in the deaths of seventy-three passengers and crew and have also been involved in numerous attempts to assassinate Castro (National Security Archive 2005). A large number of terrorist organizations exist with support from the Cuban emigrant community and the US government, including Alpha 66, Commandos L, Commandos F 4,

Democratic National Unity Party, Omega 7, Commanders of United Revolutionary Organizations, and the most important of these, the Cuban American National Foundation, which was created by the Reagan administration. At a more benign level, since 1985, Cuban Americans have also strongly supported Radio y Televisión Martí, which was established in 1985 by the Reagan administration as part of a broader effort to bombard Cuba's population with anti-Communist and anti-Castro propaganda. Cuban American representatives in the US House and Senate continually oppose attempts to facilitate trade, travel, and other activities that would benefit the well-being of the Cuban population. Because the US government is strongly opposed to the Castro regime, it historically extended substantial support to all of these types of activities, but it no longer does so. Indicative of the hostility between Cuban refugees and emigrants and the Cuban state and society, the Cuban exile community was referred to as *mariposas*, "butterflies," who left the island and became worms in the United States.

This history indicates that relations between US immigrants and their home states have long been factors in US politics. Improvements in telecommunications and the ease of international travel have made such relations both more common and more difficult to manage. Historically, the rules of diplomacy and international law empowered all states to intervene in internal US matters to ensure that the rights of their citizens in the United States were respected. This effectively has meant that immigrant-sending states were legally entitled to defend their emigrants from policies that targeted them in a discriminatory manner. These formal powers notwithstanding, historically emigrants were of little concern to the sending states. In fact, Mexico's state relations with emigrants went beyond indifferent to hostile, and this was reflected in societal discrimination against them in a variety of ways, including using derogatory labels such as *pocho* ("rotten fruit") to refer to emigrants (González 1999; Fitzgerald 2009).

Emigrant–home state relations began to change in 1962 when Colombia extended dual citizenship to its emigrants. Enacted as part of a major constitutional reform, there is no evidence that this provision influenced closer links between Colombia and its emigrants for at least three decades. Its salience as a model for other emigrant-sending states was also minimal until the 1990s, when other nations began to look to Colombia's policy as an example of similar policies they were considering. Colombia's reform, therefore, may now be seen as the signpost of a major new chapter in emigrant–home country relations that has the potential to significantly reshape US immigrant and immigration politics and policy.

This new chapter is characterized by the development of programs and policies intended to establish and strengthen ties that benefit both the home state and its emigrants. The unintended consequences of these new efforts include restructuring the political behaviors of immigrants in the United States as well as adding new complexity to the nation's immigration policies. Specifically, this development has provoked concern in regard to three issues:

1. How will the new relationships influence immigrant incorporation within the United States?
2. Will these policies result in increased family remittances and financial investments in the home country rather than in the United States? *Remittances* are financial transfers between migrants and their family members or communities in the country of origin. The World Bank estimates that globally $436 billion in funds were remitted in 2014 (World Bank 2014). The most recent country-specific estimates suggest that $123 billion in remittances were sent from the United States in 2012, approximately 23 percent of the global total for that year (World Bank 2012).
3. Will these policies serve as a link for mobilizing emigrants to become advocates or lobbyists for their home countries in the United States? If they do become advocates, will this advocacy focus on specific issues or on the breadth of the sending country's policy agenda?

This newly emerging relationship between immigrant-sending countries and their emigrants has progressed through two major stages. Initially, the focus was on promoting ties as a means to induce emigrants to remit funds to their families and to development projects in their communities of origin. This was pursued using a variety of tactics, including sponsoring cultural programs, developing special funding arrangements for development projects in sending communities, and assistance in establishing and institutionalizing immigrant clubs and associations. In recent years, the outreach has expanded to include assisting emigrants in resolving social and economic problems. Consuls in major cities with large immigrant populations have become advocates for immigrants in need of social services. In New York, for example, the Mexican, Colombian, and Ecuadorian consuls describe themselves as brokers who work with schools, hospitals, and the city's bureaucracy to arrange for immigrants, including the unauthorized, to have access to these agencies.

## Economic Ties Between Emigrants and Their Countries of Origin

Outreach regarding economic links was so successful that it led to an increased public awareness of the growth in remittances, which spurred a rise in anti-immigrant politics by generating concern that immigrants were transferring the funds they received from social service agencies to their relatives back home. Research failed to support this assumption, however (Taylor 2002). This apprehension also fueled criticisms about how, in view of the low socioeconomic status of the immigrant population, the remitted funds should be invested to improve the well-being of immigrant families in the United States (de la Garza and Lowell 2002). Additionally, critics of unauthorized immigration also argue that taxing remittances would generate funds to pay for benefits such as the education and emergency health care that the undocumented receive. Arizona, Georgia, Oklahoma, and Kansas have passed or considered such taxes. Predictably, these proposals became an irritant in relations with Mexico, which officially protested them.

In 2002, Mexico initiated the "3 x 1" program, designed to increase remittances and strengthen emigrant ties to their communities of origin. To raise funds intended to improve the infrastructure of migrant-sending areas, the program seeks to structure relations between the Mexican government and emigrant Hometown Associations (HTAs, groups of emigrants from a specific hometown or region who organize to promote social and cultural activities and/or community development projects). The "3 x 1" program provides $3 in Mexican federal, state, and local funds for each $1 contributed by HTAs for water, sewer, road, and similar infrastructure projects. HTAs propose the projects, and Mexican government agencies vet and approve them before providing the matching funds. The program operates in twenty-seven of Mexico's thirty-two states, but most "3 x 1" funds are spent in four of the highest-emigration states. Overall, family-focused remittances greatly outweigh these collective funds targeted at community development. In 2009, when remittances were down relative to 2005–2008, remittances to Mexico, for example, totaled approximately $21.2 billion, but "3 x 1" funds totaled only $38 million for 2,500 projects in 2008.

Colombia has strengthened its economic ties with emigrants by promoting business relations with emigrant communities. This has included promoting Colombian coffee sales and consumption through emigrant businesses. Much more significant is the assistance of consuls in promoting real estate and construction fairs that bring representatives of the Colombian construction industry together with Colombian immigrants to interest them in purchasing homes in their communities of origin. To date, the success of this fledgling effort suggests it will continue and expand.

### Consular Services: An Expected Quid Pro Quo?

The need for consular assistance has grown as the immigrant population has increased and the economy has gone into crisis. It should be noted, furthermore, that although the relationship between sending states and emigrants has historically been tenuous at best, sending states have long negotiated immigration policy with the United States. Sometimes they have done so primarily to assist their citizens, and other times they were principally concerned about safeguarding their own state interests. Examples of the former include El Salvador's appeal to US officials to extend the temporary US legal residency status of emigrants who came as a result of damage caused by natural disasters between 1998 and 2001. An example of the latter is Cuba's manipulation of US immigration policy to help manage its domestic problems by speeding the emigration of Cubans dissatisfied with their opportunities in Cuba.

Given its historical relationship with its emigrants, it is ironic that Mexico was the first state to develop as part of its foreign policy apparatus a specific institution devoted to improving relations with its emigrants and their descendants (González-Gutiérrez 1999). The Program for Mexican Communities Abroad (PMCA), established in 1990, was charged with the responsibility of developing and improving relations with legal and unauthorized emigrants and US-born Mexican Americans (Laglagaron 2010). This program was a major expansion of the historically intermittent efforts to defend and protect its emigrants. For example, Mexican officials had a major voice in the design of the Bracero Program and were responsible for incorporating pro-emigrant protections into its provisions during World War II, but saw their role decline, if not disappear, as the urgency of US demands for a manageable temporary labor pool diminished after the end of the war.

Reflective of this expanded approach is the more recent example of the Mexican government's involvement in the protests against California's anti-immigrant Proposition 187. In October 1994, more than 70,000 people, including large numbers of high school students who walked out of school, turned out to demonstrate against the likely passage of the statewide initiative. The demonstrators defiantly marched while carrying small Mexican flags that the Mexican consulate had distributed. The sight of the flags alienated many voters and may have convinced many undecided voters to support Proposition 187 (Ono and Sloop 2002).

A more noteworthy case of state efforts to assist immigrants was the government's publication of a brochure that was made available in 2004 to provide information regarding the risks of illegal entry and how to reduce them. The document gave rise to charges by Representative Lamar Smith of Texas that Mexico advocated unauthorized migration. A content analysis of the publication concludes that it emphasizes safety issues and does not advocate illegal migration. Nonetheless, the brochure caused such uproar among anti-immigration advocates that it was taken out of circulation in 2006.

Another significant example of Mexican officials acting on behalf of their country's undocumented emigrants and becoming implicated in US domestic politics occurred when they attempted to use a new photo ID card, the *matrícula consular,* as a substitute for legal immigration documents issued by US immigration officials for unauthorized migrants. These identity cards provided basic demographic information that Mexican officials hoped would satisfy the requirements of US authorities whenever they needed reliable information to identify immigrants involved in incidents such as auto accidents or criminal behaviors. The first *matrícula* was issued in San Francisco in 2002, and 2 million cards were issued over the following two-year period.

Banks welcomed the *matrícula.* The US Treasury Department indirectly authorized banks to accept the *matrícula* as part of how it would implement the requirements of the USA Patriot Act to verify the identity of foreign nationals. Treasury's report to Congress regarding how this requirement would be implemented states that "the proposed regulations do not discourage bank acceptance of the *matrícula consular* identity card that is being issued by the Mexican government to immigrants." US banks were in favor of using the *matrículas* because they saw them as a means of increasing deposits by immigrants and collecting fees on the $18 billion in money transfers from the United States to Mexico.

The local governments of eighty cities, including Tucson, Phoenix, Denver, Los Angeles, San Antonio, San Francisco, Chicago, Houston, and Dallas, quickly moved to accept the *matrícula* for uses such as obtaining a library card, entering public buildings, obtaining business licenses, registering children for school, and accessing a few limited public services. At the state level, the most important use of the *matrículas* is in obtaining driver's licenses. Although most states now require proof of legal immigration status or citizenship to be eligible for a driver's license, approximately thirteen states accept the *matrícula* as proof of identity when issuing a license. State and local officials, including eight hundred police departments, have accepted the *matrícula* because it is a means to help immigrants come out of the shadows and reduce the likelihood of their being abused by employers or victimized by anti-immigrant citizens or of avoiding responsibility for vehicular accidents and criminal behaviors (Dinnerstein 2003). This widespread acceptance has led several other foreign governments, including Nicaragua, El Salvador, and Brazil, to considering issuing similar cards to their own citizens who are living here illegally. Ecuador and Guatemala began issuing their own versions. The *matrícula* is still in use but remains controversial. Many states that initially accepted the *matrícula* for some purposes have since changed their stance on this. The private sector is also torn between the convenience it offers and the seeming endorsement of illegality that it provides. A banker resigned in protest, for example, when the Chevy Chase Bank, a major Washington, DC–area bank, used *matrículas* to open accounts for clients suspected of being unauthorized immigrants; the resignation did not dissuade the bank from continuing to accept the cards.

These and other examples illustrate the limited extent to which emigrant-sending states have worked to assist their citizens. Mexico's response to S.B. 1070, Arizona's new anti-undocumented immigrant legislation, however, may signal the abandonment of the more limited approach that has characterized most emigrant-sending country policies to assist their citizens. Mexico's friend-of-the-court brief before the federal court that heard the constitutional challenge to Arizona's law contended that Mexico has "a substantial and compelling interest in protecting its citizens and ensuring that their ethnicity is not used as a basis for state-sanctioned acts of discrimination" and that Arizona's new immigration law is unconstitutional and harms the interests of immigrants and of Mexico as a state. Bolivia, Colombia, El Salvador, Guatemala, Nicaragua, Paraguay, and Peru filed separate but nearly identical motions to join Mexico's legal brief. A federal judge accepted Mexico's brief. If this type of response were to become more regularized it would constitute a significant new stage in the involvement of emigrant-sending states in the politics of immigrant-receiving states.

Such pro-immigrant initiatives notwithstanding, it seems clear that such efforts are primarily intended to serve sending state interests rather than meet immigrant concerns, as the events that culminated in the creation of the PMCA demonstrate. PMCA's origins are found in the reaction of the Partido Revolucionario Institucional (PRI), Mexico's long-dominant political party, to the mobilization of emigrants in support of a leftist challenge from the Partido Revolucionario Democrático (PRD) during the 1988 presidential campaign. The PRD reached out to emigrants in Southern California, who persuaded Mexican American activists in the US Democratic Party to ask that their party pass a resolution calling for fair and honest elections in Mexico's forthcoming election. Mexican officials responded angrily and with concern to this "intrusion" in Mexican affairs. Although the request was ignored by the Democratic Party, it alerted Mexican officials to the possibility that emigrants and Mexican Americans could begin to play a role in Mexican politics and US-Mexico relations.

This realization led to an explicit effort to signal to the Mexican population in the United States that the president of Mexico and the Mexican state wanted to establish strong positive relations with emigrants and Mexican Americans. The Mexican president began meeting with prominent Mexican American leaders in the United States and in Mexico to signal his interest in and support for their concerns. Opposition leaders followed suit even though they could not offer the symbolic status of presidential invitations, nor could they afford to invite emigrants to Mexico City. This tactic was heavily employed during the Congressional debate over the North American Free Trade Agreement (NAFTA). Mexican president Carlos Salinas met with major Mexican American and Latino organizational leaders to persuade them to mobilize Mexican Americans and Latinos to support NAFTA. Additionally, the Mexican government contracted with prominent Mexican American leaders to have them lobby for NAFTA. To further strengthen the president's image as a supporter of emigrants and Mexican Americans in general, the Salinas government awarded six Mexican Americans *El Aquila Azteca*, the highest award the Mexican government can give noncitizens.

It is unclear what the overall effect of these initiatives was. Regarding NAFTA, Mexican American members of Congress insisted that the original provisions be expanded to include benefits for communities along the US-Mexico border and did not rally strongly in behalf of Mexico's preferences. Emigrants remain divided about politics in Mexico and may have preferred the opposition candidate to the PRI's nominee in 1994 and 2000. Their views were of little consequence, however, because they were not allowed to vote in those elections (they have subsequently gained some voting rights, though few take advantage of the opportunity). What is clear, however, is that Mexican officials were less motivated to pursue these policies by their concern for the well-being of emigrants than they were by their desire to benefit broader partisan and state interests in Mexico.

### Dual Citizenship

Sending states have expanded their outreach efforts to include offering emigrants dual nationality and dual citizenship. Although the two usually go together, they should be distinguished for analytical purposes. Mexico, for example, distinguishes between nationality and citizenship, with nationality rights less fundamental than citizenship rights. In principle, the rights of nationals can be changed legislatively. In most other countries, however, "dual citizenship" and "dual nationality" are the same.

In the past twenty years, Argentina, Bolivia, Brazil, the Dominican Republic, Ecuador, Honduras, Nicaragua, Panama, Peru, and Venezuela enacted dual citizenship provisions, whereas Colombia did so in 1962. Mexico established dual nationality in 1998. As dual citizens, emigrants are granted such privileges and rights traditionally reserved for people living in the homeland as government protection, access to public higher education, and the right to participate formally in their homelands' political processes by voting, becoming involved in all aspects of the electoral process, including, in some countries, holding office.

This array of rights and privileges leads to the criticism that dual citizenship fosters links between emigrants and countries of origin that may impede immigrants from developing strong allegiances to the United States, and could facilitate their mobilizing against the United States and in support of home-country interests. Virtually all research refutes this claim (DeSipio 2006; Staton, Jackson, and Canache 2007). As we have suggested earlier in this chapter, immigrants express much more positive feelings toward the United States than toward their home countries, express little interest in the day-to-day conduct of home-country politics, and are much more likely to agree with US perspectives on key issues involving relations with their home countries than with policies favored by sending states (de la Garza et al. 1992).

How, then, do immigrant relations with their communities of origin affect US politics and policy? The answer depends on factors such as how many immigrants come, why they come, how they are treated after they arrive, and their relationships with their home states. The significance of these multiple variables helps explain why some sending states find it necessary to intervene on behalf of their citizens, why some with similar needs fail to do so, and why others see no reason for engaging in such activities. Guatemala, for example, is too weak to challenge US anti-immigrant policies even though its emigrants find themselves in the same situation as Mexican emigrants. China, for reasons that are unclear, has the status to challenge US practices toward its emigrants, but does not do so. The Philippine government also voices no protest regarding how their emigrants are treated. Its silence is puzzling because the Philippine population in the United States totals between 2 and 4 million, including guest workers, legal resident aliens, naturalized citizens, and unauthorized immigrants. Together, they remit approximately $7 billion to the Philippines annually. Perhaps the government fears that any protest could jeopardize its long-standing guest worker program and diminish remittances, but this seems unlikely given that the guest workers total 6,000 annually, or only 0.2 percent of this nation's Philippine population.

As the pro-immigration reform demonstrations of 2006 and 2007 illustrate, immigrants now have the numbers as well as the organizational skills and leadership to influence US politics (Voss and Bloemraad 2011). To date, those efforts have been primarily channeled through the Democratic Party. When their policy preferences are not endorsed by the Democrats or Republicans, however, but are shared by the Mexican state, as is the case with immigration reform, immigrants may develop alliances with the Mexican government to pressure US officials to enact policies that reflect their preferences.

Interviews with sending state officials indicate that home-country governments believe their emigrants will, as Dominican officials voiced in private, become the equivalent of the "Israeli lobby," that is, become staunch advocates of home-country interests. However, the evidence suggests that immigration may be the only policy around which such an alliance could be built, as the inability of the Mexican government to rally Latinos and Mexican Americans to support NAFTA illustrates. Ethnic advocacy groups such as the National Council of la Raza and the Southwest Voter Registration and Education Project supported NAFTA because they saw it as a means of protecting Mexican American interests rather than because of their support for Mexican interests. All but one Mexican American member of Congress voted for NAFTA, but only after the agreement was modified to include provisions designed to benefit Mexican Americans in the border area. Similarly, only three of the twenty-one members of the Congressional Hispanic Caucus voted in support of the Central American Free Trade Association (CAFTA), which was considered an extension of NAFTA.

A rare example of immigrants mobilizing around foreign policy on behalf of the home country might be evident in the response by Colombian immigrants to the US decertification of Colombia in 1996. Decertification is a significant US foreign policy tool that can have severe ramifications for the decertified country. If Congress determines that a state is not complying with international anti-drug efforts or cooperating with US policy, "all US aid except anti-drug assistance" will be withdrawn. Decertification also means the Unites States will vote against that country's receiving loans from international lending institutions, and it may mean that other forms of financial penalties will be imposed. Rather than weaken him, however, the decertification decision strengthened Colombia's president Ernesto Samper, because it created the image that he was a victim of US bullying.

Colombian immigrants in the United States mobilized through their organizations to protest the decertification. Many if not most of the "protestors" were high-status professionals and businesspeople who chafed at how they were treated by INS officials when they went through US Customs at airports. When they presented Colombian passports, they were often asked to step aside so they could be questioned, and their bags were thoroughly checked. In effect, they felt as if they were suspected of being narco-traffickers. Their protest never became visible to the general public, but they communicated their dissatisfaction to the civic organizations and officials they dealt with. Given their status, these were surely numerous and important individuals. It is unclear whether they were motivated to assist their home government or to improve how they were treated by US officials. In either case, the Colombian government benefited.

In sum, emigrant–home country relations are unlikely to impact US politics and policy significantly. Short of explicit ethnic discrimination, which is unlikely to be constitutionally legitimate, the issues that concern immigrants, such as unemployment, the schools, and social services, are so clearly domestic problems that neither Mexico nor any other sending state would attempt to intervene with how they are managed. The uniqueness of the two exceptions to this rule—Cuban American influence regarding US-Cuban relations, and US immigration policy—underscores the validity of this claim. Although Cuban Americans were among its most ardent supporters, America's Cuban policy was primarily justified and continued by Cold War considerations and anti-Communist symbolism. Similarly, those who support immigration reform consist of an array of actors that includes large sectors of the business community, labor unions, civil libertarians, and immigrants themselves. None of these represents or advocates on behalf of sending states.

Because of their numbers and spatial concentration, immigrants and their children could become influential actors at all levels of the polity, especially as they naturalize and become more socialized in American politics. Indeed, their mere presence is already affecting national and state politics through their influence on reapportionment (Camarota 2005). As immigrants become more involved in politics, they are even more likely to focus on domestic issues and distance themselves from home country politics and the likelihood of becoming foreign advocates. To date, they evidence little inclination to lobby for home country interests, except when their immediate concerns are affected, as is the case with immigration issues. Thus, there is no reason to expect that emigrant–home state relations will influence the political behavior of immigrants and their descendants in the future in ways likely to threaten US national interests. Instead, as is the case historically with most immigrants, today's immigrants will focus increasingly on their domestic concerns and move into the US political mainstream.

## Conclusion

As we showed in the previous chapter, the formal requirements for making the transition from immigrant to naturalized citizen are relatively few in the United States, with the informal expectation of bureaucratic competence perhaps serving as the major barrier for immigrants who seek to become US citizens. Our national expectations, however, for being a "good" citizen are considerably higher. As a nation of immigrants, the United States has always needed to ensure that its immigrants cannot only move toward formal citizenship but also enliven the democracy with their opinions and participation. Their voice, though always necessary to ensure that the democracy lives up to its standards of representing the voices of all citizens, frequently creates concerns or fears in the native-born population. At different points in US history, natives have used their organization and their votes to slow the civic and political incorporation of immigrants.

We have shown that for today's immigrants, these fears are unsubstantiated. Immigrants are on a path to civic incorporation. Although they participate less than their native-born coethnics, immigrants clearly can be and have been mobilized around issues in their schools and communities. Without question, more effort is needed by ethnic and non-ethnic community-based institutions to ensure that participation rates increase, but that should not obscure the civic engagement of many of today's US immigrants. Similarly, naturalized US citizens on average vote at rates somewhat lower than those of their native-born coethnics, but for the newest immigrant/ethnic populations in the United States (Latinos and Asian Americans), this pattern is reversed. Again, this indicates a need for targeted mobilization, but is also evidence that mobilization can be successful among naturalized US citizens (Michelson and García Bedolla 2014).

Many immigrants maintain a parallel set of civic and political engagements with their countries of origin. The evidence clearly indicates that this transnational politics does not come at the expense of US civic involvement. For many immigrants, it serves as a democratic training ground around issues with which they may be more familiar or, initially, find to be more pressing. The increased investment that many emigrant-sending countries are making in reaching out to the emigrants and seeking to build a nation of dispersed emigrants will, in the long term, then, serve to build US-focused civic and political engagement, at least among those immigrants who engage in transnational activities.

For many in the native population, however, the relatively lower rates of immigrant civic participation and naturalized citizen voting in the face of what appears to be a growing transnational engagement renews concerns about the long-term political loyalty of immigrants. Although we find these fears to be unfounded, we recognize that they add to the opposition to some of the compromises that will be necessary for the passage of comprehensive immigration reform. In the next chapter, we return to the discussion of what will be necessary to build an immigration policy for the next generation and what compromises will have to be reached in Congress and in the population as a whole.

# 6

· · · · · · · · · · · · · · · · · · · · · · · · · · · · · · · · · · · · · · · · · · · · · · · · ·

# Conclusion: US Immigration Policy for the Twenty-First Century

WE BEGAN OUR DISCUSSION IN THIS VOLUME WITH THE OBSERVATION that many interests in American society are organizing to influence the ongoing legislative debate on immigration policy, with the hopes that this debate will result in comprehensive reform of US immigration policy for the twenty-first century. This activism has steadily increased over the past decade and a half and is now routinely considered one of the factors influencing national and local electoral outcomes.

Seeking to reverse what they saw as a disappointing—and surprising—outcome in the 2012 presidential race, Republican leaders ramped up their efforts to reform immigration policy in order to begin to build their electoral connection to the future, and so they could put the issue behind them before the next election. In that, they echoed Democratic Party leaders, who have long led legislative efforts in immigration reform, in part to build on their strong base of support among Latino and Asian American voters. To date, these efforts have failed and immigration will remain as part of the national policy debate in the 2016 elections and beyond. Immigration reform remains as distant as when President George W. Bush made initial, tentative reform proposals in the weeks before the September 11, 2001, attacks, or when the approximately 5 million immigrants, immigrant family members, and their supporters took to the streets in 2006.

We have discussed some of the causes of this stalemate throughout the book, but in this chapter we focus more explicitly on the constitutional locus of the stalemate—the Congress, and more specifically the House of Representatives—to assess the specific barriers to immigration reform. We then return to the key elements, first discussed in Chapter 1, that will make up the eventual immigration reform that is passed and enacted into law (note that we see this as an inevitability, which we will discuss in the conclusion to this chapter). We examine the action that Congress has taken thus far on each issue, and what it will need to do to address each issue in order to pass a comprehensive immigration reform bill. Finally, we conclude by discussing what will need to change in order to move from the current stalemate and achieve comprehensive immigration reform for the twenty-first century.

## The Current Stalemate

For immigrants seeking to legalize their status or the status of relatives, for employers seeking workers with the skills they need, for states seeking to control the flow of unauthorized immigrants into their communities and schools, and for native-born populations concerned about the cultural and economic changes spurred by immigrant populations, Congress's repeated inaction on immigration reform may seem inexcusable. This failure to reform immigration fits into a larger national narrative about an out-of-touch Congress and hyper-partisan division in Washington (Mann and Ornstein 2012; Jacobson 2013).

Partisanship undoubtedly plays a role in the immigration stalemate, but so does the complexity of the issue. All of the major reforms to immigration in the last century have been fought over and debated at length, both by the population as a whole and by Congress. As we discussed in Chapter 2, the National-Origin Quota Bills of the 1920s capped a fifty-year-long debate over whether or not Congress could restrict immigration and, once that question was resolved in the affirmative, who should be excluded. Even when these highly restrictive bills became law, the restrictionist effort continued for some activists who also sought to include Western Hemisphere immigrants in the quotas and thus prevent their migration in large numbers (Ngai 1999). The 1965 immigration legislation that guides today's policies emerged from a twenty-year-long effort to build targeted exceptions to the National-Origin Quota laws into a broad bill (Fitzgerald and Cook-Martín 2014: Chapter 2). The Immigration Reform and Control Act required ten years of Congressional hearings and debates prior to passage (Gimpel and Edwards 1999).

Why does immigration legislation require such extensive debate, energy, and compromise? Ultimately, it is because immigration policy shapes the future of the nation in a way that few other types of legislation do. To the degree that immigration legislation structures the question of who can immigrate, it can change the face of the nation in a very dramatic—and for some, very visceral—way. Congress engages questions of who can immigrate and under what circumstances with great care. In an era of hyper-partisanship in which party control of the Senate or House or the presidency can shift with each election, Congress takes this responsibility all the more seriously.

How has the increased partisan divide in Congress shaped the path of immigration reform? Compared to less partisan eras, Congress has generally been less willing to take on controversial issues, like immigration, that require compromise to ensure passage (Desilver 2013). And when they do vote on such bills, members are sticking with their parties at record levels. With immigration policy in the current era, Republicans are largely united in wanting a more restrictionist approach that is built on immigration enforcement, whereas Democrats, though somewhat less cohesive, are more focused on questions of maintaining diversity in the legal immigrant flow and ensuring a path to earned legal status for long-term unauthorized immigrants resident in the United States (Facchini and Steinhardt 2011). This correspondence between party and form of immigration policy is particularly evident in the House of Representatives, where, not surprisingly, the stalemate of the current era is most evident.

There are several consequences of this hyper-partisan era in Congress for immigration. First, the debate over comprehensive immigration reform, to the extent that it has taken place at all, has been in the Senate rather than in the House of Representatives. The nature of the Senate is that, with its six-year terms of office, it has more distance from electoral pressures than the House, which elects its entire membership every two years. So the Senate often begins the process of debate and reform to absorb some of the political costs of entering controversial debates. In 2006 and 2013, these debates led to the passage of legislation that the House then didn't act on, and in 2007, the Senate itself failed to pass a bill.

Second, the high levels of partisanship have ensured that moderate members of the House—including Speaker John Boehner, at least on immigration—have been unable to persuade their more restrictionist and cautious colleagues of the value of even beginning a debate over immigration reform. Certainly many of these Republican members, on principle, oppose immigration at current levels, fear the cultural change and labor market changes spurred by contemporary immigrants, and feel strongly that the failure to respect US law makes unauthorized immigrants ineligible for citizenship. These positions, however, are undoubtedly reinforced by electoral concerns, specifically the risk of being challenged in Republican primaries by candidates who take more strident positions on immigration reform (DeSipio 2011a). As we mentioned in Chapter 1, this message was made clear to many Republican House members when the then–House majority leader, Eric Cantor, lost a Republican Party primary to a largely unknown and underfunded challenger who used Cantor's tepid support for the DREAM Act as evidence that Cantor was out of touch with his district. Although it is not possible to measure members' precise motivations, both principles and electoral concerns are important factors in Republican House members' lack of interest in debating comprehensive immigration reform. Between eighty and one hundred Republican members of the House of Representatives are consistently unwilling to consider any immigration reform that includes legalization for unauthorized immigrants currently residing in the United States.

These members have a caucus in the House—the Congressional Immigration Reform Caucus (http://irc.poe.house.gov/index.cfm/about-irc). The exact membership of the caucus varies; in late 2012, it had ninety-three dues-paying members. This caucus has been able to block House consideration of Senate-passed immigration reform legislation by indicating that its members, who make up a near-majority of the Republican caucus in the House of Representatives, will not consider any immigration bill that includes a path to legal status for unauthorized immigrants resident in the United States. And because Speaker Boehner largely follows House custom and doesn't bring bills to a vote that don't have majority support from the majority caucus (in the current Congress, this means support from a majority of the Republican caucus in the Republican-controlled House), this effectively prevents debate or a vote on a comprehensive immigration reform bill. Speaker Boehner has violated this institutional custom on several occasions, such as to pass the Violence Against Women Act in 2013 and to pass increases in the debt ceiling in 2013 and 2014, but he has shown no indication that he is willing to do so for immigration reform. Were he to allow a Senate immigration bill to pass the House on Democratic votes, it would undoubtedly be the end of his speakership.

Ironically, if it weren't for this intransigence among some in the Republican caucus, Republicans would probably be able to ensure passage of a narrow bill with additional enforcement, relatively fewer opportunities for unauthorized migrants, and a circumscribed set of options for future immigration to permanent residence. Their unwillingness to engage the debate, however, maintains the status quo (which few are satisfied with) and the likelihood that in the future a more inclusive bill will pass.

Routine Republican control of the House of Representatives will likely continue through the 2010s, in part due to the redistricting that took place after major Republican state legislative victories in the 2010 election. In most states, state legislators design the House of Representatives districts, and so the post-2010 Congressional redistricting advantaged Republicans more than it did Democrats. The Brennan Center for Justice at the New York University Law School estimates that the redrawing of districts after the 2010 election gave the Republicans an advantage in eleven House seats that they would not have had if the districting process had been less partisan (Iyer and Gaskins 2012). These eleven seats made up approximately half of the majority that Republicans held in the 113th Congress. This advantage could certainly reverse itself after the 2020 redistricting. That said, the Republicans have a longer-term advantage in the House, certainly relative to their advantage in presidential elections. The Democratic electorate is concentrated in cities and along the coasts, but the Republican votes are more spread out, which is an advantage in House races (Cohn 2014). Democratic dominance in presidential elections does not ensure an ability to win a majority of House (or Senate) seats.

In sum, the House of Representatives, which has served as an effective barrier to consideration of comprehensive US immigration reform in the early years of the twenty-first century, will likely continue to be controlled by those who are opposed to the passage of a comprehensive bill for the foreseeable future. The Senate, which has been more open to immigration reform, will likely be relatively evenly divided, with each party occasionally holding the majority, making it less likely to seek to influence the House. The Constitution ensures, however, that one branch of the legislature can stall or block legislation regardless of the positions of the president and the other branch of the legislature.

# Building the US Immigration Regime of the Early Twenty-First Century

In the first chapter, we laid out the various immigration policy issues that Congress would need to address to achieve truly comprehensive immigration reform. We revisit those issues here and discuss what Congress has done, and what it will need to do, in order to reach a workable compromise in each of these areas. Briefly, as a reminder, these issues are:

- Meeting the labor needs of sectors most dependent on immigrant labor.
- Protecting the labor rights of immigrants, including the right to organize.
- Regulating unauthorized migration.
- Providing a path to legalization for unauthorized immigrants.
- Protecting the civil and human rights of immigrants.
- Safeguarding US national security interests and global responsibilities.
- Restructuring fiscal policy so that costs of immigration are shared equitably by local, state, and federal authorities.
- Developing programs to ensure that immigrants have the training and encouragement needed to speed their entry into American society—what we characterize as *immigrant incorporation policy* in this book.

## *Meeting the Labor Needs of the US Economy and Ensuring the Labor Rights of Immigrants*

US immigration policy has always been designed to ensure that the nation's economy will grow. For the business community to support immigration reform—and they are a key advocate for reform—national labor needs must be met. Given this, immigration reform will not reduce the volume of immigration to the United States; in fact, it will likely increase overall levels of immigration, at least in periods of economic growth. This would seem to conflict with the public opinion data that we presented in Chapter 3, which show a plurality of the American people prefer a policy in which fewer immigrants migrate to the United States. However, Congress is unlikely to propose anything that would have the effect of reducing legal immigration, and if they were to do so, we could expect support for the status quo—the stalemate—to grow. The nation's labor needs ensure that any eventual immigration reform bill will maintain or increase current immigration levels.

However, a future immigration reform bill could likely cause a few major changes to the current flow of migrants. It could alter the criteria for immigration eligibility, it could shift the status of some immigrants from permanent residents with a path to citizenship to guest workers, or it could limit some of the economic and social rights of immigrants to permanent residence. Congress will need to reevaluate the balance between migration eligibility based on having an immediate family member in the United States versus possessing skills needed by the economy. It will also need to debate the appropriate level of guest worker migration, the sectors of the economy in which guest workers can work, and the rights of those migrants.

The Senate debated these issues in 2006, 2007, and 2013, and with each proposed bill the number of guest worker visas increased. Under these bills, new guest workers would have also gained *labor mobility*—the ability to change employers—not held by previous or current guest workers. However, only one of the bills provided a direct path for guest workers to permanent residence. And only the 2007 bill addressed the balance between family preference and labor market contributions in the allocation of permanent resident visas. However, the Senate was unable to pass that bill.

Questions of guest worker policies and the allocation of permanent resident visas remain controversial. As Congress debates these issues, it will need to address popular concerns about the volume of immigration to the United States. Because reducing the overall number of immigrants is unlikely, Congress will need to make the argument that the changes it makes will bring immigrants to the United States who can better build and strengthen the nation's economy. Congress will also need to assure native workers that they will not face added competition from immigrant labor, and assure organized labor that guest workers and new permanent residents will have workplace protections and the right to organize.

The Congressional stalemate has spurred the formation of new coalitions to advocate for comprehensive immigration reform. One of the most interesting of these new coalitions has been an alliance between the business community, through the US Chamber of Commerce, and organized labor, through the American Federation of Labor–Council of

Industrial Organizations (AFL-CIO). The business community has long advocated expansive immigration and the opportunity for migration by both permanent residents and guest workers. Organized labor, on the other hand, has historically been more cautious about immigration, concerned about the competition native workers might face from immigrant workers entering the labor market, and fearing the likelihood that business owners would find it expedient to exploit immigrant labor, particularly guest workers and unauthorized immigrants.

Unions—particularly the service unions—have changed their tune considerably over the past two decades. In part, this is due to a compositional change in their memberships (Schmitt and Warner 2010). The fastest-growing unions are in the service sector and the membership of these unions is increasingly comprised by first- and second-generation immigrants. The leadership of these unions has also changed and now better reflects the membership. In other words, many union leaders now have close ties to the immigrant community. Many unions are now advocates for immigration reform, and in particular, for expansive legalization. Their support for immigration, however, is contingent upon receiving workplace protections comparable to those of native workers for new immigrants—including guest workers—should they seek to unionize (Milkman 2000). Unions also brought new tactics to the immigration reform campaign, including mass rallies; in fact, they were central to ensuring the high levels of mass participation in the 2006 immigrant rights rallies nationwide (Sziarto and Leitner 2010; Wang and Winn 2011).

This alliance between organized labor and the business community challenges the partisan divide in Congress over immigration reform. To date, however, unions have had more success with their frequent partisan allies, the Democrats, than business leaders have had with the Republicans. As a result, unions have been able to increase the salience of their demands, both for expansive legalization of immigrants and for protections for labor, and specifically protections for union organizing, in any new guest worker program established as part of comprehensive immigration reform.

### New Regulation and Enforcement to Eliminate Future Unauthorized Migration

Comprehensive immigration reform can succeed only to the degree that it assures the American public that unauthorized migration will slow considerably with the passage of the bill. As we discussed in Chapter 1, this is the area of immigration policy that Congress and the executive branch have been most able to find agreement on over the past two decades. Enforcement along the US-Mexico border has increased considerably, and interior enforcement and deportation of unauthorized immigrants living and working in the United States have also increased significantly over the past decade.

However, the electorate will likely not be swayed by evidence of the effectiveness of the new enforcement strategies implemented since the 1990s. Despite demographic analysis of the US population that shows that the number of unauthorized immigrants resident in the United States has remained largely unchanged since 2009 (Passel et al. 2014), and despite the Obama administration's willingness to deport unauthorized immigrants at unprecedented levels, over the increasingly vocal opposition of many who otherwise support the administration (Peralta 2014), the perception of unauthorized immigration as out of control continues to trump any evidence of the increasing effectiveness of immigration enforcement.

Consequently, any future comprehensive immigration reform bill will need to increase enforcement of unauthorized immigration even more. This will likely include expanded staffing for border control and interior enforcement, new physical barriers along borders, and new technologies both to impede unauthorized border crossing and to prevent work in the United States without legal status. This expanded enforcement will be expensive and will increasingly impinge upon the freedoms of US citizens and permanent residents. To date, there has been only limited backlash from US citizens, mostly from residents of the area around the US-Mexico border, in response to this steady increase in immigration enforcement. This opposition could grow, however, if Congress is forced to move to the next step—one that it has been unwilling to consider seriously thus far. The pressure to assure the American public that unauthorized immigration will stop with the passage of a new immigration bill could mean that Congress might try to implement a non-counterfeitable national identification card and require its use for certain activities, such as starting a new job or obtaining health care.

A final hurdle in assuring the American public that unauthorized migration will no longer be an issue stems from what will likely be an expansion in guest worker programs. Such programs, if they do not have effective ways to monitor and control unauthorized workers, would simply create a longer-term problem: guest workers and the employers who hire them tend not to want to sever the relationship at the end of the contract, which then creates new unauthorized immigrants. This will add to the pressure to create a non-counterfeitable identification that only US citizens and permanent residents would have.

### Legalization of Unauthorized Immigrants in the United States

A path to legal status for unauthorized immigrants in the United States and a path for these newly legalized residents to attain citizenship within a reasonable time frame are as necessary as new enforcement strategies in any comprehensive immigration reform bill. There is a political dimension to this necessity: no reform can pass without the votes of Democrats, and they will likely support only a bill that includes some form of legalization. There is also an ethical component. As we discussed in Chapter 2, when the United States has previously faced large numbers of unauthorized immigrants in the 1920s, 1940s, 1950s, and 1980s, it has created a path to legal status. Today's unauthorized immigrants have arguably made more of a commitment to the United States than have the unauthorized immigrants of the twentieth century who were eventually given legal status. More than 60 percent of unauthorized immigrants in 2013 had resided in the United States for more than 10 years and the median length of residence for all unauthorized immigrants grew to 12.7 years (Passel et al. 2014). Nearly half live with US citizen family members.

If the premise that comprehensive immigration reform requires some form of legalization is accepted (though this is not the case for many House Republicans), the focus of the debate then becomes what, exactly, the path to legalization should look like. That is, who should be eligible for legalization and what should be required to attain legal status? As 2006, 2007, and 2013 Senate debates demonstrate, there is no consensus on these questions yet. The specifics of legalization that Congress must address, which we detailed in Chapter 1, are undoubtedly complicated. However, the complexities of legalization shouldn't obscure the fact that when the question is asked dispassionately and without using the word *amnesty*, the American public is generally supportive of creating opportunities for unauthorized immigrants in the United States to legalize their status and, eventually, move toward US citizenship (Jones et al. 2014). As we indicated in Chapter 3, this support is fluid, depending on the political environment and on how the question is asked. Recognizing the political imperative of some form of legalization in order to ensure passage of comprehensive immigration reform, Congress will need to establish enough barriers, standards, and requirements for legalizing immigrants to ensure sufficient popular support.

## *The Protection of Immigrants' Civil and Human Rights*

Congress's long delay in passing immigration reform has allowed for extensive organizing in both the pro- and anti-reform communities. The tangible consequences of the anti-immigration reform mobilization are evident in the continued Congressional stalemate. What is perhaps less clear are the increasing expectations of immigrants and their allies for a widespread and inclusive reform that addresses the needs of most undocumented immigrants in the United States and ensures that the immediate relatives of US citizens and permanent residents will continue to be able to immigrate.

Pro-reform advocates are increasingly concerned not just about policy issues but also about the civil and human rights of immigrants in the United States (Risse 2008; Benhabib 2012). Congressional advocates of immigration reform are also increasingly raising these same concerns, though this is somewhat tactical on their part. The growing concern over civil and human rights reflects a changing American society in which an increasing share of the public sees immigration in more than economic or cultural terms. Immigrants and their children are changing the public debate and highlighting the idea that immigrants are moral actors who have fundamental rights that must be respected in immigration law (Hing 2006).

Recognition of immigrant rights will likely never be the dominant narrative of immigration in the United States, so how it will be addressed in comprehensive reform legislation is less clear. Certainly, Congress will be attentive to the practices of the Department of Homeland Security and reprimand the agency for any excesses. Over time, however, immigration enforcement will increasingly challenge citizens as well as immigrants, which could cause some tensions in US society. As we have suggested, any comprehensive immigration reform will undoubtedly include increased border and interior enforcement, including new procedural requirements for US citizens and permanent residents.

We anticipate that immigration reform will increase the nation's focus on the civic training of immigrants. At least in part, this will be because any legalization program will require immigrant candidates for legalization to demonstrate some civic knowledge or to take classes to gain that knowledge. That requirement alone will spur a huge demand for civics classes and necessitate the combined efforts of school districts, community college boards, and civic organizations to provide that training on a scale unprecedented in American society.

We suspect that the eventual path to immigration reform will also spur new waves of mass mobilization. As Congress eventually debates, and nears, a final decision on an immigration reform bill, mass protests and civic engagement, like those seen in 2006, will likely reemerge to take a stance on policy issues (e.g., supporting or opposing particular proposals). However, a broader moral claim will likely be necessary to spur mass mobilization, much like the opposition to the criminalization of unauthorized status that galvanized many of the 2006 marchers (Ramírez 2013). The increasing demands for ensuring the civil and human rights of immigrants could play this role. And when a comprehensive reform bill passes, it will demonstrate to immigrant communities the civic value of collective action and be a powerful reminder of their power in the American democracy.

## US Immigration Policies and US National Security Needs

As we discussed in Chapter 1, immigration reform proposals were briefly considered in the summer of 2001, but they quickly disappeared from the policy debate after 9/11. As important as immigration policy is to the nation, it will always be tied to national security imperatives, that is, it will need to serve US geopolitical interests and ensure that immigrants—whether legal, unauthorized, guest workers, or visitors—are not a threat to the nation's security or safety.

Asylum and refugee policy is one element of immigration and national security that has long been debated by Congress, but without a resolution satisfactory to either Congress or the executive branch. Historically, the United States has awarded refugee status or asylum to political migrants from countries that were once supported by the United States but that had undergone changes that put them in opposition to US interests. The current law delegates refugee and asylum decisions to the executive branch (the Department of State), but limits the overall number of refugees regardless of geopolitical circumstances. Comprehensive immigration reform will likely include refugee and asylum policies that place less of an emphasis on the political connections of refugees and more of an emphasis on their fear of persecution, which is the standard used by the United

Nations. In addition, Congress will likely, at least initially, seek to shape the implementation of these policies.

Since 9/11, policymakers have increasingly questioned the political loyalty and organizational connections of immigrants in the United States. Undoubtedly, this would continue whether there is comprehensive immigration reform or not. What could change, though, is the range of beliefs and organizational loyalties that would cause an immigrant to be scrutinized or put at legal risk once in the United States. Immigrants seen as national security threats or who violate US law are subject to deportation. In the years since 9/11, the number of deportations has grown and many of these are based on the commission of crimes by the deportees (US Immigration and Customs Enforcement 2014). Comprehensive immigration reform will likely not change this pattern.

As we indicated in Chapters 4 and 5, most if not all naturalized US citizens are loyal to the United States and adopt its civic and political culture willingly and quickly. With a very few exceptions, naturalized US citizens do not face the risk of deportation that non-naturalized immigrants do. However, Congress and the executive branch have begun to question this distinction and may well reduce some rights of naturalized citizens when it next takes up immigration legislation (Thiessen 2012). And unlike other issues in the immigration reform debate, it is doubtful that there will be organized voices speaking up to defend the breadth of rights that immigrants and naturalized citizens have traditionally exercised.

### Immigration, Federalism, and Fiscal Policy

The best evidence indicates that immigrants are a net financial plus to government. However, comprehensive immigration reform will also need to remedy what has become an increasing irritant for immigrant-receiving states and cities: the fiscal benefit (i.e., taxes) is disproportionately paid to the federal government by immigrants, even though many of the costs of providing services—public education, public safety, and social services—are borne by the states and localities (Congressional Budget Office 2007; Institute on Taxation and Economic Policy 2013). Central to any successful immigrant incorporation policy would be recognizing that immigration is a federal policy and that the costs as well as the benefits of immigration should rest with that level of government. The conversation has to focus on the cost being an investment in the future of the nation that will take many years to realize, just as public education for US-born children does not pay off immediately; immigrant children and the children of immigrants will be part of US society for many years to come and can become either a liability or an asset depending on the investment.

It will be difficult to resolve this issue fully, particularly in tight budget times, for a couple of reasons. First, it is unlikely that the federal government will be willing to pay all of the costs for providing education and social services to immigrants. Second, this element of immigration reform differs in an important way from other issues: partisan division will not shape the Congressional debate in this area. Instead, this component of comprehensive immigration reform pits the interests of immigrant-receiving states, which generally are larger states, against those of the smaller states with fewer immigrants.

One way to address this issue is through a legalization program. Estimates suggest that a large-scale legalization program would increase the state and local tax base by as much as $2 billion annually (Institute on Taxation and Economic Policy 2013). Although legalization would undoubtedly also increase the demand for some state services, the Congressional Budget Office estimates that legalization along the lines proposed by the US Senate in S. 744 would generate at least $200 billion in additional federal revenues after controlling for the new costs of services provided to the newly legalized immigrants (Congressional Budget Office 2013). The states—at least those with income taxes—would see similar fiscal gains from legalization.

### Ensuring Immigrant Incorporation

The story of US immigration policy is not simply one of numbers. Although no nation has welcomed as many immigrants as the United States has over the 225 years since independence, the story of immigration is also one of successful political, social, and cultural incorporation of immigrants and their children. Ultimately, if immigrant incorporation is successful, then the other questions of immigration policy are of less concern. On the other hand, failure, or even perceived potential failure, is noted quickly by the native-born population and serves to undermine popular support for immigration, as we saw in the period just after 9/11.

All available evidence suggests that incorporation of the post-1965 immigrants has been successful, if uneven. The current system may be failing among some unauthorized immigrants and their children, but even these migrants, who entered the United States with considerable disadvantages, are adapting to American society fairly successfully, albeit more slowly than other immigrants (Portes and Rumbaut 2001; Bean and Stevens 2003). Past successes, of course, are no guarantee of future success, and Congress will need to be attentive in the design of a new immigration system to select immigrants who meet national needs and are also likely to succeed in US society. It will also need to ensure that the federal government and the states provide the training and opportunities necessary for immigrants' successful incorporation.

As we discussed in Chapters 2 and 4, there have been few immigrant-specific policies and programs to ensure the incorporation of immigrants—naturalization being the exception. States have historically been the locus of immigrant incorporation policies, but even so, these state programs, such as public K–12 and higher education, were not designed specifically with immigrants in mind. And in recent years, states have increasingly reduced their provision of services to their residents. Although the federal government has little ability to challenge these reductions, it needs to be attentive to the consequences of these service reductions on immigrants and the long-term effects on immigrant incorporation.

It may not be debated as part of the next comprehensive immigration reform bill, but we anticipate that some immigrant incorporation policies that had traditionally been the responsibility of states will shift to the federal government, specifically language training, job training and retraining, and programs to assist with conversion of professional licensing and professional degree requirements earned abroad. These programs may well continue to be administered by the states but paid for by the federal government as part of the shift in the fiscal costs and benefits of immigration policy. Immigrant incorporation policies will also need to be attentive to the children of immigrants, some of whom are US citizens by birth and others of whom are not.

Incorporation policies have rarely been central to policymaker discussions of immigration policy and, as such, will likely remain less dominant in any future Congressional debates of US immigration policy. Of course, this is a somewhat vicious cycle, as policymakers' biases and impressions about the relative success or failure of today's immigrants will undoubtedly shape their thinking about the other immigration policy issues that must be resolved in order to have comprehensive immigration reform.

Ultimately, the native population must perceive that immigrants are a net plus to US society and that we as a society can afford to add them to our numbers.

## What Needs to Change for the Nation to Adopt Immigration Reform?

Since the turn of the twenty-first century, the nation has had three moments when Congressional passage of comprehensive immigration reform seemed possible: early in the first term of the George W. Bush administration, in the months before 9/11; in 2006, when the Senate passed bipartisan immigration reform legislation; and soon after President Barack Obama's reelection in 2012. In each case, observers were confident that President Bush or President Obama would be able to sign a bill that passed Congress with bipartisan support. However, none of the periods of executive and legislative attention to immigration reform ultimately led to a signed bill. On the contrary, each period led to a steady widening of the legislative divide over a comprehensive solution to the nation's twenty-first-century immigration needs.

This might lead to the conclusion that a comprehensive immigration reform is not possible in the current political environment. Without question, the early twenty-first century is a period of extreme partisanship in American government and, with the exceptions of the period just after 9/11 and the first two years of the Obama presidency, Congress has been less productive in this period than in any period since the New Deal (Desilver 2013; Cillizza 2014). Ultimately, however, as we have demonstrated throughout this volume, immigration is too important to the nation, and the current system of immigration regulation has too many critics in American society, for the current system to survive indefinitely. Whatever its form, immigration reform is an inevitability. So, the question that we end our discussion with is, what must change in Congress (and, perhaps, in the executive branch) to allow for the enactment of a comprehensive immigration reform bill?

We approach this discussion with some caution. The social sciences are notoriously poor at predicting *when* things will happen. Public policy, in particular, is difficult to predict because unexpected events can shift the debate overnight—for example, immigration reform looked like only a modest challenge for a popular first-term president in the summer of 2001 but became a political impossibility for several years following the morning of September 11, 2001. We also take for granted in our discussion a continued demand for both the labor of immigrants from economic interests in US society and the ongoing desire of residents of the United States to reunite with family members who live abroad, as each of these incentives to migration has been present throughout the nation's history (Zolberg 2006). We also anticipate that alliances and movements that have developed either to support immigration reform (e.g., between the Chamber of Commerce and the AFL-CIO) or to oppose immigration reform, particularly legalization of unauthorized immigrants (e.g., the Tea Party), will remain active and influential in the policy debate (Parker and Barreto 2013).

With those caveats in mind, what then is necessary to break the stalemate and allow the nation to develop a successful immigration policy for the twenty-first century? In our minds, two characteristics of the contemporary political structure must remain and a third must shift its focus. The two that must maintain their current approach to immigration reform are that the executive branch must remain broadly supportive of comprehensive immigration reform and that the Senate must maintain its willingness to engage bipartisanship to seek compromises on immigration policy. However, in order to see immigration reform legislation, the House of Representatives must move away from its intransigence on comprehensive reform and enter into a meaningful dialogue with the Senate. It can certainly influence the design of the bill in this scenario, but it must be open to compromise on all elements identified above, including the opportunity for many or most of today's unauthorized immigrants to legalize their status and, eventually, be eligible for naturalization. As we will suggest, this necessary piece of the puzzle will occur only after significant shifts in the House's membership, which are unlikely to occur before the early 2020s.

Of these three necessary elements, the most likely is that the president—regardless of who holds the office—remains an advocate of comprehensive immigration reform. This is not a foregone conclusion. Certainly, some of the national leaders who appear to have presidential aspirations, such as Texas senator Ted Cruz or Kentucky senator Rand Paul, are vocal opponents of legalization—what they characterize as amnesty. More moderate Republicans are a bit more tempered in their opposition to legalization, but would need to win the votes of Republican primary voters in order to win their party's presidential nomination and would consequently be encouraged to take positions that would make support of a comprehensive immigration bill more difficult, if elected to the presidency. Senator John McCain's challenges in winning the Republican presidential nomination after cosponsoring the 2006 and 2007 Senate bills show the difficulties that national Republican leaders might well face in balancing the interests of Republican primary voters and the national interest on immigration policy (DeSipio 2011a).

For several reasons, however, we anticipate that the president will remain more supportive of comprehensive immigration reform than either the Senate or the House of Representatives. Some of this confidence comes from a reading of electoral math. Democrats have a relative advantage over Republicans in national politics. Democrats, for example, have won the popular vote in five of the last six elections and have carried a majority in the Electoral College in four of those elections. The electoral constituencies that support Democrats are growing more rapidly than the core Republican constituencies. Republicans are also more divided than the Democrats on this issue and this division plays itself out in national politics more than it does at the Congressional or local level (Aberbach and Peele 2011).

That electoral math, of course, does not preclude a Republican victory. Ultimately, the relative strength of a candidate and the skill with which the campaign is conducted can overcome any electorate disadvantages. To win the presidency in the contemporary era, however, any Republican would need to attract moderate voters in the general election, regardless of whatever bargains had been made to win the party primary. A candidate's message on issues like immigration is critical to winning those moderate votes, so whether Democrat or Republican, the winning candidate would likely need to adopt a position that makes the passage of comprehensive immigration reform possible (Jones et al. 2014). Once in office, the newly elected president would face encouragement from the interests in US society—including business interests and ethnic leaders—that have long advocated comprehensive immigration reform (Facchini et al. 2011). Presidents Bush and Obama have both advocated comprehensive reform.

Our assertion that the Senate will maintain its bipartisan support for immigration reform is perhaps more controversial. In 2007, the Senate was unable to reach any sort of agreement and many Democrats as well as most Republicans gave up on immigration reform. In 2010, the Senate was unable to overcome filibuster to support the DREAM Act, which had passed in the House of Representatives (it did receive a majority vote in the Senate, but not the necessary sixty votes to overcome filibuster). Despite these periods of Senate intransigence, it has more consistently sought a bipartisan compromise on immigration. In 2006, it passed a relatively inclusive bill; the vote to pass this legislation included many Republican senators (DeSipio 2011a). In 2012 and 2013, the bipartisan "Gang of Eight" crafted a more restrictive bill that was able to pass on the votes of all Democratic senators and fourteen Republican senators (US Senate 2013). This majority is particularly remarkable considering the hyper-partisanship of the 113th Congress.

Senators also look to national constituencies more than members of the House of Representatives do. While formally representing a state in the Senate, senators seek to become national leaders on specific issues and build national constituencies. Many also envision an eventual run for national office. This greater national focus of senators, regardless of party, ensures that senators will be more attentive to interests in the broader US society seeking comprehensive immigration reform. Some—particularly Republican senators—fear primary challenges by anti-immigration candidates, but incumbency is generally a greater value in the Senate primaries than in the House primaries. As a result, we anticipate that the Senate—regardless of which party is in the majority—will remain responsive to societal demands for immigration reform. However, we do believe that the intensity of this responsiveness will vary. Senate sessions in which the Democrats are in the majority will be more likely to make comprehensive immigration reform a priority than sessions in which the Republicans hold the majority.

The primary locus of the current stalemate is the House of Representatives. We anticipate that this will remain the case at least until the early 2020s, and potentially beyond. Republicans are likely to remain in the majority until the House is redistricted after the 2020 census. Republicans in the House will retain today's plurality, or perhaps a majority, that for principled and political reasons opposes any immigration reform that includes a path to legal status for unauthorized immigrants. Neither Speaker Boehner nor his successor will be likely to pass an immigration reform bill with mostly Democratic votes, and so the Republican House majority ensures that no comprehensive reform bill will become law.

This stalemate may well remain beyond 2022 (the first congressional election after the 2020 redistricting), even though Democrats will likely do better in state legislative races that largely shape the redistrictings that follow in 2020 than they did in 2010. It will also be a presidential election year—when more Democrats turn out—and Congress will be unlikely to have passed as controversial a bill as they had before the 2010 election— the Affordable Care Act, or Obamacare—which angered and mobilized many Republican voters. However, by itself, more success in redistricting may not be enough for the Democrats to overcome the Republican congressional geographic advantage. Instead, Congress will be won or lost by each party based on its success in reaching out to voters, speaking to the issues that drive them, and communicating why their party will be better for the nation. At this writing, it isn't possible to anticipate which party will have won this battle for the nation's hearts and minds in the distant future. We can, however, say with confidence that a careful reading of the political tea leaves suggests that the House membership will not change sufficiently before 2020 to create a likely path to comprehensive immigration reform.

House Republicans suggest a different path: to abandon comprehensive reform and instead break up the pieces of immigration policy. They would gauge which of the major immigration issues gets majority support, pass legislation dealing with just that issue, and call whatever passes "immigration reform." We think that this path is politically unlikely. As is evident, almost all elements of immigration reform are controversial, and each piece requires compromise. Organized labor, for example, finds guest worker programs abhorrent, but nonetheless will accept some expansion of guest worker programs in exchange for labor protections for those workers and a path to legalization for unauthorized workers in the United States, many of whom are union members or in union families. Business interests are ambivalent about legalization, but realize that their support of legalization wins them critical support on issues they do care about (expanding legal immigration of skilled workers and guest worker programs) from immigrant ethnic community activists and from organized labor. We could go on, but the point is that comprehensive reform requires a coalition of diverse interests often conceding some of their interests to achieve their larger goals. Breaking up immigration reform, as suggested by some House leaders, would likely dissolve this coalition and ensure that little or no legislation passes—except, perhaps, more money for immigration enforcement. As a result, it is not in the interest of any of the interests supporting reform to seek narrow and targeted solutions

(Kelly 2014). The ultimate effect of breaking up the bill would be to maintain the status quo, which clearly dissatisfies so many.

## Conclusion

We conclude by acknowledging the contradiction of our argument: comprehensive immigration reform is inevitable, yet it is stuck in a stalemate that lasts into the foreseeable future. How can it then be inevitable?

We would answer this question by returning to the discussion in the Introduction and Chapter 1. The nation is ultimately too dependent on immigrants, for both their labor and their relationships with US citizens and residents, to allow for a significant reduction in future immigration. If this is the case, then, the nation has a responsibility to itself and to its citizens to create an orderly system of immigration. This was the challenge that the nation faced when it first decided that it could, and should, regulate immigration in the late nineteenth century, and it continues to face this same challenge today. Business leaders assert (and economists and demographers largely agree) that the native labor force cannot meet the needs of the nation's economy. US citizens and permanent residents want to reunite with family members abroad and to ensure that family members living in the United States without proper documentation can come out of the shadows. The nation has obligations under international treaties and bilateral relationships to welcome refugees and asylees who face fear of persecution abroad. Each of these demands might be met on a piecemeal basis, and the current immigration system, usually called "broken," can adapt in part. Or, instead, the nation can pass comprehensive immigration reform, as called for by Presidents Bush and Obama, the majorities of both a Republican and Democratic Senate, business and labor leaders, and immigrant advocates.

The model of what will eventually become law is available. Senate Bills 2611 (2006) and 744 (2013) have many differences, but in broad strokes they are more similar than different. In those models is a foundation for a compromise. The nature of that compromise is that many pieces of the model are distasteful or abhorrent to different groups in American society, but each also contains the positive elements that will make support for the overall bill possible. Ultimately, Congress can, and must, identify the compromises necessary to move the nation's immigration forward into the twenty-first century.

# Bibliography

Aberbach, Joel D., and Gillian Peele, eds. 2011. *Crisis of Conservatism? The Republican Party, the Conservative Movement, and American Politics After Bush*. New York: Oxford University Press.

AFL-CIO. 2013. "Joint Statement of Shared Principles by U.S. Chamber of Commerce President and CEP Thomas J. Donohue and AFL-CIO President Richard Trumka." Press Release, February 21. Washington, DC: AFL-CIO.

Aguirre, Benigno E., and Rogelio Saenz. 2002. "Testing the Effects of Collectively Expected Durations of Migration: The Naturalization of Mexicans and Cubans." *International Migration Review* 36 (1) (Spring): 103–124.

Alba, Richard, and Victor Nee. 2003. *Remaking the American Mainstream: Assimilation and Contemporary Immigration*. Cambridge, MA: Harvard University Press.

Altman, Ida, and James Horn. 1991. *"To Make America": European Emigration in the Early Modern Period*. Berkeley and Los Angeles: University of California Press.

Alvarez, Robert. 1987. "A Profile of the Citizenship Process Among Hispanics in the United States." *International Migration Review* 21 (2) (Summer): 327–351.

Anbinder, Tyler G. 1992. *Nativism and Slavery: The Northern Know-Nothings and the Politics of the 1850s*. New York: Oxford University Press.

*Arizona et al. v. United States*. Supreme Court of the United States. 2012. 11–182. Decided June 25, 2012.

Asian American Justice Center, APIA Vote, and the National Asian American Survey. 2013. *Behind the Numbers: Post-Election Survey of Asian American Voters*. Washington, DC: Asian American Justice Center and APIA Vote.

Bada, Xóchitl, Jonathan Fox, and Andrew Selee. 2006. *Invisible No More: Mexican Migrant Civic Participation in the United States*. Washington, DC: Woodrow Wilson Center for Scholars.

Bahrampour, Tara. 2012. "Documentation for Deferred Action Leads to Confusion Among Illegal Immigrants." *Washington Post* (September 13).

Balderama, Francisco E., and Raymond Rodríguez. 1995. *Decade of Betrayal: Mexican Repatriation in the 1930s*. Albuquerque: University of New Mexico Press.

Balistreri, Kelly Stamper, and Jenifer Van Hook. 2004. "The More Things Change the More They Stay the Same: Mexican Naturalization Before and After Immigration Reform." *International Migration Review* 38 (1) (Spring): 113–130.

Barkan, Elliot R., and Nikolai Khokhlov. 1980. "Socioeconomic Data as Indices of Naturalization Patterns in the United States: A Theory Revisited." *Ethnicity* 7: 159–190.

Barreto, Matt A., Sylvia Manzano, Ricardo Ramírez, and Kathy Rim. 2009. "Mobilization, Participation, and Solidaridad: Latino Participation in the 2006 Immigration Protest Rallies." *Urban Affairs Review* 44 (5) (May): 736–764.

Bean, Frank D., and Gillian Stevens. 2003. *America's Newcomers and the Dynamics of Diversity*. New York: Russell Sage Foundation.

Benhabib, Seyla. 2012. "The Morality of Migration." *The New York Times* (July 29).

Benjamin-Alvarado, Jonathan, Louis DeSipio, and Christine Montoya-Kirk. 2009. "Latino Mobilization in New Immigrant Destinations: The Anti-H.R. 4437 Protest in Nebraska's Cities." *Urban Affairs Review* 44 (5) (May): 718–735.

Bloemraad, Irene. 2006. *Becoming a Citizen: Incorporating Immigrants and Refugees in the United States and Canada*. Berkeley: University of California Press.

Bredbenner, Candice Lewis. 1998. *A Nationality of Her Own: Women, Marriage, and the Law of Citizenship*. Berkeley: University of California Press.

Broder, Tanya, and Jonathan Blazer. 2011. *Overview of Immigrant Eligibility for Federal Programs*. Los Angeles, CA: National Immigration Law Center.

Brookings-Duke Immigration Policy Roundtable. 2009. *Breaking the Immigration Stalemate: From Deep Disagreements to Constructive Proposals*. Washington, DC, and Durham, NC: The Brookings Institution and The Kenan Institute for Ethics, Duke University.

Bumiller, Elizabeth. 2004. "Bush Would Give Illegal Workers Broad New Rights." *New York Times* (January 7).

Calavita, Kitty. 1992. *Inside the State: The Bracero Program, Immigration, and the I.N.S.* New York: Routledge.

Camarota, Stephen. 2005. "The Impact of Non-Citizens on Congressional Apportionment." Testimony prepared for the House Subcommittee on Federalism and the Census, December 6. Washington, DC: Center for Immigration Studies.

Camayd-Freixas, Erik. 2013. *US Immigration Reform and Its Global Impact: Lessons from the Postville Raid*. New York: Palgrave-Macmillan.

Castles, Stephen. 1985. "The Guests Who Stayed: The Debate on 'Foreigners Policy' in the German Federal Republic." *International Migration Review* 19 (3): 517–534.

Castles, Stephen, with Heather Booth and Tina Wallace. 1984. *Here for Good: Western Europe's New Ethnic Minorities*. London: Pluto Press.

Chavez, Leo R. 2008. *The Latino Threat: Constructing Immigrants, Citizens, and the Nation*. Stanford, CA: Stanford University Press.

Chishti, Muzaffar, and Claire Bergeron. 2010. *Obama Administration's Steps Point to Significant Shift in Immigration Enforcement Policy.* Washington, DC: Migration Policy Institute.

Cillizza, Chris. 2014. "Yes, President Obama Is Right: The 113th Congress Will Be the Least Productive in History." *The Washington Post* (April 10).

CNN. 2012. "President: Full Results." http://www.cnn.com/election/2012/results /race/president#exit-polls. Accessed December 19, 2012.

CNN/ORC Poll. 2014. *CNN/ORC International Poll.* Atlanta, GA: CNN (July 24).

Cohn, Nate. 2014. "Why the Democrats Can't Win the House." *New York Times* (September 6).

Congressional Budget Office. 2007. *The Impact of Unauthorized Immigrants on the Budgets of State and Local Governments.* Washington, DC: Congressional Budget Office.

———. 2013. *S. 744, Border Security, Economic Opportunity, and Immigration Modernization Act Cost Estimate.* Washington, DC: Congressional Budget Office.

Congressional Quarterly. 2006. "House Seeks to Tighten Borders." *CQ Almanac 2005.* CQ Press Electronic Library. Washington, DC: Congressional Quarterly.

———. 2008. "Immigration Rewrite Dies in Senate." *CQ Almanac 2007.* Washington, DC: Congressional Quarterly.

Corbin, Cristina. 2010. "N.C. Congresswoman Calls for American to Be Stripped of Citizenship over Al Qaeda Website." FoxNews.com, July 20. http:// www.foxnews.com/politics/2010/07/20/nc-congresswoman-calls-american -stripped-citizenship-al-qaeda-website/. Accessed July 28, 2010.

Cornelius, Wayne A., and Jessa M. Lewis. *Impacts of Border Enforcement on Mexican Migration: The View from Sending Communities.* La Jolla, CA: Center for Comparative Immigration Studies.

Crul, Maurice, and John H. Mollenkopf, eds. 2012. *The Changing Face of World Cities: Young Adult Children of Immigrants in Europe and the United States.* New York: Russell Sage Foundation Press.

de la Garza, Rodolfo O. 2011. "Neither Walls nor Open Borders: A New Approach to Immigration Reform." *The New Labor Forum* 20 (1): 65–71.

de la Garza, Rodolfo O., and Louis DeSipio. 1993. "Save the Baby, Change the Bathwater, and Scrub the Tub: Latino Electoral Participation After Seventeen Years of Voting Rights Act Coverage." *Texas Law Review* 71 (7) (June): 1479–1539.

———. 1998. "Interests Not Passions: Mexican American Attitudes Toward Mexico, Immigration from Mexico, and Issues Shaping U.S.-Mexico Relations." *International Migration Review* 32 (2) (Summer): 401–422.

———. 2006. "Reshaping the Tub: The Limits of the VRA for Latino Electoral Politics." In David L. Epstein, Richard H. Pildes, Rodolfo O. de la Garza, and Sharyn O'Halloran, eds. *The Future of the Voting Rights Act,* pp. 139–162. New York: Russell Sage Foundation Press.

de la Garza, Rodolfo O., Louis DeSipio, Angelo Falcón, F. Chris García, and John A. García. 1992. *Latino Voices: Mexican, Puerto Rican, and Cuban Perspectives on American Politics.* Boulder, CO: Westview Press.

de la Garza, Rodolfo O., Louis DeSipio, and David Leal. 2010. *Beyond the Barrio: Latinos in the 2004 Elections.* Notre Dame, IN: University of Notre Dame Press.

de la Garza, Rodolfo O., Angelo Falcón, and F. Chris García. 1996. "Will the Real Americans Please Stand Up: Anglo and Mexican-American Support of Core American Political Values." *American Journal of Political Science* 40 (2) (May): 335–351.

de la Garza, Rodolfo O., and Briant Lindsay Lowell. 2002. *Sending Money Home: Hispanic Remittances and Community Development.* Lanham, MD: Rowman and Littlefield Publishers.

de la Garza, Rodolfo O., and Harry Pachon. 2000. *Latinos and U.S. Foreign Policy: Representing the "Homeland"?* Lanham, MD: Rowman and Littlefield Publishers.

De León, Arnoldo. *In re Ricardo Rodríguez: An Attempt at Chicano Disenfranchisement in San Antonio, 1896–1897.* San Antonio, TX: Caravel Press.

Derby, Lauren H. 2009. *The Dictator's Seduction: Politics and the Popular Imagination in the Era of Trujillo.* Durham, NC: Duke University Press.

Desilver, Drew. 2013. *Congress Ends the Least-Productive Year in Recent History.* Washington, DC: Pew Research Center.

DeSipio, Louis. 1996a. "Making Citizens or Good Citizens? Naturalization as a Predictor of Organizational and Electoral Behavior Among Latino Immigrants." *Hispanic Journal of Behavioral Sciences* 18 (2) (May): 194–213.

———. 1996b. *Counting on the Latino Vote: Latinos as a New Electorate.* Charlottesville: University Press of Virginia.

———. 2001. "Building America, One Person at a Time: Naturalization and Political Behavior of the Naturalized in Contemporary U.S. Politics." In Gary Gerstle and John Mollenkopf, eds. *E Pluribus Unum? Contemporary and Historical Perspectives on Immigrant Political Incorporation,* pp. 67–106. New York: Russell Sage Foundation Press.

———. 2006. "Transnational Politics and Civic Engagement: Do Home-Country Political Ties Limit Latino Immigrant Pursuit of U.S. Civic Engagement and Citizenship?" In Taeku Lee, S. Karthick Ramakrishnan, and Ricardo Ramírez, eds. *Transforming Politics, Transforming America: The Political and Civic Incorporation of Immigrants in the United States,* pp. 106–126. Charlottesville: University of Virginia Press.

———. 2011a. "Drawing New Lines in the Sand: Evaluating the Failure of Immigration Reform from 2006 to the Beginning of the Obama Administration." In Kim Voss and Irene Bloemraad, eds. *Rallying for Immigrant Rights: The Fight for Inclusion in 21st Century America,* pp. 215–232. Berkeley: University of California Press.

———. 2011b. "Immigrant Incorporation in an Era of Weak Civic Institutions: Immigrant Civic and Political Participation in the United States." *American Behavioral Scientist* 55 (9) (September): 1189–1213.

DeSipio, Louis, and Rodolfo O. de la Garza. 2005. "Between Symbolism and Influence: Latinos and the 2000 Elections." In Rodolfo O. de la Garza and Louis DeSipio, eds. *Muted Voices: Latinos and the 2000 Elections*, pp. 13–60. Lanham, MD: Rowman and Littlefield Publishers.

DeSipio, Louis, and David Leal. 2010. "Introduction. A View from the Battleground's Periphery: Latinos and the 2004 Elections." In Rodolfo O. de la Garza, Louis DeSipio, and David Leal, eds. *Beyond the Barrio: Latinos in the 2004 Elections*, pp. 1–71. Notre Dame, IN: University of Notre Dame Press.

DeSipio, Louis, Natalie Masuoka, and Christopher Stout. 2008. "Asian American Immigrants as the New Electorate: Exploring Turnout and Registration of a Growing Community." *Asian American Policy Review* XVII: 51–71.

DeSipio, Louis, Harry P. Pachon, and W. Andrew Moellmer. 2001. *Reinventing the Naturalization Process at INS: For Better or Worse?* Claremont, CA: The Tomás Rivera Policy Institute.

DeSipio, Louis, and Carole Jean Uhlaner. 2007. "Immigrant and Native: Mexican American 2004 Presidential Vote Choice Across Immigrant Generations." *American Politics Research* 35 (2) (March): 176–201.

Dinnerstein, Marti. 2003. *IDs for Illegals? The "Matrícula Consular" Advances Mexico's Immigration Agenda*. Washington, DC: Center for Immigration Studies.

Dugan, Andrew. 2013. *Passing New Immigration Laws Is Important to Americans: Major Parts of the Senate Immigration Bill Popular Among Different Racial/Ethnic Groups*. Princeton, NJ: Gallup Poll.

Erie, Stephen. 1988. *Rainbow's End: Irish Americans and the Dilemmas of Urban Machine Politics, 1840–1985*. Berkeley: University Press of California.

Espenshade, Thomas J., and Maryann Belanger. 1997. "U.S. Public Perceptions and Reactions to Mexican Migration." In Fran D. Bean et al., eds. *At the Crossroads: Mexico and U.S. Immigration Policy*, pp. 227–262. Lanham, MD: Rowman and Littlefield Publishers.

Facchini, Giovanni, Anna Maria Mayda, and Prachi Mishra. 2011. "Do Interest Groups Affect U.S. Immigration Policy?" *Journal of International Economics* 85: 114–128.

Facchini, Giovanni, and Max Friedrich Steinhardt. 2011. "What Drives U.S. Immigration Policy? Evidence from Congressional Roll Call Votes." *Journal of Public Economics* 95: 734–743.

FitzGerald, David. 2009. *A Nation of Emigrants: How Mexico Manages Its Migration*. Berkeley: University of California Press.

FitzGerald, David Scott, and David Cook-Martín. 2014. *Culling the Masses: The Democratic Origins of Racist Immigration Policy in the Americas*. Cambridge, MA: Harvard University Press.

Foner, Nancy. 2000. *From Ellis Island to JFK: New York's Two Great Waves of Immigration*. New Haven, CT: Yale University Press.

Fraga, Luis R., John A. García, Rodney Hero, Michael Jones-Correa, Valerie Martinez-Ebers, and Gary M. Segura. 2008. *Latino National Survey (LNS), 2006* (computer file). ICPSR20862-v1. Miami, FL: Geoscape International, 2006. Ann Arbor, MI: Inter-university Consortium for Political and Social Research.

———. 2012. *Latinos in the New Millennium: An Almanac of Opinion, Behavior, and Policy Preferences*. New York: Cambridge University Press.

Gallup. 2014. *Immigration: Gallup Historical Trends*. Princeton, NJ: Gallup Poll.

Gamm, Gerald H. 1986. *The Making of New Deal Democrats: Voting Behaviors and Realignment in Boston, 1920–1940*. Chicago: University of Chicago Press.

García, John A. 1987. "Political Integration of Mexican Immigrants: Explorations into the Naturalization Process." *International Migration Review* 15 (4): 608–625.

García Bedolla, Lisa, and Melissa R. Michelson. 2012. *Mobilizing Inclusion: Transforming the Electorate Through Get-Out-the-Vote Campaigns*. New Haven, CT: Yale University Press.

Gardner, Martha. 2005. *The Qualities of a Citizen: Women, Immigration and Citizenship, 1870–1965*. Princeton, NJ: Princeton University Press.

Gavit, John Palmer. 1971 [1922]. *Americans by Choice*. New York: Harper Brothers Publishers.

Gibson, Campbell J., and Emily Lennon. 1999. "Historical Census Statistics on the Foreign-born Population of the United States: 1850–1990." Washington, DC: US Census Bureau. http://www.census.gov/population/www/documentation/twps0029/twps0029.html. Accessed September 16, 2010.

Gimpel, James G., and James R. Edwards, Jr. 1999. *The Congressional Politics of Immigration Reform*. Boston, MA: Allyn and Bacon.

Givens, Terri, Gary P. Freeman, and David Leal, eds. 2009. *Immigration Policy and Security: U.S., European, and Commonwealth Perspectives*. New York: Routledge.

González, Gilbert G. 1999. *Mexican Consuls and Labor Organizing: Imperial Politics in the American Southwest*. Austin: University of Texas Press.

Gonzalez-Barrera, Ana, Mark Hugo Lopez, Jeffrey S. Passel, and Paul Taylor. 2013. *The Path Not Taken: Two-Thirds of Legal Mexican Immigrants Are Not U.S. Citizens*. Washington, DC: The Pew Research Center.

González-Gutiérrez, Carlos. 1999. "Fostering Identities: Mexico's Relations with Its Diaspora." *Journal of American History* 86 (2): 545–567.

Gorman, Anna. 2010. "Arizona's Immigration Law Isn't the Only One." *Los Angeles Times* (July 16).

Grant, Madison. 1916. *The Passing of the Great Race, or The Racial Basis of European History*. New York: Charles Scribner's Sons.

Guest, Avery. 1980. "The Old-New Distinction in Naturalization: 1900." *International Migration Review* 14 (4): 492–510.

Gyory, Andrew. 1998. *Closing the Gate: Race, Politics, and the Chinese Exclusion Act.* Chapel Hill: University of North Carolina Press.

Hajnal, Zoltan, and Michael U. Rivera. 2014. "Immigration, Latinos, and White Partisan Politics: The New Democratic Defection." *American Journal of Political Science* 58 (4) (October): 773–789.

Handlin, Oscar. 1951. *The Uprooted: The Epic Story of the Great Migrations That Made the American People.* Boston, MA: Little, Brown and Company.

Haney Lopez, Ian. 1996. *White by Law: The Legal Construction of Race.* New York: New York University Press.

Hayduk, Ron. 2006. *Democracy for All: Restoring Immigrant Voting Rights in the United States.* New York: Routledge.

Hernández, Kelly Lytle. 2010. *Migra! A History of the Border Patrol.* Berkeley: University of California Press.

Hessick, Carissa Bryne, and Gabriel J. Chin, eds. 2014. *Strange Neighbors: The Role of States in Immigration Policy.* New York: New York University Press.

Hing, Bill Ong. 2004. *Defining America Through Immigration Policy.* Philadelphia, PA: Temple University Press.

———. 2006. *Deporting Our Souls: Values, Morality, and Immigration Policy.* New York: Cambridge University Press.

Hoefer, Michael, Nancy Rytina, and Bryan Baker. 2012. *Estimates of the Unauthorized Immigrant Population Residing in the United States: January 2011.* Washington, DC: US Department of Homeland Security.

Horowitz, Carl F. 2012. "The 'Noncitizen' Voting Rights Deception." *The Social Contract* 23 (1) (Fall).

Horsley, Scott. 2010. "Under Obama, More Illegal Immigrants Sent Home." Washington, DC: National Public Radio (July 28).

Hotline on Call. 2008. "Obama: Immigration Will Be a Year One Priority." *Hotline on Call.* Washington, DC: National Journal (July 8).

Huntington, Samuel P. 2004. *Who Are We? The Challenges to America's National Identity.* New York: Simon and Schuster.

ICF International. 2011. *U.S. Citizenship and Immigration Services' Records Study on Pass/Fail Rates for Naturalization Applicants.* RFQ/Project No. HSS-CCG-09-Q-00228. Fairfax, VA: ICF Incorporated.

Immigration Policy Center. 2013. *A Guide to S.744: Understanding the 2013 Senate Immigration Bill.* Washington, DC: Immigration Policy Center.

Institute on Taxation and Economic Policy. 2013. *Undocumented Immigrants' State and Local Tax Contributions.* Washington, DC: Institute on Taxation and Economic Policy.

Isacson, Adam, and Maureen Meyer. 2012. *Beyond the Border Buildup: Security and Migrants Along the U.S.-Mexico Border.* Washington, DC: Washington Office on Latin America.

Iyer, Sundeep, and Keesha Gaskins. 2012. *Redistricting and Congressional Control: A First Look*. New York: Brennan Center for Justice at New York University Law School.

Jacobson, Gary C. 2013. "Partisan Polarization in American Politics: A Background Paper." *Presidential Studies Quarterly* 43 (4) (December): 688–708.

Jasso, Guillermina, and Mark Rosenzweig. 1987. "Using National Recording Systems for Measurement and Analysis of Immigration to the United States." *International Migration Review* 21 (12): 1212–1244.

———. 1990. *The New Chosen People: Immigrants in the United States*. New York: Russell Sage Foundation.

Johnson, Kevin R. 2013. "The Beginning of the End: The Immigration Act of 1965 and the Emergence of Modern U.S./Mexico Border Enforcement." *UC Davis Legal Studies Research Paper Series*. Research Paper 360 (December). Davis: University of California–Davis.

Jones, Robert P., Daniel Cox, Juhem Navarro-Rivera, E. J. Dionne, Jr., and William A. Galston. 2014. *What Americans Want from Immigration Reform in 2014: Findings from the PRRI/Brookings Religion, Values, and Immigration Reform Survey, Panel Call Back*. Washington, DC: Public Religion Research Institute and the Brookings Institution.

Jones-Correa, Michael. 2004. "Under Two Flags: Dual Nationality in Latin America and Its Consequences for Naturalization in the United States." *International Migration Review* 35: 997–1029.

Kandel, William A. *U.S. Naturalization Policy*. Washington, DC: Congressional Research Service.

Kelly, Erin. 2014. "Tech Industry Creates Fears Among Immigration Advocates." *USA Today* (April 29).

Kerwin, Donald. 2014. "Creating a More Responsive and Seamless Refugee Protection System: The Scope, Promise and Limitations of US Temporary Protection Programs." *Journal on Migration and Human Security* 2 (1): 4–72.

Kim, Seung Min. 2014. "Eric Cantor Loss Kills Immigration Reform." *Politico* (June 10).

Laglagaron, Laureen. 2010. *Protection Through Integration: The Mexican Government's Efforts to Aid Migrants in the United States*. Washington, DC: Migration Policy Institute.

Lake, David. 2010. "The Practice and Theory of US Statebuilding." *Journal of Intervention and Statebuilding* 4 (3): 257–284.

Latino Decisions. 2012. *impreMedia-Latino Decisions Election Eve Poll 2012*. Seattle, WA: Latino Decisions. http://www.latinodecisions.com/files/7613/5234/2212/Latino_Election_Eve_Poll_-_By_state.pdf. Accessed December 19, 2012.

Lee, Esther Yu-Hsi. 2014. "On Tax Day, a Reminder That Undocumented Immigrants Pay Billions in Taxes," *Think Progress* (April 15).

Lee, James. 2013. *U.S. Naturalizations 2012.* Washington, DC: US Department of Homeland Security.

Lipsky, Michael. 2010. *Street Level Bureaucracy: Dilemmas of the Individual in Public Services,* 30th Anniversary Expanded Edition. New York: Russell Sage Foundation.

Liptak, Adam. 2012. "Blocking Parts of Arizona Law, Justices Allow Its Centerpiece." *New York Times* (June 26).

Magaña, Lisa, and Erik K. Lee, eds. 2013. *Latino Politics and Arizona's Immigration Law SB 1070.* New York: Springer Press.

Mahler, Sarah J., and Myer Siemiatycki. 2011. "Diverse Pathways to Immigrant Incorporation: Comparative Canadian and U.S. Perspectives." *American Behavioral Scientist* 55 (9): 1123–1130.

Mann, Thomas E., and Norman J. Ornstein. 2012. *It's Even Worse Than It Looks: How the American Constitutional System Collided with the New Politics of Extremism.* New York: Basic Books.

Martin, Daniel C., and James E. Yankay. 2012. *Refugees and Asylees: 2011.* Washington, DC: US Immigration and Naturalization Service, Office of Policy and Planning Statistics Division.

Masuoka, Natalie, and Jane Junn. 2013. *The Politics of Belonging: Race, Public Opinion, and Immigration.* Chicago: University of Chicago Press.

Maxwell, Rahsaan. 2010. "Evaluating Migrant Integration: Political Attitudes Across Generations in Europe. *International Migration Review* 44 (1) (Spring): 25–52.

Meissner, Doris, and Donald Kerwin. 2009. *DHS and Immigration: Taking Stock and Correcting Course.* Washington, DC: Migration Policy Institute.

Meissner, Doris, and James W. Ziglar. 2010. "Why the U.S. Had to Challenge Arizona on Immigration." *Washington Post* (July 22).

Menchaca, Martha. 2011. *Naturalizing Mexican Immigrants: A Texas History.* Austin: University of Texas Press.

Michelson, Melissa. 2000. "Political Efficacy and Electoral Participation of Chicago Latinos." *Social Science Quarterly* 81 (1): 36–50.

———. 2002–2003. "Political Efficacy Among California Latinos." *Latino/a Research Review* 5: 1–15.

Michelson, Melissa R., and Lisa García Bedolla. 2014. "Mobilization by Different Means: Nativity and GOTV in the United States." *International Migration Review,* 1–18.

Migration Policy Institute. 2012. "As Many as 1.4 Million Unauthorized Immigrant Youth Could Gain Relief from Deportation Under Obama Administration Grant of Deferred Action." Press Release (June 15). Washington, DC: Migration Policy Institute.

Milkman, Ruth. 2000. *Organizing Immigrants: The Challenge for Unions in Contemporary California.* Ithaca, NY: Cornell University Press.

Motomura, Hiroshi. 2006. *Americans in Waiting: The Lost Story of Immigration and Citizenship in the United States*. New York: Oxford University Press.

Muller, Thomas. 1993. *Immigrants and the American City*. New York: New York University Press.

NALEO (National Association of Latino Elected Officials). 1986. *Proceedings of the First National Conference on Citizenship and the Hispanic Community*. Washington, DC: NALEO Educational Fund.

National Conference of State Legislatures. 2014. *2013 Immigration Report*. Denver, CO: National Conference of State Legislatures.

National Immigration Forum. 2009. "Immigrant Integration and Immigration Fees in the Department of Homeland Security Appropriations Bill." Washington, DC: National Immigration Forum (July 9).

National Security Archive. 2005. *Luis Posada Carriles: The Declassified Record*. Washington, DC: National Security Archive.

———. 2006. *Letelier-Moffitt Assassination Thirty Years Later*. Washington, DC: National Security Archive (September 30).

Newport, Frank, and Joy Wilke. 2013. "Immigration Reform Proposals Garner Broad Support in U.S." Washington, DC: Gallup Poll (June 19).

Newton, Lina. 2008. *Illegal, Alien, or Immigrant: The Politics of Immigration Reform*. New York: New York University Press.

Ngai, Mae M. 1999. "The Architecture of Race in American Immigration Law: A Reexamination of the Immigration Act of 1924." *The Journal of American History* 86 (1) (June): 67–92.

———. 2003. *Impossible Subjects: Illegal Aliens and the Making of Modern America*. Princeton, NJ: Princeton University Press.

Nicholls, Walter J. 2013. *The DREAMers: How the Undocumented Youth Movement Transformed the Immigrant Rights Debate*. Stanford, CA: Stanford University Press.

Omi, Michael, and Howard Winant. 1994. *Racial Formation in the United States: From the 1960s to the 1990s*. Second Edition. New York: Routledge.

Ono, Kent A., and John M. Sloop. 2002. *Shifting Borders: Rhetoric, Immigration, and California's Proposition 187*. Philadelphia, PA: Temple University Press.

Opportunity Agenda, The. 2012. *Millennials' Attitudes Toward Immigrants and Immigration Policy*. New York: The Opportunity Agenda.

Pachon, Harry P., and Louis DeSipio. 1994. *New Americans by Choice: Political Perspectives of Latino Immigrants*. Boulder, CO: Westview Press.

Pallares, Amalia, and Nilda Flores-González, eds. 2010. *Marcha! Latino Chicago and the Immigrant Rights Movement*. Urbana: University of Illinois Press.

Pantoja, Adrian, Ricardo Ramírez, and Gary Segura. 2001. "Citizens by Choice, Voters by Necessity: Patterns in Political Mobilization by Naturalized Latinos." *Political Research Quarterly* 54 (4) (December): 729–750.

Pantoja, Adrian, and Gary Segura. 2003. "Fear and Loathing in California: Contextual Threat and Political Sophistication Among Latino Voters." *Political Behavior* 25 (3) (September): 265–286.

Parker, Christopher S., and Matt A. Barreto. 2013. *Change They Can't Believe In: The Tea Party and Reactionary Politics in America*. Princeton, NJ: Princeton University Press.

Passel, Jeffrey S. 2007. *Growing Share of Immigrants Choosing Naturalization*. Washington, DC: Pew Hispanic Center.

Passel, Jeffrey S., and Rebecca L. Clark. 1998. *Immigrants in New York: Their Legal Status, Incomes and Tax Payments*. Washington, DC: The Urban Institute.

Passel, Jeffrey S., and D'Vera Cohn. 2009. *Mexican Immigrants: How Many Come? How Many Leave?* Washington, DC: Pew Hispanic Center (July).

Passel, Jeffrey, D'Vera Cohn, and Ana Gonzalez-Barrera. 2012. *Net Migration from Mexico Falls to Zero—and Perhaps Less*. Washington, DC: Pew Hispanic Center.

———. 2013. *Population Decline of Unauthorized Immigrants Stalls, May Have Reversed*. Washington, DC: Pew Research Center.

Passel, Jeffrey S., D'Vera Cohn, Jens Manuel Krogstad, and Ana Gonzalez-Barrera. 2014. *As Growth Stalls, Unauthorized Immigrant Population Becomes More Settled*. Washington, DC: Pew Research Center's Hispanic Trends Project.

Passel, Jeffrey, and Mark Hugo Lopez. 2012. *Up to 1.7 Million Unauthorized Immigrant Youth May Benefit from New Deportation Rules*. Washington, DC: Pew Hispanic Center.

Pear, Robert. 1993. "U.S. to Encourage Legal Immigrants to Get Citizenship." *New York Times* (November 26).

Peralta, Eyder. 2014. "National Council of La Raza Dubs Obama 'Deporter-in-Chief'." National Public Radio, *The Two Way* (March 4).

Pew Research Center. 2013. *Most Say Immigration Policy Needs Big Changes: But Little Agreement on Specific Approaches*. Washington, DC: Pew Research Center.

———. 2014a. *Public Divided over Increased Deportation of Unauthorized Immigrants*. Washington, DC: Pew Research Center.

———. 2014b. *Surge of Central American Children Roils U.S. Immigration Debate*. Washington, DC: Pew Research Center.

Pew Research Hispanic Trends Project. 2013. *A Nation of Immigrants: A Portrait of the 40 Million, Including 11 Million Unauthorized*. Washington, DC: Pew Research Center.

Portes, Alejandro, and John Curtis. 1987. "Changing Flags: Naturalization and Its Determinants Among Mexican Immigrants." *International Migration Review* 21 (2) (Summer): 352–372.

Portes, Alejandro, and Rafael Mozo. 1985. *Latin Journey: Cuban and Mexican Immigrants in the United States*. Berkeley: University of California Press.

Portes, Alejandro, and Rubén G. Rumbaut. 2001. *Legacies: The Story of the Immigrant Second Generation*. Berkeley and New York: University of California Press and Russell Sage Foundation.

Preston, Julia. 2009. "Firm Stance on Illegal Immigrants Remains Policy." *New York Times* (August 4).

———. 2011. "Some Cheer Border Fence as Others Ponder the Cost." *New York Times* (October 19).

Putnam, Robert D. 2000. *Bowling Alone: The Collapse and Revival of American Community*. New York: Simon and Schuster.

Ramakrishnan, S. Karthick. 2005. *Democracy in Immigrant America: Changing Demographics and Political Participation*. Stanford, CA: Stanford University Press.

Ramakrishnan, S. Karthick, and Irene Bloemraad, eds. 2008. *Civic Hopes and Political Realities: Immigrants, Community Organizations, and Political Engagement*. New York: Russell Sage Foundation Press.

Ramakrishnan, S. Karthick, Jane Junn, Taeku Lee, and Janelle Wong. 2012. *National Asian American Survey, 2008*. ICPSR31481-v2. Ann Arbor, MI: Inter-university Consortium for Political and Social Research, 2012-07-19. doi:10.3886/ICPSR31481.v2.

Ramírez, Ricardo. 2013. *Mobilizing Opportunities: The Evolving Latino Electorate and the Future of American Politics*. Charlottesville: University of Virginia Press.

Rasmussen Reports. 2010. "64% in Arizona Say Children of Illegal Immigrants Should Not Automatically Become U.S. Citizens." Rasmussen Reports (July 5, 2010). http://www.rasmussenreports.com/public_content/politics/general _state_surveys/arizona/64_in_arizona_say_children_of_illegal_immigrants _should_not_automatically_become_u_s_citizens. Accessed July 13, 2010.

Reitz, Jeffrey, and commentaries by Don J. DeVoretz and Harold Troper. 2004. "Canada: Immigration and Nation-Building in a Transition to a Knowledge Economy." In Wayne A. Cornelius, Takeyuki Tsuda, Philip L. Martin, and James F. Hollifield, eds. *Controlling Immigration: A Global Perspective*. Second Edition, pp. 97–139. Stanford, CA: Stanford University Press.

Renshon, Stanley. 2005. *The 50% American: Immigration and National Identity in an Age of Terror*. Washington, DC: Georgetown University Press.

Risse, Mathias. 2008. "On the Morality of Immigration." *Ethics and International Affairs* 22 (1) (Spring): 25–33.

Rosberg, Gerald. 1977. "Aliens and Equal Protection: Why Not the Right to Vote?" *Michigan Law Review* 75 (April–May): 1092–1136.

Rytina, Nancy. 2002. "IRCA Legalization Effects: Lawful Permanent Residence and Naturalization Through 2001." Washington, DC: US Immigration and Naturalization Service, Office of Policy and Planning Statistics Division.

Saad, Lydia. 2014. "More Would Decrease Immigration Than Increase: Support for Increasing Immigration Is Up, Yet More Would Still Curb It." *Gallup Poll* (June 27). Princeton, NJ: Gallup Poll.

Schlozman, Kay Lehman, Sidney Verba, and Henry E. Brady. 2012. *The Unheavenly Chorus: Unequal Political Voice and the Broken Promise of American Democracy.* Princeton, NJ: Princeton University Press.

Schmitt, Eric. 2001. "Bush Aides Weigh Legalizing Status of Mexicans in U.S." *New York Times* (July 14).

Schmitt, John, and Kris Warner. 2010. "The Changing Face of U.S. Labor, 1983–2008." *Working USA: The Journal of Labor and Society* 13 (June): 263–279.

Schneider, Jens, Leo Chávez, Louis DeSipio, and Mary Waters. 2012. "Belonging." In Maurice Crul and John Mollenkopf, eds. *The Changing Face of World Cities*, pp. 206–234. New York: Russell Sage Foundation Press.

Schrag, Peter G. 2000. *A Well-Founded Fear: The Congressional Battle to Save Political Asylum in America.* New York: Routledge.

———. 2010. *Not Fit for Our Society: Immigration and Nativism in America.* Berkeley: University of California Press.

Schuck, Peter H., and Rogers M. Smith. 1985. *Citizenship Without Consent: Illegal Aliens in the American Polity.* New Haven, CT: Yale University Press.

Seller, Maxine Schwartz. 1988. *To Seek America: A History of Ethnic Life in the United States.* Rev. and enlarged. Englewood, NJ: Jerome S. Ozer Publisher.

Silver, Nate. 2014. "Eric Cantor's Loss Was Like an Earthquake." *FiveThirtyEight .com* (June 11).

Simanski, John, and Lesley M. Sapp. 2012. *Immigration Enforcement Actions: 2011.* Washington, DC: US Immigration and Naturalization Service, Office of Policy and Planning Statistics Division.

Singer, Audrey. 2013. *Implementation Facts: Deferred Action for Childhood Arrivals* (DACA). Washington, DC: Brookings Institution.

Spiro, Peter. 2008. *Beyond Citizenship: American Identity After Globalization.* New York: Oxford University Press.

Staton, Jeffrey K., Robert A. Jackson, and Damarys Canache. 2007. "Dual Nationality Among Latinos: What Are the Implications for Political Connectedness?" *The Journal of Politics* 69 (2) (May): 470–482.

Sterne, Evelyn S. 2001. "Beyond the Boss: Immigration and American Political Culture, 1880–1940." In Gary Gerstle and John Mollenkopf, eds. *E Pluribus Unum? Contemporary and Historical Perspectives on Immigrant Political Incorporation*, pp. 33–66. New York: Russell Sage Foundation Press.

Sziarto, Kristin M., and Helga Leitner. 2010. "Immigrants Riding for Justice: Space-time and Emotions in the Construction of a Counterpublic." *Political Geography* 29: 381–391.

Takaki, Ronald. 1993. *A Different Mirror: A History of Multicultural America.* New York: Little, Brown and Company.

Taylor, J. Edward. 2002. "Do Government Programs 'Crowd In' Remittances?" In Rodolfo O. de la Garza and Briant Lindsay Lowell, eds. *Sending Money Home: Hispanic Remittances and Community Development*, pp. 189–214. Lanham, MD: Rowman and Littlefield Publishers.

Thiessen, Marc. 2012. "Yes, U.S. Citizens Can Be Held as Enemy Combatants." *AEIdeas*. Washington, DC: American Enterprise Institute.

Tichenor, Daniel J. 2002. *Dividing Lines: The Politics of Immigration Control in America*. Princeton, NJ: Princeton University Press.

Tichenor, Daniel J., and Marc R. Rosenblum. 2012. "Poles Apart: The Politics of Illegal Immigration in America." In Marc R. Rosenblum and Daniel J. Tichenor, eds. *The Oxford Handbook of the Politics of International Migration*, pp. 614–638. New York: Oxford University Press.

Triay, Victor Andres. 2001. *Bay of Pigs: An Oral History of Brigade 2506*. Gainesville: University of Florida Press.

United Nations. 2010. *Population Density and Urbanization*. http://unstats.un.org/unsd/demographic/sconcerns/densurb/default.htm. Accessed July 28, 2010.

US Census Bureau. Various years. *Voting and Registration in the Election of November [various years]*. Series P-20. Washington, DC: US Census Bureau.

———. 2010. *2010 Statistical Abstract of the United States*. Washington, DC: US Census Bureau. http://www.dhs.gov/xlibrary/assets/statistics/yearbook/2010/ois_yb_2010.pdf. Accessed August 26, 2010.

US Census Bureau, American Community Survey Reports. 2012. "The Foreign-Born Population in the United States: 2010." *American Community Survey Reports*. Washington, DC: US Census Bureau.

US Citizenship and Immigration Services. 2009. "Pathway to U.S. Citizenship." Washington, DC: US Citizenship and Immigration Services.

———. 2010a. "Administrative Alternatives to Comprehensive Immigration Reform." Draft Memorandum to Alejandro N. Mayorkas, Director. Washington, DC: US Citizenship and Immigration Services.

———. 2010b. *A Guide to Naturalization*. Washington, DC: US Citizenship and Immigration Services. http://www.uscis.gov/files/article/M-476.pdf. Accessed July 8, 2010.

———. 2014. *Number of I-821D, Consideration of Deferred Action for Childhood Admissions Arrivals, by Fiscal Year, Quarter, Intake, Biometrics, and Case Status: 2012-2014*. Washington, DC: US Citizenship and Immigration Services.

US Customs and Border Protection. 2014. United States Border Patrol. Washington, DC: US Customs and Border Protection. http://www.cbp.gov/sites/default/files/documents/U.S.%20Border%20Patrol%20Fiscal%20Year%20Staffing%20Statistics%201992–2013.pdf. Accessed April 15, 2014.

US Department of Homeland Security. 2013. *2012 Yearbook of Immigration Statistics*. Washington, DC: Office of Immigration Statistics.

———. 2014. *U.S. Lawful Permanent Residents: 2013*. Washington, DC: Office of Immigration Statistics.

US Department of State. 2005. *Trafficking in Persons Report*. Washington, DC: US Department of State. http://www.state.gov/g/tip/rls/tiprpt/2005/46606.htm. Accessed July 28, 2010.

US Immigration and Customs Enforcement. 2014. *FY 2013 ICE Immigration Removals*. Washington, DC: Department of Homeland Security, Immigration and Customs Enforcement.

US Immigration and Naturalization Service. 2000. *1998 Statistical Yearbook of the Immigration and Naturalization Service*. Washington, DC: US Immigration and Naturalization Service.

US Senate, Committee of the Judiciary. 1980. *History of the Immigration and Naturalization Service*. Washington, DC: Congressional Research Service.

US Senate. 2013. "Outline of the Border Security, Economic Opportunity, and Immigration Modernization Act of 2013." Unpublished manuscript.

Van Hook, Jennifer, Susan K. Brown, and Frank D. Bean. 2006. "For Love or Money? Welfare Reform and Immigrant Naturalization." *Social Forces* 85 (2) (December): 643–666.

Voss, Kim, and Irene Bloemraad, eds. 2011. *Rallying for Immigrant Rights: The Fight for Inclusion in 21st Century America*. Berkeley: University of California Press.

Wang, Ted, and Robert C. Winn. 2011. "Groundswell Meets Groundwork: Building on the Mobilizations to Empower Immigrant Communities." In Kim Voss and Irene Bloemraad, eds. *Rallying for Immigrant Rights: The Fight for Inclusion in 21st Century America*, pp. 44–59. Berkeley: University of California Press.

Wong, Janelle S. 2006. *Democracy's Promise: Immigrants and American Civic Institutions*. Ann Arbor: University of Michigan Press.

Wong, Janelle, S. Karthick Ramakrishnan, Taeku Lee, and Jane Junn. 2011. *Asian American Participation: Emerging Constituents and Their Political Identities*. New York: Russell Sage Foundation Press.

Woodrow Wilson Center for Scholars. 2007. "Immigrants' Rights Marches, Spring 2006." http://www.wilsoncenter.org/sites/default/files/2006_immigrant_marches_database_0.xls. Accessed October 21, 2014.

World Bank. 2012. "Bilateral Remittance Matrix 2012." Washington, DC: The World Bank. http://econ.worldbank.org/WBSITE/EXTERNAL/EXTDEC/EXTDECPROSPECTS/0,,contentMDK:22759429~pagePK:64165401~piPK:64165026~theSitePK:476883,00.html. Accessed April 29, 2014.

———. 2014. "Remittances to Developing Countries to Stay Robust This Year, Despite Increased Deportations of Migrant Workers, Says WB." Press Release. Washington, DC: The World Bank (April 11).

Wyman, Mark. 1993. *Round-Trip to America: The Immigrants Return to Europe, 1880–1930*. Ithaca, NY: Cornell University Press.

Yang, Philip Q. 1994. "Explaining Immigrant Naturalization." *The International Migration Review* 28 (3): 449–477.

———. 2002. "Citizenship Acquisition of Post-1965 Asian Immigrants." *Population and Environment* 23 (4) (March): 377–404.

Ziegelman, Jane. 2010. *97 Orchard: An Edible History of Five Immigrant Families in One New York Tenement.* New York: HarperCollins.

Zolberg, Aristide M. 2006. *A Nation by Design: Immigration Policy in the Fashioning of America.* Cambridge, MA, and New York: Harvard University Press and Russell Sage Foundation Press.

# Index

Made in the USA
Middletown, DE
12 February 2017